*Praise for Adam Davidson's*

# THE PASSION ECONOMY

"Davidson's case studies are excellent, but the heart of the book is a set of rules worthy of committing to memory. . . . Fine inspiration for entrepreneurs that should be required reading in any business school curriculum."

—*Kirkus Reviews* (starred review)

"[Davidson's] anecdotes are captivating, with shrewd lessons on management, marketing, and strategy. . . . Readers with a start-up yen will find useful and inspiring insights here."

—*Publishers Weekly*

"I love Adam Davidson's book. This is the golden moment for the marriage of passion and excellence, a time for optimism, not pessimism. The opportunity to create great businesses you love and that your customers come to love lies around every corner. The heart of every economy is small enterprise, not large. We have waited a long time for this book, and brother, does it deliver. Bravo!"

—Tom Peters, author of *The Excellence Dividend*

ADAM DAVIDSON

# THE PASSION ECONOMY

Adam Davidson is the cofounder of NPR's *Planet Money* podcast and has been an economics writer for *The New Yorker* and
*The New York Times Magazine*. He has won many of journalism's most prestigious awards, including a Peabody for his cov-
erage of the financial crisis. He is now the CEO and cofounder
of Three Uncanny Four, a passion-based podcast production
company.

www.adamdavidson.com

# THE PASSION ECONOMY

# THE PASSION ECONOMY

### THE NEW RULES FOR THRIVING
### IN THE TWENTY-FIRST CENTURY

## ADAM DAVIDSON

**VINTAGE BOOKS**

A DIVISION OF PENGUIN RANDOM HOUSE LLC

NEW YORK

FIRST VINTAGE BOOKS EDITION, NOVEMBER 2020

The Library of Congress has cataloged the Knopf edition as follows:
Names: Davidson, Adam, author.
Title: The passion economy : the new rules for thriving in the
twenty-first century / Adam Davidson.
Description: First edition. | New York : Alfred A. Knopf, 2020. |
Includes index.
Identifiers: LCCN 2019022771 (print) | LCCN 2019022772 (ebook)
Subjects: LCSH: Economic history—21st century. | Businesspeople—Case
studies. | Economic forecasting.
Classification: LCC HC59.3 .D38 2020 (print) | LCC HC59.3 (ebook) |
DDC 330.9—dc23
LC record available at https://lccn.loc.gov/2019022771

**Vintage Books Trade Paperback ISBN: 978-0-8041-7277-6**
**eBook ISBN: 978-0-385-35353-3**

Author photograph © Michael Lionstar
Book design by Soonyoung Kwon

www.vintagebooks.com

Printed in the United States of America
10  9  8  7  6  5  4  3  2  1

For Jen,
without whom there would be nothing

Always remember that you are absolutely unique.
Just like everyone else.

Often attributed to MARGARET MEAD


You must learn from the mistakes of others—
you will never live long enough
to make them all yourself.

*Human Engineering,*
BY HARRY MYERS AND MASON M. ROBERTS, 1932

# CONTENTS

# PREFACE

When I think about the change in the economy, the change that has shifted the United States and most of the rest of the world from one sort of economic system to an entirely different one, I think about my dad and my grandfather and how hard it was for them to understand each other.

My father's father, Stanley, was born in 1917 and died a century later, still a tall, proud man with a thick head of hair that was naturally black until his last decade. Stanley looked to me like Superman: strong chin, chest pushed forward, posture erect. He didn't have time for frivolity. He was a serious man who did serious work. With his young grandchildren, he had a routine: a firm handshake followed by a gift of a twenty-dollar bill and some vague homily about doing good work, after which we were dismissed. I cannot remember ever speaking to him when I was young; I only recall smiling, shaking hands, and rushing off. When I became an adult and, to his surprise and mine, a reporter covering economics, I was able to talk with him about the one topic he truly loved: business.

My dad (also named Stanley, though he has always gone by his middle name, Jack) could not be more different. He is an actor who, for as long as I can remember, has told me that the most wonderful part of his profession is that you remain child-like your entire life. As I write this, my dad is eighty-three and has maintained an imaginative, exuberant view of the world. He is riveted by children and loves to hear every word my young son says, after which he calls out, "Did you hear that? He made up an amazing story!" My dad has always been fascinated by pretty much everything—science, the news, art, history, sports. There is only one subject he has always found unbearably boring, perhaps a bit evil, and entirely unworthy of discussion: business.

In a sense, this book is a reconciliation of the conflict between these two Stanleys, these two men who lived in the same country at the same time but might as well have been on entirely different planets. For most of the twentieth century, the overwhelming majority of men and women were forced to make a choice when it came to work: follow the money or follow their passion; become like my grandfather or become like my dad. But now, more than ever before, business and art, profit and passion, are linked. They have come together in a way that would have made no sense to either of the Stanleys in the past.

To illuminate the transition I describe and celebrate in this book, let me tell you more about my grandfather, since he is a pretty representative stand-in for the entire twentieth-century economy. Stanley Jacob Davidson, Sr., was born in New England to young parents who were cut off from their own families. His father was a Jewish immigrant whose parents had disowned him—even practiced mourning rituals as if he had died—when he impregnated and then married a Christian dance-hall girl. The dance-hall girl was, herself, alienated from her family—a rough clan barely eking out a living in a remote corner of Maine. The new broke and broken family in Worcester, Massachusetts, faced unending crises, culminating in Stanley's father's death of tuberculosis when my grandfather was only five. His mother, overwhelmed, put Stanley and his brother in an orphanage for much of a year before taking them out again with the provision that, even as grade schoolers, they would need to work and bring money to the family. Decades later, Stanley was still prouder of his childhood business (he bought hens, built an incubator, and sold eggs to neighbors) than of anything else he would go on to accomplish in his life.

Before he was twenty, while the Great Depression was ravaging the country's economy, Stanley was married with a young son (my dad), soon to be followed by three more children. He was lucky to get a factory job that paid sixteen dollars a week. The factory made external grinders: large machines that spin two parallel cylinders of metal, coated with an abrasive, sandpaper-like surface. The cylinders could grind a metal cube into a perfectly smooth sphere in seconds. This is how ball bearings are made. It was brutal, dangerous work. This was the era of big men in blue overalls working in hot factories dodging sparks, their bodies covered in a mix of sweat and grease. For those who worked alongside Stanley, the tiny particles of metal dust made coughing and sneezing a sharp, painful, often bloody agony.

But overall, the ball bearing business was good for Stanley, especially with the start of World War II. "You can't fight a war without ball bearings," Stanley used to say. And it's true. Every moving piece on every war machine—the tires, the guns, the gun turrets, the tank treads, the tank rifles—moves because it has ball bearings at its joints. Stanley worked two shifts a day, often six days a week.

The postwar economic boom was even better for the ball bearing business and for Stanley. America had a lot of building to do—the interstate highway system; suburbs filled with houses, roads, and sewers; cities that grew much bigger; factories getting larger and more efficient—and every bit of building required ball bearings. They were in the wheels and gears of tractors and cranes and the machinery inside the factories and in the elevators and escalators in those tall buildings.

Stanley worked hard and was promoted, again and again, and eventually ran the factory. He was smart and good at strategic thinking. But his core management ability was that he was tough. He saw a factory floor as a machine and each man (it was almost entirely men) as a cog in that machinery. They could be annoying cogs, always complaining about this or that, but a strong manager knew how to shut their complaining down and get them back to work.

Did Stanley love ball bearings? Did he have a particular passion about them? No, he most certainly did not. He got the job because his father-in-law knew a guy, and he stayed in the job because that's what you did when you had a job: you stayed and tried to get promoted. He retired after fifty-four years, having worked at the same company his entire adult life.

Every moment of his life reinforced the same lesson: hard work is how people take care of their loved ones, how countries stay free, how life improves for everybody. Stop working, even for a moment, and everything will fall apart. He worked. His wife took care of the kids. And those kids barely knew the man who was rarely at home and, when there, was often angry and impatient. My dad says he had no idea what Stanley did for a living, only that whatever it was seemed awful.

From an early age, my dad had passions. He loved telling stories; he loved making people laugh; he loved daydreaming about a life much more fun and expansive than the grim, plodding one of his father. In the Worcester of the 1940s, a boy like Jack—a bright but indifferent student who cracked jokes and hung out with friends instead of working—could be assessed only one way: he was trouble. He would either be tamed or become a lifelong loser: broke, drunk, maybe in prison. My father internalized this view. He drank and smoked and got into fights and was suspended a dozen times before the principal expelled him. When Stanley learned of the expulsion, he told my dad that he could no longer live at home. He washed his hands of him.

My dad was on his own, working at a shoe factory, at sixteen. It was miserably boring work, nailing heels onto shoes one after the other, all day long. He can remember saying to himself, "My life is over. Already." His father, it seemed, had been right. Men who follow their passions go nowhere. My dad certainly couldn't think of any grown man he had met who had successfully built a life of fun and personal expression. That was for wealthy people and drunks.

Over the next several years, my dad had a series of unlikely experiences that led to precisely the life he wanted. He joined the marines, thinking it would transform him into the man his father wanted him to be. After his discharge, he managed to get into the University of Massachusetts at Amherst. He didn't do well and was about to flunk out when a friend asked for a favor. The friend was putting on a play in the school's theater department, and one of the actors had pulled out at the last minute. Could Jack, please, fill in? It was an easy role: my dad just needed to act like he was drunk and lurch across the stage. His first step in front of the curtain drew a huge laugh from the audience, and that was that. My dad had found his life's work. He would be an actor. He had never met a professional actor. He had never seen a play. But he transferred to Boston University and entered the theater school.

For Stanley, the announcement of this career was absurd, enraging. *Why not be a butterfly chaser or a unicorn rider? An actor? You're going to pretend that you are someone else for a living? You're going to play dress-up as a job? That is not what a man does. A man works, for money, and then uses that money to pay for a home for his wife and children. Who ever told you work was supposed to be fun? Who is going to pay you? Actors make no money. They don't get regular paychecks. They are not men.*

My dad nonetheless pursued his dream and has been a working actor for almost sixty years. We were never rich, and there were some worrisome months here and there, but for the most part, he made enough of a living to raise two children in New York City. We understood—because he told us all the time—that he had made a conscious choice to pursue his passion, his dream, instead of pursuing money. And he would say he did that to be a good father, to be a model for his children, to show them that they, too, could pursue their passions and their dreams, even if they were never going to get rich or, at times, maintain financial stability at all.

We lived in Westbeth Artists Housing, a building in the Greenwich Village neighborhood of New York City. It was created in 1970, the year of my birth, by a group of philanthropists and the federal government to offer subsidized housing for artists. It's still there—my dad lives in the same apartment I grew up in—and houses about one thousand people: painters and dancers and poets and musicians and actors, other artists and their families who pay rent far below the market rate. It is a special place, a community of people doing, roughly, the very opposite of what Stanley believed was right.

When I began my adult life in the 1990s, I believed the stories the two Stanleys told. I believed that I had a choice to make: money or passion, financial comfort or fulfillment. It made sense. That was the economic reality of the previous hundred years and a message I had received over and over. I wanted to be a playwright, but I also wanted more financial stability than that life could offer. So I took what felt like a middle-ground job: I became a journalist. I could write and learn, travel and explore. But I could also get a paycheck and have a retirement account and all those sensible things. Growing up in artists' housing in the 1970s, I had heard from grown-ups that everything is worthy of exploration—sex and drugs and personal expression. There was only one area of inquiry to be avoided: money. Money was the opposite of art, the opposite of passion. So I rebelled in, perhaps, the only way I could. I became an economics reporter, covering business, finance, markets, and other forbidden topics.

As I learned how the economy works, I came to understand the world of my Stanleys with even more rigor. There is a clear economic logic to the twentieth-century triumph of ball bearings over acting. Ball bearings are a fundamental product, necessary for almost all other economic activity. They don't require passion or invention. A ball bearing in 1999 had the same essential function as a ball bearing in 1919. The difference was that companies had gotten better at making more of them more quickly and cheaply and reliably. That was the heart of my grandfather's career: removing inefficiencies so that the same thing could be made more cheaply and overseeing research and development so that the products became ever so slightly better each year. That was, in fact, the heart of the twentieth-century economy. Economists call it production-side growth, which means that most companies, most of the time, made their profit by cutting the cost of production.

This efficiency extended to the ways our economic goods spread around the country and the world. At the beginning of the twentieth century, most markets were local; most people bought things made nearby. But with the expansion of rail and then the highway system and then commercial air travel and the hyperefficiency of containerized shipping, markets became national and, eventually, global. Increasing trade across state and then national boundaries meant that one ball bearing maker could sell ball bearings all over the world and would have to compete with other ball bearing makers all over the world, so everybody worked even harder to become even more efficient at making the same thing more quickly and cheaply. If a worker proved an ability to do this routine work and to spot inefficiencies and get rid of them, that worker would make a better living. That's what my grandfather did. The widget economy excluded people like my dad. A factory can't be efficient if each worker is pursuing a distinct passionate view of how best to work. The economic logic fed our culture and our educational system. People who followed the rules and accommodated the needs of a large organization thrived; those who didn't, failed.

Of course, there have always been passionate outsiders like my dad. A few of them did remarkably well. Bob Dylan, Diana Ross, Marlon Brando, and Joan Rivers, for instance, were able to pursue their own passions, be unrelentingly themselves, and still thrive economically. But, tellingly, they succeeded through a very widgetized distribution system. The music and television industries had a lot in common with ball bearings. They transformed creative work into mass production, distributing the work to as many people as possible at the lowest production cost.

Most creative, passion-fueled people lived lives roughly equivalent to my dad's. He spent most of his career on the stage, performing roles in relatively small theaters off-Broadway or at various regional stage companies around the country. It is a rough way to make a living, traveling from job to job, going to auditions, getting rejected, hoping a casting person says yes. Even when you get work, it doesn't pay a lot. Live theater isn't scalable in the way that a television show is. Performing on a stage in front of real people is intimate, personal, and, at its best, incredibly passionate. But it can reach only those physically present. (His income was sporadic, although there were enough big paydays from movies, commercials, and the occasional Broadway show or guest spot on a television program that, as I said earlier, we never suffered. Still, he was an exception. Few of the actors he started with are acting today. When he went to the fifty-year reunion for the Boston University School of Theatre class of 1963, he learned he was the only graduate there still making his living from acting.)

My father and his father had an uneasy relationship for most of my life. Each man looked at the other with pity and disappointment, and they rarely spoke or spent time together. I became a bit of a translator. I understood both worlds—business and art, responsibility and passion—well enough that

I could talk with both men and feel proud of both of them, even if they had succeeded in such radically different ways. But they never really understood each other. How could they?

Now the era of the warring Stanleys is over. That is what this book is about. Our economy can no longer be described with the simple binary of the twentieth century, where on one side is money, stability, and routinization and on the other is passion, personal expression, and financial uncertainty. The two Stanleys are now one. To succeed financially we must embrace our unique passions. We have to pay close attention to those interests and abilities that make each of us different. Becoming diligent about doing the same thing in the same way as others is the surest path to financial mediocrity or even ruin. That does not mean that this is now the era of my dad, where self-expression is sufficient for a successful career. We need a fair bit of my grandfather's business sense, too. Simply pursuing one's passion is not enough. We must pay close attention to the marketplace, seeking out novel ways to match our particular set of passions with those people who most value them. At the core of this book are stories of people who have figured this out and have been able to model an entirely new way of living, one that combines the financial goal of my grandfather's work with the personal passion and joy of my dad's.

The widget economy that gave my grandfather so much became too widgetized—it scaled up so much that it left most of the workers behind. Walk into a factory, any factory, today and you won't see a bunch of men like Stanley, wearing blue overalls, covered in grease, going home exhausted but proud of a day's work. Instead, you'll see machines—big, clean, white machines. There are only a handful of people. Those people don't lift things or bend metal. They wear clean white coats and are specially trained to program the computers that tell the machines what to do. Manufacturing in America never died. America makes more stuff worth more money than ever before. But American manufacturing *employment* disappeared, almost entirely, and the widget-type jobs that replaced it are worse. They are low-paying retail jobs that offer little chance for advancement. The Stanley of today, a young man with a growing family and no college degree, would have little hope of retiring—as the actual Stanley did—with three nice homes, a few million dollars in the bank, and the pride of a successful career. The world that gave my grandfather, Stanley, so much opportunity was destroyed by two forces: technology and trade. Computers and the machines they run are much better at performing routine tasks than humans are. Today, robots make the robots that make ball bearings. At the same time, increasing global trade means that those tasks that do require human labor are increasingly often performed in low-wage countries. This is not a one-time transition. Countless hundreds of thousands of consultants, engineers, and business strategists are constantly studying technology and global markets to figure out how to make more things with fewer people.

This is not all bad news. The same forces—technology and trade—that destroyed the widget economy have given birth to what I call the Passion Economy. The Internet allows people who want to sell a unique product or service to find customers all over the world. Automation makes it possible for people to manufacture their unique products without needing to build a factory first. Advances in trade mean that those unique products can be delivered to the people who most value them, wherever they happen to be.

This book lays out the economics of how this change happened and how you can take advantage of it. I have always found abstraction hard to follow, hard to apply to my own life, so this book is made up chiefly of stories, stories about regular folks who aren't geniuses and who weren't born to wealthy, connected families. I find it most helpful to learn from people whose stories are relatable, people who overcame familiar struggles by applying simple, accessible lessons. Many of the people in this book took a long, rough journey to reach their success, and every one of them hopes that their story can make your journey less challenging. They want you, like them, to unlock your secret passion and turn it into a thriving business and a good life.

So here we go: on to the Passion Economy. For me, this book is the culmination of years of research, during which I have been shadowing entrepreneurs. I have spent many hours discussing theories with professors, reading academic journal articles, calling skeptics, arguing through fine points.

So many people in the media, politics, and the general public seem convinced that the American Dream has collapsed, that our economy will work only for the very few and the rest are screwed.

Well, I disagree. You're not screwed. Yes, there are new challenges, but virtually everyone can have a richer life, in every sense of the word. Perhaps most radically of all, I believe that this better life is not all that hard to achieve. It's within reach for tens of millions of Americans who, right now, are very nervous about their economic future. Thriving won't require an Ivy League degree or any inherent genius. On the contrary, with a handful of easy-to-learn rules, a shift of perspective, and a bit of hard work, a meaningful marriage of passion and business can be forged, and far more people can do a whole lot better.

# THE PASSION ECONOMY

# CHAPTER 1

# A SHOE SALESMAN'S SON AT MIT

*The son of a brilliant failed entrepreneur learns that anybody who follows a few simple rules can thrive in our new economy*

The central building of MIT's Sloan School of Management is designed to send the powerful signal that it is a place where people look to the future. It is all curved, with steel and glass, with a massive, multistory atrium, marble walls, and a clean, modern look that suggests that it is a temple for the efficient exploration of new technology. I had gone to MIT to meet with Scott Stern, whose official title is "professor, technological innovation, entrepreneurship, and strategic management."

I had come across Scott while researching a hunch. At NPR's *Planet Money* and then at *The New York Times Magazine*, my job was to report about the economy. During the financial crisis and the years immediately after, much of my work was, frankly, quite depressing. I kept interviewing people whose lives had been devastated, their homes repossessed, their credit shot. I reported on entire industries that had collapsed. Now and then, though, I came across someone who was thriving. Taken together, these were people who didn't stand out as brilliant or credentialed or well connected. These were regular folks—an accountant in South Carolina, some Amish guys in Ohio, a lesbian couple in Brooklyn, a fellow making brushes on Long Island—who had somehow figured out that the very forces that were wreaking havoc around them also brought new opportunities. Each of them had looked at a traditional and struggling industry and invented a new way of succeeding in it. These were not billionaires or people featured on the covers of magazines or individuals who had become household names, but they were all earning a good living, building wealth, and providing a better life for their families than they had once thought possible.

I read pretty much every business book that becomes well known, and one thing about them has always struck me. Countless books explain how to be the CEO of a massive corporation or how to create a Silicon Valley start-up that will make you unimaginably rich. There are so many books that recount how once-in-a-generation geniuses made their fortune. But there are so few books about the kinds of folks I was discovering, those who looked at a terrifying economy and found a clear path to stability and wealth when, all around them, their peers were anxious. I collected these people; I published stories about some and kept details about others in a file on my computer. Eventually, I had found so many of these folks that I became convinced that this was a widely known trend, and I was the last to learn of it. But as I called around to business school professors and small business associations and thumbed through every book and searched every website I thought could be useful, I found that there didn't seem to be anybody looking at them.

That is, until I discovered Scott Stern. I was making my hundredth (or was it thousandth?) call to a business school professor in a failing attempt to find someone, anyone, who could explain how regular folks can succeed in this economy. I kept rediscovering the same thing. Business and economics professors don't, generally, think about this. They have lots of research and advice for people who want to launch billion-dollar start-ups or become heads of banks. They know how to analyze labor market data to identify trends. As a group, though, they don't have an answer to the question most of us most want them to address: How can a regular person do well in a rapidly changing economy? Then, one day, I was talking to one of these professors and asking this question yet again when the professor said, "Oh, I think Scott knows about this. You should talk to him."

I wonder how many people have met and quickly dismissed Scott. He looks like he could be cast in a movie as "generic business guy." He wears the same outfit every day: a white button-down shirt, dark pants, and dark shoes, with a cell phone strapped to his belt. He has neat dark hair (though it becomes unruly when he gets excited, which is often). He could be an accountant, a computer programmer, a dentist.

Scott also has a particular vocal tic that, at first, I found a bit maddening. In the middle of a sentence, he will repeat the same phrase three, four, ten times in a row: "I just mean to say. I just mean to say. I just mean to say." Or, "I thought it might be helpful. I thought it might be helpful. I thought it might be helpful. I thought it might be helpful." At our first meeting, I noticed that he would interrupt me when I was in the middle of a sentence, repeating one of his phrases: "I just mean to say. I just mean to say. I just mean to say. I just mean to say. I just mean to say . . ." *If you just mean to say something*, I thought, *then say it! Or let me finish what I was saying.*

During that meeting, *I* almost dismissed Scott. But some instinct told me to stay, be patient, listen. When I got past first impressions, I (like a lot of people) learned that Scott is an exciting, inspiring business thinker. His mind combines nimble experimentation—hurtling all over the place as it explores the contours of a thought—with a tightly focused precision, allowing him to zero in on the core issue and lay it out with granular clarity. The verbal tic, I came to realize, is a sign that the Stern brain machinery is working, the functional equivalent of a blinking light showing that a computer's hard drive is being accessed. If I wait a bit, let the tic run its course (it takes only a few seconds, even if it seems a lot longer), he will come out with something brilliant.

Having now spent many hours with him, I realize that our most fruitful talks were those that veered quickly and seemingly randomly from topic to topic, open ends left unresolved. I sometimes found these exchanges stimulating but would be frustrated by the lack of a conclusion, assuming that I would soon depart with nothing to take away. *What, exactly, did we talk about? How did we get from wondering about McDonald's all-day-breakfast strategy to that assessment of medieval castle defenses to that story about a former student who now makes clothing?* The fact is, though, Scott doesn't leave these threads unresolved. All of a sudden, he stands up, saying, "I thought it might be helpful. I thought it might be helpful. I thought it might be helpful. I thought it might be helpful." As he repeats this, he grabs a marker and starts drawing a diagram on a whiteboard. Soon he reveals that we haven't been having an aimless, wandering bull session. We have been constructing a careful argument, a precise view of the world, one whose logic Scott will then lay out in stunning clarity.

Someone once told me that there are two kinds of geniuses. One is the person who says things you could never have thought of and don't fully understand after hearing them. That genius reveals the massive gulf between you and him or her. Albert Einstein describing his theory of relativity is the ultimate example. The other type of genius is a person who can take a jumble of confused thoughts and reassemble them so clearly, so simply, that it makes you feel as if you, yourself, are the genius, since you now fully understand something that was in there, in confused form, in your brain, all along. Scott Stern is that second kind of genius.

Scott has done an awful lot in his career. But his most important contribution and the one that makes him an essential part of this book is his most recent. Scott, along with some friends, has revealed the previously unknown rules of entrepreneurship, something that many had thought impossible. This is no small thing. Entrepreneurship has, historically, been the realm of a tiny group of outliers, a brilliant, privileged few who can build new businesses on the force of their will, daring, and access to capital. No more. Scott has shown that entrepreneurship—like swimming or speaking French—can be taught to almost anybody willing to spend some time and expend some effort. If his conclusions are accepted broadly, they might be able to transform the world. How many people continue in jobs they don't love, working for insufficient wages, because they don't believe they have the inherent gifts necessary to follow their dreams and take control of their economic lives?

I wonder—as does Scott—if he would have ever unlocked the secret of entrepreneurship if it weren't for those damn Striker sneakers his dad made him wear. When Scott was in junior high school in the 1980s, his father, in one of his unsuccessful schemes, bought a container load of about ten thousand pairs of sneakers from a factory in Korea at a ridiculously cheap three dollars each and imported them to Long Island. His dad was sure he would sell them quickly. After all, these sneakers, he said, came from the same factory as Nikes, which were going for ten times as much. But nobody wanted off-brand, super-cheap sneakers, so they stayed in the family garage, in huge piles, sorted by size. Whenever Scott or one of his siblings needed a new pair of shoes, they would beg their father to let them buy Nike or Adidas or any shoe that their friends wouldn't mock. Generic shoes, with a big dumb S on them, were humiliating. Everyone else had swooshes or stripes, signaling that their parents could afford shoes with style. Their dad, of course, would point to the garage and tell them to find whatever size they needed. When I visited Mr. Stern a full thirty years later, he asked me my shoe size and offered me a pair, from the pile still in that garage. (I politely declined.)

Scott's dad, Eitan Stern, was born in Israel, the son of parents who had fled Germany just before the Holocaust. In Germany, they had been wealthy, but in their haste to escape the Nazis they lost everything. Israel, during Eitan's youth, was still a poor, socialist country struggling to build itself. Surrounded by nations that objected fiercely to the new country's presence in the Middle East, Israelis understood that the possibility of war was never very far off. Having fled one conflagration, Eitan's parents decided to leave before finding themselves in the midst of another.

The family moved to the United States and settled on Long Island. Eitan, a teenager who spoke no English, felt lost. A biology teacher took an interest in him and offered guidance. To Eitan, the teacher (who had his students call him by his first name, Hank) was the perfect American man. He was athletic, a hunter, and he spent his weekends running a fishing charter out in the Atlantic. Before long, Eitan was there all weekend long, serving as Hank's mate on the ship. Hank would be up on the bridge steering the ship, and Eitan would be on the deck helping their customers—six or ten or, when it was really crowded, twenty businesspeople going out for the day. Eitan quickly became a fishing expert and would effortlessly bounce from one customer to the next, baiting their hooks or helping reel in a fish. "I would yell at these guys," Eitan remembers. "I was seventeen or eighteen or nineteen, and I was hollering at the chief executive of E. F. Hutton, 'You're not doing things right. Keep the tip of the rod up!'"

Hank and Eitan developed a great routine. Back in those days, the 1960s, there were still huge schools of fish twenty or so miles off the coast. Hank would pilot the ship right to the center of a big school. Eitan would dump chum off the side of the boat, inspiring a feeding frenzy. "You could catch dozens of fish in a matter of minutes," he remembers. The clients loved it; they felt like pros. Eitan would efficiently slice the fish into fillets. Usually, the clients wanted, at most, six or so servings for dinner. The rest—hundreds of pounds of fresh fish—were Eitan's to do with as he pleased, so he sold them to restaurants near the port. Add in the generous tips the clients gave him, and Eitan was pulling in over a thousand dollars a week. "I was making more money than I knew what to do with," he said.

As it turned out, those summers were the high point of Eitan Stern's business career. He never again made more money than he knew what to do with, though not for lack of trying. Eitan spent his entire career in the fishing industry, selling fishing tackle and fishing rods. At first, he was a salesman, working for a local company that imported fishing tackle from South Korea and Taiwan. He traveled all over the eastern United States, throughout the South and the mid-Atlantic and much of the Midwest, developing relationships with small bait shops and big sporting goods stores. He also traveled frequently to Asia to visit the factories where the products were made. After a while, he grew tired of working for others, especially when his employer, the owner of the import business, retired and his indifferent son took over. So when Scott was seven years old, Eitan went out on his own.

For most of Scott's childhood, Eitan was an entrepreneur, starting and running a series of businesses, all with the same basic premise: he would buy decent-quality products in Asia at a discount and bring them to the United States; then he would sell them for about half the price of the competing products made by big-name brands. He could undercut Berkley, Wright & McGill, Penn Fishing, and all the other high-end brands, and would attest that his products were just as good. Having started with the small, cheaper stuff—lures and weights—he eventually moved into the rods and reels themselves, the more expensive and higher-margin parts of the industry. He bought a brand name, Striker—he loved how it sounded—and would visit the Asian factories he hired to produce the Striker goods so he could guide them in custom-making the perfect fishing gear, designed for performance, durability, and cost. He even visited auto shows each year, to see what the hottest new car colors were and then use those colors on his rods.

Today, although Eitan is a heavyset man with a white Santa Claus beard who walks with some difficulty, his bearing still hints at the young, handsome athlete he once was. Even as he describes failures in his career, he speaks with a confident, booming voice. Hearing Eitan describe the business, even now, decades after it failed, it's easy to be seduced by his enthusiasm. How could it not have worked?

His most reliable customers were small bait shops—particularly in Florida—where he had developed good relationships with the owners. They would tell their more thrifty customers about the great deal available with Striker rods, reels, and tackle. These loyal customers gave Eitan enough business that he did fine for a while. He bought a small but comfortable house and was able to afford the occasional vacation for his family. But he never made enough to get ahead.

He never could scrape up the funds for a marketing campaign, and the one or two additional salespeople he could afford to hire had enough work maintaining the company's current customers, so there was no chance of extending his customer base outside of those small Florida shacks and his other clients. He would borrow and save to pay for another container load of rods and reels, and then spend months hustling, trying to move them through a supply chain controlled by others. He never got a celebrity sponsor the way other companies did. (Indeed, a handful of wildly popular fishing celebrities make their livings promoting various fishing gear brands.)

Then there was his brief foray into sneakers. The sneakers laid out the flaws in his business model quite neatly (if disastrously). In his mind, Eitan had found a product that he knew was just as good as the competition. He was on the factory floor; he saw how they were made. He knew which materials went into them. He knew that anybody paying more than he was charging was a fool. Anybody who took the time to compare products would realize that he was offering them a bargain. But, of course, nobody took the time. Nobody else knew how great his products were. Nobody distinguished them from cheap, shoddily made knockoffs.

There are a lot of Eitan Sterns in America. There are more than thirty million officially registered small businesses, most of which are sole proprietorships—a house painter, an accountant, a beautician working for him- or herself—and nearly six million have employees. About two out of three new jobs are in small businesses, not large ones. If it weren't for small businesses, our economy would be in far more dire shape.

Many of these small firms, like Eitan's, struggle to grow and survive. It's a puzzle. Eitan is quite smart. "My dad is much smarter than I am," said Scott, one of the smartest people I know. His dad worked incredibly hard—too hard, probably, spending months of the year on the road and in the air, visiting factories in Asia and meeting his clients all over the United States. He knew just about everything there was to know about the fishing industry. He could spend hours explaining how different types of lures are made and which features attract more fish and which ones do nothing for the fish but do seem to lure overpaying customers. His knowledge was encyclopedic. He knew about the raw materials that went into fishing rods, reels, and tackle; he knew about the factories that made the items, the supply chain, and the different types of retailers who delivered the items to the end customer. He also knew a lot about those customers. He knew the difference among hobbyists, fishing club members, and those for whom fishing was a central part of their lives. For all of this, he never could figure out how to thrive. He was never, as Scott said, able to jump above "somewhere between being middle-class and not."

Scott never much liked fishing, though by ten years old he was a frequent fisher. He could have done a great job on a fishing charter boat, like his dad, but that wasn't for him. He was a math prodigy. When he was eight, his third-grade teacher told Eitan that they had a genius on their hands. When Scott was ten, in 1979, he began writing computer programs, even though most people then, including Scott's parents and teachers, had no idea what a computer program was. By twelve, Scott was creating software that could help Eitan keep track of his business.

It is striking that Scott, this young math and computer genius, was honing his interest in studying business just as his father's business was crumbling. Scott's analytic acuity would have allowed him to be an accomplished engineer, software developer, mathematician, or physicist. Instead, once at New York University, he decided to study economics, which combined all of his interests: math, history, and even the confounding riddle of why his dad had failed when others succeeded.

As an undergraduate, Scott didn't find the answers to his questions about his dad. His economics classes were abstract—lots of graphs about supply and demand and something called "the efficient frontier." No specific human beings were mentioned in any of his economics classes. His courses were entirely about these purely theoretical "agents" who reacted to prices the way robots would react to a software command. There was nothing that explained why some people thrived and others didn't or why truly brilliant, hardworking people could fail while much dumber, lazier folks succeeded. Having been admitted to the prestigious Stanford University graduate program in economics, Scott hoped to get his answers there.

He arrived in Palo Alto only a few weeks after graduating from college and saw, immediately, that he was one of the youngest graduate students. Most of his classmates had spent a few years in the business world or had already earned a master's degree in economics. All entering graduate students were required to take the same advanced math course, and Scott quickly realized that he was way behind the others. One phrase came up in almost every class: "comparative statics." It's a technical term that most people have never heard of, but it is essential to any economic analysis. Scott had no idea what the words meant and was too embarrassed to ask. He decided that he would drop out of graduate school, move back to his parents' place on Long Island, and figure out something else to do with his life.

In a deep funk, Scott went to the basement of the dorm he was living in to do his laundry. Another graduate student, Joshua Gans, was there. Joshua is a brilliant, intense Australian who had published some serious economic papers while still in college. He was comfortable with the math and other technical details. He was good at everything that Scott felt incapable of doing well. Scott told Joshua he was giving up. Joshua, who would become Scott's lifelong intellectual partner and close friend, has a remarkable ability to remove emotion from a question and structure a series of objective criteria with which to analyze a problem. He laid out the many reasons Scott should, indeed, quit. He was lousy at math, at least when compared to the other graduate students. He was far too young. He was a bit emotional and struggled to push himself through challenges. Joshua told Scott he had been watching him, paying attention to the comments he made in class and while sitting around the dorm discussing economic issues. He said that Scott might not realize it, but he possessed a stunning ability to link economic theories to the real world. Scott was always asking how all those graphs and math formulas reflected the actual behavior of human beings. Joshua told him that being good at math was helpful, sure, in economics, but having Scott's ability was far more important. He might struggle a bit in graduate school, but if he held on to his big, important questions, he could make a real difference in people's lives.

Thanks to that fateful laundry room talk, Scott decided to stay in graduate school. Before long, he met his first mentor, Nathan Rosenberg, who seconded Joshua's opinions about him. Rosenberg's office was a quiet sanctuary, a reprieve from the highly competitive graduate school program and the general vibe of lively ambition on Stanford's campus. Rosenberg, nearing seventy, provided an almost perfect model for the kind of career Scott wanted. He had grown up in New Jersey, in a working-class family, and, like Scott, had done all right in school but had never been a superstar. He graduated from Rutgers, got his economics PhD at the University of Wisconsin, and went on to a career spent writing thoughtful analyses of the Industrial Revolution. While nobody would suggest that Rosenberg's books were entertaining thrillers, they were much closer to popular history than traditional economics tomes. His books had no mathematical formulas and few abstractions. Instead, he carefully studied the history of specific fields—metallurgy, electricity, aircraft engines—and analyzed their social and political contexts. He wrote about real people and explored why some innovations and businesspeople thrived and others did not.

Finally, Scott thought, he had found someone who shared his passion for applying economics to real-world situations. Scott and Rosenberg worked together on a major paper about a seemingly obvious idea: that businesspeople face a lot of uncertainty. Specifically, when someone has a new idea that she would like to bring to the market, she doesn't know if it will work or not and can't foretell if anybody will be willing to pay for it. This was such a basic and obvious idea that few economists had spent time thinking about it. It certainly wasn't factored into their various models of how the economy works.

Scott and Rosenberg dug deep into the complicated histories of the development of the laser, the radio, the computer. They observed that the initial inventors had no way of knowing whether or not their inventions would ever become popular products. For example, the laser, one of the most consequential inventions of the 1950s, was conceived by brothers-in-law Charles Townes and Arthur Schawlow as a side project, a bit of hobbyist fun they could do when not engaged in their serious work at Bell Labs.

According to traditional economics, there was little incentive for these innovators to spend long hours in their labs, year after year, developing ideas that had a good chance of being worthless. Indeed, why would these people have spent so much time and effort seeking to invent something they thought was worth so little?

It was hard to answer these questions through historical accounts about long-dead businesspeople and inventors. Scott wanted to find living people who were making these same sorts of decisions. He learned about some inventors who had worked to synthesize an artificial form of insulin. Insulin, of course, is an essential medicine for people with diabetes. Before its discovery in the 1920s, people with diabetes had died quickly and painfully. Doctors had devised ways of extracting insulin from the pancreas of dogs, cows, and pigs. This was expensive and did not produce enough of the substance to keep everyone with diabetes alive. In the late 1970s, several groups of medical researchers and biotech firms had been in a race to come up with an inexpensive, reliable synthetic insulin. It was a perfect case study. Scott was able to learn why scientists had made specific choices. Why did some stay at a company that paid them less money and had a slimmer chance of success? Why did one group focus obsessively on narrow areas of research while others pursued a wide range of different possible paths? This work eventually became a key component of Scott's PhD dissertation, which, when made public, caused a minor sensation in the field of economics.

Scott's paper showed that scientists and entrepreneurs take into account a whole host of considerations that are not explicitly economic before they launch a new company or a new research project. Some highly value the ability to work with the smartest people in the field, others prize the creative freedom to follow their hunches wherever they may go, and still others want to make as much money as possible. Scott also found a fascinating interplay between new start-ups, entrepreneurial companies created to find synthetic insulin, and the large pharmaceutical companies—the so-called Big Pharma firms—which were likely to pay top dollar to whichever small entrepreneur first cracked the secret. For his dissertation research, Scott took a page from his mentor, Nathan Rosenberg, using journalistic techniques to report on specific people at specific companies—something economists rarely do. He also used mathematical models and systematic empirical data to give the entire story more rigor.

To a non-economist, Scott's work may seem obvious. Of course different human beings want different things. But economists had, for a long time, believed that individual differences don't matter. Yes, maybe one person likes scientific discovery, doesn't care so much about money, and prefers chocolate ice cream to strawberry; someone else loves money above all things and hates chocolate. But when you look at a population of millions or billions of people, you can average out all these individual differences and assume that they don't matter in the aggregate.

Since at least World War II, economists had become obsessed with mathematical models. They built models that calculated the interplay of inflation, employment, interest rates, economic growth, and other considerations. The economists who thrived, the ones who got prestigious tenured jobs at the top universities and who received Nobel Prizes, were the brilliant mathematicians who came up with ever more complex theoretical models of the economy. There's no question that they, as a group, did valuable work. By the time Scott came along in the 1990s, though, this old model was beginning to fray. There was a new hunger among economists—and, more important, in the general public—for economic answers to questions that had nothing to do with math and abstract "agents" in a theoretical framework. Americans and people around the world wanted answers to the same question Scott had: Why do some people thrive in the economy and others fall so far behind?

It is no coincidence that the abstraction phase of economics coincided with a period that the field came to call "the Great Compression." For several decades in the middle part of the twentieth century, the American economy worked remarkably well for so many people. It was the only time in history that, for a large population, the poor became richer more quickly than the rich did. It was a period of widespread prosperity, economic stability, and, after the Depression and the First World War, general optimism. Of course, America had many poor people, many people who struggled. Still, nearly everybody in nearly every part of the country was doing much better in 1970 than they had been in 1950. (Of course, some did much better, and there was rampant racial and gender discrimination, yet all demographic groups were, on average, richer in 1970 than they had been in 1950.) Nearly everybody was making more money than their parents had and fully expected that their children would make more money than they did. With such broad-based economic growth, the details of how some people were different from others didn't matter all that much. Who cares if you love risk and I hate it, you like scientific research and I prefer a reliable flow of cash—if we're both making considerably more money than we did a decade ago, we have no reason to zero in on these picky details.

This period of benign, widely shared economic prosperity began to fall apart in the late 1970s. By the time Scott was finishing his dissertation, in 1996, it had become abundantly clear to some people in America (and other wealthy nations) that while some portion of the population was getting very rich indeed, a very significant group of people were struggling. In this period of rising inequality, the economics field was struggling to catch up. Suddenly, the small differences between people mattered a whole lot, because it became increasingly crucial to figure out which of those differences led some to succeed and others to fail. Scott's obscure question about his father's fishing (and shoe) business had become one of the central questions in the field of economics. And he had, by luck, positioned himself to be among the few who might be able to answer the essential question of why some people thrive and others don't, because it required the kind of grounding in both the literature of difference and mathematical economics that Scott possessed in spades.

It is odd that economists and business school professors spend shockingly little time studying the economic and business issues that affect most Americans: the drivers of success and failure in small business. At any given time there are no more than a few thousand large, publicly traded companies and maybe another few thousand technology start-up firms seeking (mostly in vain) to become huge. There are also those tens of millions of small businesses. Only that handful of large or wannabe-large businesses, however, get nearly all the academic attention. With so much focus on the large firms, we know surprisingly little about how small businesses succeed or fail; there is little evidence-based, rigorous study of them. The tools that do exist tend to focus on three areas. The first, and by far the most dominant, is the self-help idea that wealth and opportunity are available if you can just learn to believe in yourself (*Entrepreneur* magazine, June 2015: "6 Actions You Can Take Every Day to Build Your Self-Confidence"; *Forbes*, January 2014: "How to Increase Self-Esteem and Success in Business"; *Inc.* magazine, March 2015: "6 Tips to Build Self-Confidence for Business Success"). The second area of advice centers on coming up with a unique product or service that people will crave. If you create the next iPhone, say, or just a better slice of pizza, you will leave your competition in the dust and make a fortune. The last area of common advice focuses on the basic nuts-and-bolts routines of a decently run business. You should have a business plan and a budget. You should save money when you start and make sure you pay your taxes on time.

For Scott Stern, this is all perfectly reasonable advice. *Of course* you need to provide a product or service people want to buy. *Of course* you should do a decent job of keeping track of money flowing in and flowing out. But after two decades of carefully studying who succeeds and who fails at starting a new business, the key difference between new businesses that succeed and those that don't is *strategy*. All the other issues are important, but they are tactics, and tactics matter only if the strategy is right.

These days, it's common to hear the word "strategy" used in business circles. *What's your innovation strategy? What do you think of Apple's mobile strategy?* All business schools teach a strategy course. There are tens of thousands of books on the subject of business strategy and several organizations devoted to it, including the Association for Strategic Planning and the Strategic Management Society. Every major consulting group, from McKinsey to Bain to PricewaterhouseCoopers, has a strategy arm complete with thousands of strategic advisers.

Nonetheless, the term, "corporate strategy"—this central piece of business thinking—is quite young in the world of commerce. It first appeared in the 1960s, gained some traction in the 1970s, and became a central component of nearly every large business only after 2000. In the fast-growing years after World War II, there was little need for strategy. Simply being a company that sold something was often enough to keep growing. It was only with the rise of global trade and the appearance of computer technology and automation that competition sped up so much that companies couldn't just do the same thing, with minor tweaks, year after year. They had to make careful, difficult decisions about where to put resources and which projects to abandon.

Google's Ngram viewer, which can show the use of a word

or phrase in millions of books, reveals that "corporate strategy" appears only after 1960 and becomes far more commonplace after 1980. No doubt, this is because of the transformative book, *Corporate Strategy*, by Harvard's Michael Porter, which provided the first widely used system for implementing a strategy. The book was focused on the concerns of large businesses and, for years, strategy was mostly something big companies or entire countries did. Small businesses couldn't easily use most of Porter's tools—such as influencing the pricing of widely traded goods—because they were, well, too small.

Strategy was more akin to some form of mystical shamanism than it was to a learnable business tool. This was deliberate. People who, somehow, knew "strategy" made a lot of money because they were seen as wizards, practitioners of a secret art form. This is common in business. Once upon a time, basic accounting was something that only the elite used (in the Middle Ages, basic accounting was a carefully guarded trade secret). Similarly, buying and selling stocks and bonds were, for a long time, the purview of a well-connected privileged class.

After the financial crisis of 2008, Scott assessed his collective body of research and concluded that he had been—without entirely realizing it—translating the work of Porter and others to the concerns of smaller businesses and entrepreneurs. He was ready to turn strategy into a tool like so many others: a clear set of instructions that anybody—including people less smart than his dad—could learn how to use. He knew who he wanted to partner with in this endeavor: his old friend Joshua Gans, the brilliant mathematical economist he had met in the laundry room. Scott called Gans and suggested that they do something audacious, something that no one else had done before. He wanted to create a general theory of success for the small entrepreneurial businessperson. Scott had a lot of big ideas; Gans could help him develop those thoughts and base this general theory on research and mathematical proof. Scott thought they could do it rather quickly.

For two years, the friends worked intensely together. During much of that period, they called each other every day and exchanged a never-relenting flurry of e-mails. Their conversations would often go late into the night, filled with both arguments and laughter. A few times the arguments became too intense—the worst being a blowup over different interpretations of the impact of government funding on insulin research—after which the two men wouldn't speak to each other for weeks. They would each swear off the partnership and pout, and then, inevitably, one would e-mail the other with some new theory and the conversations would immediately resume.

This period was, intellectually, the most thrilling of Scott's life. He laid it out to me at one of our many meetings at his office at MIT. Scott's office has massive windows with a perfect view of the Charles River and the city of Boston. With his verbal tics dialed up, Scott grew increasingly animated as he described the work he and Gans did. He paced the room, his voice loud, as he told me about how all of the various elements of his research and the research of others he admired clicked into place.

Part of what makes Scott and Joshua's ideas so compelling is that, once you hear them, you immediately realize two things: first, that these ideas are good ones and every business should follow them; and second, that almost nobody is following them. You—in your own business or your job—aren't following these rules.

Scott and Joshua broke down these ideas into a series of four steps that force you to ask difficult but crucial questions, precisely the questions Scott's dad—like nearly every other businessperson—never thought to ask or avoided desperately.

Step one: understanding how your business adds and captures value. This crucial step is worth elaborating on. Think of any business that has a shot at success. Someone is doing something that creates value. She is buying raw material and transforming it—like wheat, salt, milk, and eggs into bread, or plastic, leather, and cotton into sneakers. Or he is performing a service, like accounting or fishing guidance. There is a process in which the businessperson creates value. Then, in a distinct step, the value is captured: some person decides to spend money on that thing. He buys a loaf of bread, pays for a fishing charter, sends a check to his accountant. Most businesses that struggle do so because they fail to understand the value they are (or should be) creating or fail to capture the value they have created. Often, a business fails in both ways.

Take Eitan Stern. He created real value by manufacturing a quality sneaker at a lower price. But he was creating a value few people wanted. Sneaker buyers—especially in the 1980s—didn't want a functional shoe at the lowest possible price. They wanted flash and excitement, a brand that would bestow identity upon them. They wanted trusted Nikes, even if they cost one hundred dollars, and not Striker brand white shoes, even if they cost twelve bucks. Eitan thought the value was the physical thing: the rubber and cotton and leather that make up a shoe. If that were the case, his strategy of selling a nearly identical thing for less money would have been sound. But Nike knew that the value it was creating wasn't physical. Nike's marketing people generated a sense of excitement around their shoes, whatever the price. Only a tiny bit of the value they created was in the physical thing; most was in its cultural resonance.

Eitan also misunderstood how he could best capture value. In those pre-Internet days, with far fewer big-box retailers, small shoe stores sold most shoes. Mom-and-pop shoe store owners didn't want to sell super-cheap shoes, because there wasn't much profit in them. They would never want to talk some kid desperate for the latest Nikes into spending less money on a low-cost, no-name brand. In addition to marketing, Nike had developed deep expertise in distribution. Nike understood who was selling shoes and what would best incentivize those people to sell Nikes.

As Scott explained to me, Nike showed that value creation and value capture are two parts of the same strategy. By creating value that included a large premium, Nike could also capture more value by sharing some of that premium. Eitan didn't realize that selling cut-rate sneakers—even ones as good as Nike's—meant he had no budget for marketing and, furthermore, that he couldn't be generous with store owners who saw no incentive in making a tiny profit off Strikers when they could make a lot more pushing the far more popular Nikes.

Strategy is a clear line that links value creation and value capture. It is easy to look at wildly successful companies, like Nike, and see what works. It's also easy to look at failed business efforts—like Eitan's—and see what didn't. Scott and Joshua point out that people making decisions about their business aren't able to look backward. They have to pick a strategy before they know if it will work, and this generally means that they have to make difficult decisions about which of many paths they should follow. The shoe example is telling. One of the first decisions for many businesses is the same one Eitan faced: whether to embrace a high-cost, high-margin strategy or a low-cost, high-volume one.

Eitan tried to compete in a high-margin market by using a low-cost strategy. This doesn't work. Imagine if, instead, he had recognized that he wasn't in the same market as Nike—he was in the bargain shoe business, where value comes from creating a physical product at a low cost. A low-cost strategy is entirely different; everything is driven by cutting prices to the bare bones. In that market, nobody is thinking about Nike; they're thinking about squeezing every penny out of production, shipping, and marketing. Value, there, comes from volume, from selling more shoes in more stores for less money than any competitor. Eitan's product was too expensive for this world and too cheap for the other. By not clearly picking a market strategy, Eitan had doomed his business to failure.

It bears noting that Nike has shifted strategies over its

more than fifty years. In the early days, Nike's strategy was to convince athletes that it was worthwhile to spend more on a high-quality product that would allow them to perform better and longer. Only after it dominated the athletics field did Nike shift to a new strategy rooted in cultural cachet. Scott believes that you are allowed to switch strategies, though you must do so very carefully and thoughtfully. In Nike's case, it made sense, because after a certain point, it had achieved total market dominance in athletic shoes and needed to shift toward non-athletes if it wanted to continue to grow.

The word "strategy" can be intimidating (at least it is to me). It connotes a form of knowledge that professors at the best business schools and partners at elite consulting businesses impart to their select underlings. Happily, Scott shows that it can be straightforward and rooted in basic questions: What are you selling? Who most wants it? Why do they want it? How do they pay for it? Strategy is more important now than it was in the widget economy of the twentieth century because the answers to these questions are more complex and change more often. If you were selling toothpaste, say, in 1950, the answers were simple: people wanted to clean their teeth, so they bought one of a smaller number of national toothpaste brands in a local store. Today, toothpaste (like most products) is exponentially more complex. You can buy any one of dozens of brands of toothpaste, each with multiple formulations and target markets. Colgate alone boasts more than fifty distinct toothpaste formulations, including specialty products for people with a condition known as dry mouth, and those designed for children, and a range of others for people who crave one of several different levels of whitening power. The reasons we choose our toothpaste are more complex now, and the ways we buy it are more varied—local store, chain store, online, subscription service. Any new toothpaste entrepreneur needs to explore the strategy questions and their answers more thoughtfully. That holds, as well, for all new businesses. The sharper the answers, the better positioned you will be for success.

Scott offers some helpful good news. There is a clear path for an entrepreneur or a small businessperson or working man or woman who wants to develop an entrepreneurial mind-set: look inside yourself and make a thoughtful assessment of your abilities, interests, particularities, and weaknesses. Do you love to work hard, every day, and put all distractions aside? Do you instead crave a quieter, more comfortable life, one where you have ample time for family and friends? Are you quick to make decisions or slow with them? Do you enjoy cutthroat combat and high-pressure moments of intense competition? Do you want to get along with everybody you work with? Are you great at attention to detail, the big picture, or assembling a team? What do you hate? What skills do you not have that you could easily hire others who do? Which skills will you never be able to acquire? Knowing yourself is crucial when trying to figure out which paths to take as you proceed. To linger on the tooth-paste example: Do you want to do whatever it takes to make the world's top-selling toothpaste? Or would you prefer to focus on a narrower niche customer who you know uniquely well? Will you find joy and be successful in optimizing the perfect flavor formulation for a toothpaste? Or do your strengths lie more in assessing distribution and identifying new ways to get products to customers? In all likelihood, you will be able to quickly eliminate most options and focus on a small handful of potential strategies. Typically, Scott says, there will be two or three options that seem equally valid. That should be happy news, not a cause of frustration; it means you have choices in how to maximize your business.

The second step is to pick your customer. This might seem odd. One would think that either customers show up or they don't. But Scott points out that customers are not one undifferentiated mass of identical people. They have different interests, different levels of hunger for your product or service. A business needs to identify the customers it wants, and it should figure out who wants its product enough that it can charge whatever it needs to in order to make the business sustainable. If your passion is especially narrow and there is no market for it, it's good to know that before you launch. There is no guarantee that your passions will find a market. That's why you do some market testing.

Market research, much like the word "strategy," can seem discouragingly difficult, a secret science known to only a select few. But Scott says it can be much easier than people imagine, especially when you're first formulating a business idea. Start with a hypothetical ideal customer. Imagine a person or business who would most appreciate and benefit from your product or services. Then find real people who match that profile and ask them what they think of your idea and how they evaluate your competition. This can be done informally by reaching out to friends and friends of friends, or by visiting places in person or online where such people congregate. You can approach industry groups and find lists of businesses to cold-call. You might be surprised how willing people will be to speak with you when they realize you could help them improve their business or their life. By talking to at least twenty potential customers, you are likely to learn about any major flaws in your "ideal customer" theory, which will help you further refine your hypothesis.

Scott also encourages a rough guesstimate of how many people fit the customer criteria. If you plan to sell vinyl recordings of medieval flute music, you can assume that very few people will want your offering and that you will need to charge a huge amount and capture nearly the entire market to make that business work. If you believe you have discovered an incredibly delicious form of chocolate, though, you have some options. There is a huge market of chocolate lovers, and you can choose between a low-cost, high-volume strategy or a higher-cost, premium-product strategy, confident that the market is big enough—and broken up into sufficient numbers of submarkets—that you have a good chance for success at either.

The third step, the one that Scott says most people find confusing, is to pick your competition. How can you pick who you'll compete with? Scott points out that every company has a variety of options in the ways they take their product or service to market. Eitan, again, provides an example. He framed his entire sneaker business around Nike. He talked about Nike. He designed the shoes to look a bit like Nikes. He ordered them from the same factory Nike used. He felt Nike was his competition. That meant that people saw his shoes as cheap Nike knockoffs, and nobody wants to buy cheap Nike knockoffs. He could have chosen a different competitor—for example, the lousiest of discount sneakers. He could then have argued that his product was more durable, more stylish, better performing than the bottom of the barrel. By choosing that competitor and framing his business around capturing its share of the market, he would then have had an easier time seeing his subsequent choices. He would have needed a low-margin, high-volume business strategy.

Scott would argue that there is no single right answer for everybody; the right path is shaped by your product or service as well as your passions and goals. Typically, your business will have a few potential competitive paths. You could focus on stealing market share from massive industry leaders, or you could identify a narrower niche market. You will also need to choose the distribution channels you want to sell through—in person or online, direct or through intermediaries. In each case, you are picking your competition; you are deciding how your product or service will be viewed by your potential customer and what other products and services they will compare it to. By definition, passion-based businesses do not sell widget-like commodities with little differentiation from other products or services. Still, there will be some comparison, some frame of reference for the customer, even for new and unique products. By choosing the context in which you will sell, you are also choosing your competition. It's a crucial—and helpful—decision.

When zeroing in on your competitors, you also are choosing who you will cooperate with. Often, potential competitors can become partners. If you're selling online, will your site compete with Amazon, or will you partner with Amazon to sell and distribute your product? Will you make and sell your handmade soda directly to consumers or license your recipe to Coca-Cola?

Once you identify your abilities and weaknesses, what kind of value you are going to create, how you will capture that value, who you are competing with, and the broad strategy you plan to employ, step four is to focus on all the specific details of how you will capture the value from your customer. If you are planning to sell hand-knit sweaters at farmers' markets, it's not that hard. You will be talking directly to your buyers. But most businesses flow through a value chain, and you need to become expert at how that value chain works. Are you selling to a wholesaler who sells to local stores? Are you selling directly to local stores or to the end customer? Are you selling individual units or bulk? How many different sizes and shapes will your physical products come in? What is the unit of engagement for the services you will provide? Will you charge hourly or for a project? Will you require long-term commitments or do your work on demand?

Scott encourages businesspeople to spend as much time thinking about how they will sell their products and services as they do thinking about what they will sell and who they will sell to. You should experiment with and explore a variety of ways of bringing ideas to customers, pricing them, evaluating and selecting partners, and studying your competitors. Too many people assume that the way some other company does things is the only way, so they copy that standard before exploring whether there is a new or unexpected way of capturing value.

Once an entrepreneur has crafted his approach, says Scott, he needs to accept that the approach will work only if he embraces its constraints. He needs to cut off other paths. Pursuing every approach is the same as pursuing no approach at all. One can't sort of cooperate and sort of compete with another firm. You have to be all in. And one can't simultaneously price a product high (because it's of the top quality) and low (to attract more customers).

As I became closer to Scott and better understood his ideas, I began to wonder about something. He wanted to help people like his dad, businesspeople who didn't have the best education or lacked connections. Yet he was doing his work at MIT's business school, one of the most elite and expensive institutions in the world. Wasn't he helping the already fortunate become even more successful? Why was he not searching out people like his dad?

So one day I sat down with Scott and asked him.

"No," he said, softly but firmly and with finality, "I am not selling out my father. I am not selling out America's entrepreneurs. I see how lucky I am to be part of MIT. This is an amazing place that has the resources to support my research. It has the resources to support the latest research into diseases, robotics, artificial intelligence, and so many other things that will make life better for people all over the world. But the research I am doing is not for the people here. It's for everybody. I believe that I am—and a lot of people here are—constructing a solid base upon which more people can thrive than ever before. These basic ideas—adding value, capturing value, figuring out your strategy—these apply everywhere and to everyone. You don't have to have a 1600 SAT or an Ivy League education. The

whole idea is simple, straightforward: know what you are selling, who you are selling it to, and how to structure a relationship with your customers that will endure. It's simple. But it's
also proven. It's based on massive amounts of data and research
and the ability to pore through that data. That is what you get
in a place like MIT."

My other concern as I sat down with Scott that day was
that his work applied only to entrepreneurs. Most people, of
course, don't work for themselves, don't start their own companies. Most people work for someone else. Employees don't,
generally, decide what strategy their bosses will use. They don't
decide what products or services their employers should offer
or how those products or services should be priced or sold.
Employees don't determine whether to compete against or
partner with other companies. Employees get a job, are told
what to do, and then succeed or fail based on how well they do
at executing someone else's strategy.

"No," Scott said to me, for the second time in a few minutes. This time he was even more firm, more emphatic. "That
is the old way of thinking." Every company—especially the
large ones that have been around for a long time—needs to
answer these questions, he explained. What is the value they
are uniquely creating? Who most wants that value and is willing to pay for it? How do you capture that value? Who is
your competition and with whom are you cooperating? These
weren't irrelevant questions in the twentieth-century widget
economy; every company needed an answer for each of them.
But back then, the answers rarely, if ever, changed. Today, they
constantly change because of the rapid growth in technology
and trade. Just when manufacturers adjusted to China's domi-
nation of the global low-wage labor market, wages there grew,
and the country became a more high-tech producer; the low-
wage factories moved to Bangladesh and Vietnam and other
nations. Just when big firms adapted to the world of Web-based
shopping on desktop and laptop computers, they learned that

customers were doing more buying on their phones. Every major shift transforms every aspect of the creation and capture of value, often in unexpected ways.

I was working at NPR in 2005 when podcasting began maturing. At first, it was terrifying for those of us trained in traditional broadcast radio. The fundamental technology had hardly changed since the industry's dawn, in the 1920s. Radio stations and networks would create content and broadcast it to radio receivers. Everybody heard the same broadcasts at the same time. Since there was a limited number of government-allocated frequencies, the competition was fairly stable. Podcasting, in contrast, would mean that each person could choose their mix of shows and that the number of shows and podcast-producing entities could grow toward infinity. Those of us who were old radio pros feared we'd lose our jobs as listeners migrated to this new, chaotic market. That happened for a bit. Listenership to traditional radio fell, as did employment. Eventually, though, many of us realized that something even better was replacing the old system. Now there were far more people listening to a lot more produced audio in a lot of different ways. Value was captured differently, as well.

Broadcast radio captures almost all of its value through advertising; public radio supplements ads with listener donations and government and foundation grants. Podcast producers make money in many different ways: advertising, subscriptions, using the podcast to promote some other line of business. I wanted to understand this new technology and its many implications, so I created NPR's *Planet Money*, its first major news podcast. It soon became clear that a podcast listener is "worth" a lot more than a broadcast listener. Broadcast listeners are a wide mix. Some are paying close attention; others have the radio on in another room and barely know what's on the air. By its nature, broadcast is designed to reach the largest number of people. Creating passionate connections with broad audiences is hard. Podcast listeners, by contrast, are actively choosing to listen to the shows they most like, which means they are more engaged than the average broadcast audience. Advertisers learned this quickly and began to pay a huge premium to reach podcasting audiences. This meant that a podcast could be profitable with a much smaller audience than a broadcast show. This fueled the proliferation of a rich ecosystem of podcasts, each targeting a specific type of listener. For audio reporters and storytellers, this has largely been a boon. We can make more money doing work that is more satisfying because it is more closely tied to our passions. Our relationship with our audiences—albeit smaller ones—is more intimate and engaged.

Podcasting upended traditional radio in ways reminiscent of the transformation of print newspapers, film cameras, Xerox machines, broadcast television, and countless other industries whose core logic had been stable for decades and then shifted, often more than once, in a few short years. I noted, throughout my firsthand observations of the podcast transition, that some people were more attuned to these changes than others. Some—without knowing of Scott Stern—intuitively asked his core questions: What is the value we are creating? Who most wants it? How do they pay for it? Who is our competition? With whom should we cooperate? The answers changed as technology did. As with toothpaste, there was much less of a single, mass audience whose value was captured in one way. Instead, a growing and ever-changing understanding of value and value capture developed. Those who paid attention did well. When I first worked in radio, nobody I knew was getting rich and few of us, other than a small handful of celebrity hosts, were able to express our unique selves. I was trained not to find my voice but to learn how to create programming that would be familiar and not jarring to our regular listeners. Radio shows offered solid, comfortably middle-class jobs with little risk of firing and little likelihood of wealth. Today, I know more than a dozen people who started in public radio, never imagining they would be wealthy, and are now podcast millionaires. There are also a huge number of people who are not quite that rich but are making decent money creating content they love and that allows them to express themselves far more fully.

Many radio veterans, though, have still not understood how the basic questions about value have changed. They continue to make the same sorts of shows in the same ways. The audience is not growing. Young people don't own radios and have little interest in shows geared to a mass audience, because they grew up with customized niche content.

Everybody—even people who have never considered entrepreneurship and have no interest in pursuing such a path—should spend at least some time thinking through the basic value questions for their industry. You will become a more valuable employee, or you will figure out, before others do, that your employer is stuck in old thinking and it's time to find a job at a more promising, strategy-oriented firm.

Throughout this book, you will continue to see the value of Scott Stern's—and his colleagues'—findings. Significantly, the entrepreneurs I profile in these pages have never studied with Scott, nor even heard of him. Rather, they have followed similar and successful entrepreneurship paths through a combination of trial and error and, crucially, a willingness to define their roles within the Passion Economy. This often requires a scary leap, necessitating both faith in their unique abilities and a willingness to remake their business to position them for success in this new economy. But each one of these people has a lesson to teach.

When I think of the economic transformation we are now experiencing, I picture a middle-aged couple living on a farm somewhere in the Midwest in, say, 1900. They've got a bunch of kids in their teens and twenties, and they are deeply worried. This couple is making a living the same way their parents did and as their grandparents and great-grandparents did, and even as their ancestors thousands of years ago did. They are farmers. The business is plain: tend a field and live off what grows. There have been gradual changes in technology, but the fundamental logic has never altered. Work hard, all day, every day (except, maybe, parts of Sunday), and hope for good weather. If your kids work hard, they'll do fine, just like you. And, like you, they will live alongside their family and a handful of neighbors they've known their whole lives.

Suddenly, though, the kids are talking about all sorts of new things. They want to move to the city, work in a factory, drawn by a promise of payment from some businessperson they've never met. They'll have to move far from every source of stability and protection, away from family, from community, from their church. How in the world are there going to be enough jobs for everybody? These parents must have said that going to the city was a step into a terrifying unknown with enormous risk.

It was indeed a dangerous step in 1900. Many of the rules we now take for granted hadn't been established yet. Child labor and wage theft were rampant; people were forced to work twelve-hour days for minimal pay, and if they got injured, there was no workers' compensation. If a worker died on the job, the family got nothing. And the food available in the city, prepared by factories, was far more dangerous than what Mom made on the farm.

The new rules, the twentieth-century rules, came about slowly. A public education system developed, and then unions pushed for better working conditions. Child labor was outlawed (though only nationally as late as 1938), and some minimal protections were implemented for the families of those injured or killed on the job. Eventually, these new rules provided something the world had never seen before: a large, stable middle class and an economy that brought economic growth and certainty to a larger percentage of the population than any economic system ever before devised.

We are at a similar turning point. We have shifted from one sort of economy to a new one that works according to entirely different rules. We don't yet have all the institutions, the protections, the common expectations that allow us to see how to thrive in this new system. But what we do have are some visionaries, some people who have figured out the logic of this new system and have found a path forward. We can study them, learn from them, and then apply those lessons to our own lives.

There were such people in 1900—maybe even one or two of the children of that farmer couple—who, similarly, intuited the new opportunities available in the transition from farming to industry. Many of the people we think of today as creators of the modern world grew up in a largely agrarian country but were able to predict the entirely new opportunities brought by industry. These include Milton Hershey and his great competitor, Forrest Mars, who developed the modern candy industry; John Jakob Raskob, who helped Pierre S. du Pont invent the modern corporation; and countless others.

In this book, we will meet and learn from the people who see the future today. I have deliberately sought out people whose stories are accessible and include lessons anybody can apply. To help guide you through these lessons, I would like to begin with the new rules, the rules of the Passion Economy.

# CHAPTER 2

# THE RULES OF THE PASSION ECONOMY

### RULE #1: PURSUE INTIMACY AT SCALE.

To thrive in the twenty-first century, combine the best of
the nineteenth century with the best of the twentieth.

**Identify** the set of things that you love to do and that you
do well. You don't need to be the best in the world at something. People often succeed because they have a set of various
skills that don't normally go together.

It may be obvious, in an instant, what your particular passion and set of abilities are. Are you great at making vegan food
for a crowd? Passionate about finding no-longer-manufactured
auto parts? Love to take photos of homes? There is an infinite
number of these passion + ability pursuits. You might need to
take time and do some soul-searching and experimentation to
identify yours. I didn't learn about mine until I was in my thirties. That special set of skills may not be obvious or something
that everyone around you sees. It can be something small—an
odd interest or combination of interests, a little voice with a
hunch that you can barely hear. The identification of your
unique passion is the single most crucial and, often, the hardest
part of embracing the Passion Economy. It might be something
you make, it might be a kind of service you excel at, or it might
be a way to further excel as an employee in a field in which you
already work.

**Match** your passion to the people who most want it. When you have identified that specific passion and set of skills you can offer, you can easily find the people who most want it. They are already self-identified in groups. You may find them through trade magazines or trade groups, online message boards or Instagram accounts. I will give you lots of examples of people turning their passions into profitable businesses and employment. As you'll see, you may need to get creative and experimental and be willing to reach out to a lot of people—who might, at first, seem uninterested in whatever it is you have to offer. But once you put your passions and abilities together with the right kind of customers, you'll be amazed by how easy it can be to carve out a profitable niche in this economy.

Once you have those customers (or colleagues), the next step is to **listen** very closely to their feedback—as well as feedback from those who choose not to be your customers. We no longer live in a "one size fits all" economy. It's imperative that you constantly hone your products and your skills in response to your customers' needs.

**Listening** and **matching** are both closely related and also sometimes at odds. If you find yourself listening to customers who aren't right for you and trying desperately to adjust your offering to fit their needs, you are wasting your time and skills. Instead, you should seek other customers, those who are far better matches and whose feedback will help move your business forward or strengthen it. On the other hand, you don't want to spend all your time seeking a perfect customer match without realizing that it would be better to listen to the near matches, adjust your offering, and make the sale.

### RULE #2: ONLY CREATE VALUE THAT CAN'T BE EASILY COPIED.

In the Passion Economy, you can capture value—sell and distribute things—on an unimaginable and unprecedented scale. It's as simple as selling products on a website or using Twitter to get customers. But you should be careful not to produce value—create a thing that people want—at scale. Creating value at a large volume is something only huge companies can do profitably. They have factories that manufacture countless sneakers or candy bars, studios that produce music or movies, giant firms that consult all over the world. Your value should be created slowly and carefully. Absorbing the significance of this point can be hard. Only focusing your attention on those things that reach a relatively small and strongly opinionated customer base, things that are hard to do, will be worth your while. This is precisely why passion matters so much in this economy. Fortunately, our passions enable us to spend time doing things that we love but others would find hard, even maddening, to focus on. This is perhaps the single most counterintuitive idea in this book: in the current economy, you want to do the opposite of what in the past has usually been considered good business sense. The moment one of your products or services takes off and becomes widely copied, you should begin abandoning it and looking for the next thing.

The more stuff you make or the more clients you take on, the harder it is to maintain excellence and to adapt your products and services in a way that both you and your customers want. Leave scale for the mass market. The Passion Economy is about quality and the conversation you have with your clients.

### RULE #3: THE PRICE YOU CHARGE SHOULD MATCH THE VALUE YOU PROVIDE.

**Price should drive costs, not the other way around.** It took me a long time to understand the significance of this rule. We are wired to think that price is connected to cost. You calculate the cost of the raw materials you use, the time it takes to produce a good or service, you add some amount for profit, and that's your price. With intangibles, like our time, we look to competitors and charge around whatever it is they do.

This is precisely backward. Think of making a luxury car. You would prefer to have a sense of how much people would pay for a certain degree of luxury before you began choosing the materials to go into the vehicle. You determine the price point, and then you reverse engineer the vehicle in line with those costs that can justify the price. You include the smooth leather but recognize that hand-tooling might bump the car's cost beyond your optimal price.

This is especially true for our time, though this fact seems particularly hard for people to understand. Think of your accountant. You would probably want that person to be extremely knowledgeable about aspects of tax law that apply to you. You might also hope that this person spends time being creative, thinking of new ways for businesspeople like you to thrive. Those things take time. Now, no accountant can charge people an hourly rate for the minutes he spends wandering through a park thinking creatively. But he can charge an amount, to the right mix of clients, that allows him to spend this time. Knowledge, creativity, time to think: these are the Corinthian leather of the services world. So, rather than complain that the hourly rate you charge doesn't allow you to spend time improving your knowledge and creativity, charge more and earn that higher amount by spending your time appropriately.

**Value is a conversation.** In the iconic marketplace, described by Adam Smith in his 1776 book *The Wealth of Nations*, price is determined by fierce competition. Many producers are creating the same goods and many buyers are looking them over. No buyer or seller controls the process. The price is the result of all those people haggling.

You shouldn't charge market prices. Market prices are based on the idea that whatever it is you are selling is a commodity that is no better and no worse than what everyone else is selling. Your products and, especially, your services should be unique—so special to your customers that there is no obvious reference point. You should spend time with your clients, pointing out how you are saving them money in other ways, helping them make more money, or making their lives considerably more enjoyable. The price you charge should be the opposite of a fixed amount on a price tag. It should come from frequent discussions with your client.

**Passion pricing *is* a service.** The very process of discussing pricing can often be a central part of the service you are providing. When talking with a client about how much value your product or service delivers—how much more money the client makes, how much cost they eliminate—you are helping that client better understand her own business and needs. This is true when an architect or a website designer helps a client understand the value of design choices. We all become better off when we have a richer understanding of the impact of our choices. Part of your expertise, part of what you uniquely know because you have spent so much time thinking about it, is the way your particular passion can add value to your customers' lives. This value can be calculated in dollar terms or emotional benefit. And helping customers understand the value that your products and services provide is a real service in and of itself.

**Pay attention to BATNA.** Businesspeople sometimes use the phrase "best alternative to a negotiated agreement," or BATNA, to understand the implications of not reaching a deal. This is helpful when setting prices. If you have a passion business and are fully in the Passion Economy, then you are offering something unique with no exact competitor. Still, no customer needs to go with you. They can go with someone else—someone, perhaps, not offering the full Passion Economy value but whose product or service is priced so much cheaper that it's worth it. In setting prices, you should be ambitious, be confident, and, almost certainly, go far higher than you initially imagined possible. You must also pay attention to the alternatives. You should even ask people who don't choose to use your products or services what they decided to use instead.

**Charge a lot and then earn it.** A good way to thrust your thinking toward the Passion Economy is to imagine doubling your prices, rates, or salary. This can feel shocking, obnoxious, but it forces you to start imagining what you would need to do—and who you would need to do it for—to deserve twice as much. In some cases, people can immediately double their rates without losing much business. In other cases, the thought experiment of imagining far higher prices helps a person realize that they are selling to the wrong customers. For still others, considering doubling their prices is a prod, prompting someone to realize that she needs to acquire more skills, more education, or a better mix of products.

**Realize that your pay may come in things other than money.** I know many journalists who could easily earn far more money doing public relations or some other job, but they choose to remain journalists because they love the work, the influence they have, the opportunity to uncover secrets. My parents are both in the arts, and they never made as much money as they might have had they pursued other careers, but they had wonderful, emotionally satisfying working lives, and they wouldn't have exchanged them for money.

**The price you charge should change constantly.** Your skills, abilities, and passions shift. Your customers' needs shift. The nature of the world changes. These are the things that affect price, and since they are constantly changing, you should change your prices with them. By continually evaluating price, you are also forced to examine the products and services you provide, the value they bring to the people who pay you for them, and the potential customers who might value them even more. Price is a simple number, but it tells you how well you are engaging the Passion Economy.

**The price you quote shouldn't change unless the services**

**and products offered change.** While your prices should adapt to changes in the value you create, when you quote a price to a customer, you should stick with it. This is more tactical than strategic. One helpful strategy is always to offer three tiers of pricing: a medium tier for the specific set of services the client requested at a price that feels right; a lower tier, which subtracts some of the services but has the advantage of a lower price; and a higher tier at a higher price for far more access. This frames the pricing conversation with your clients, showing them that if they want to pay less, they will get less in exchange.

There is a delicate balance in this process. An initial phase of open conversation makes the value of the relationship clear to the customer. Then comes the moment of price setting, in which the sophisticated pricer shows far less flexibility. In the initial "value conversation," in which you talk with the person paying you, it makes sense to be open, fluid, and creative, exploring how different price levels will guide the relationship. The second and distinct "pricing conversation," however, needs to be firmer, less flexible, even filled with some degree of tension and awkwardness. Even when pricing is rooted in value, it can still be a shock to a customer to face the specific numeric reality of the value they have just agreed on. If the pricing conversation isn't a little bit tense and the price isn't a bit shocking, you might be pricing too low, in order to avoid even a hint of conflict; you also might not, yet, fully understand or feel confident in the value you provide.

**Salary is a price.** If you have a job in a company, you are still charging a price; it's called your salary. All of the pricing rules apply here, too. If you got a job that came with a set salary, then you are being treated as a commodity, equal in value to everyone else who might qualify for that job. Imagine demanding that your salary be doubled. How could you justify such an aggressive request? You probably can't, because the company that would recognize that value would not be paying you your current salary. This means that you likely have to do two things: go to another company that recognizes your value and find ways to articulate your value more clearly.

The Passion Economy rules for businesses also apply to people with jobs. There are universal qualities that everyone recognizes as having value—being on time, getting along with your colleagues, doing assigned tasks promptly and thoroughly—but that will never differentiate you from your peers. It's like making a perfectly serviceable but unexceptional loaf of bread. I would never suggest that you start showing up late, acting rudely, and failing in your assignments. Instead, you should identify your unique passions and skills, analyze the needs of others within the company and among your company's customers, and pinpoint special projects that you, and you alone, can imagine and execute. Some corporate cultures don't allow for such internal entrepreneurship, but most do, at least to some extent.

**The price you charge should feel good to you.** We are habituated to thinking of prices as an external fact, like the temperature, that we have little control over. That is because standardized pricing was a central component of standardizing everything in the twentieth-century scale economy. It would have been absurd in any business context to argue that a price is wrong because it just doesn't feel good. In the Passion Economy, though, price is emotional. The entire point is to match your internal passions and skills with the specific needs and desires of a customer. The passion price is whatever you and a customer agree is right. Emotions are not soft, silly things that are irrelevant in the tough world of business. Emotions are the whole thing: if you are priced below what feels fair to you, you won't be able to engage your full passion, and you will be letting your customer down. If the customer can't pay the amount that feels good, then you have the wrong customer or you have the wrong product.

One surprising factor in emotion-based pricing is that prices can change based on your feelings. You might charge less for a project that is thrilling to do because you will learn a great deal from doing it. A year later, the same project is far less exciting because you have already learned everything you can from that activity. You might not want to do the project at any price, or you might want to increase the price dramatically. Similarly, your life might change. If you have kids who have grown up and no longer occupy as much time, you might want to lower your prices so that you have more work to do.

For some, the hardest thing about emotion-based pricing is that, at its best, it matches the feelings of a buyer and a seller. This might feel weak, to some. We have been trained to view pricing as a battle of wills, each side hoping to force the other to bend and the final price being some number that the buyer thinks is too high and the seller thinks is too low. Passion Economy deals are different. A price comes from extensive conversation, complete with real data about the work required of the seller and the benefits received by the buyer. If either side is unhappy, it means that either the conversations weren't thorough enough or the match is not a good one.

**Pricing low is _not_ a strategy.** One of the most common errors people make is finding out what the competition is charging and then pricing their own goods or services a bit lower. This is not a strategy; it is the abdication of strategy to the competition. It avoids asking the crucial Passion Economy question: What is the value I am creating that is beyond that of similar businesses or services, and who am I creating it for?

It is possible that after you properly assess your value for your customers, your prices will be lower than some of your competitors'. That is quite different from starting with an externally defined price.

**Pricing _is_ your value.** Pricing is often an afterthought. A businessperson creates a product or service, looks at what her competitors are charging, and charges somewhere around the same amount. Instead, pricing should be at the very center of your business, your job, your way of understanding your role in the world. Pricing is your value, at least in commerce. (I don't recommend coming up with prices for the time you spend with your children or spouse or friends.) You should get your full value, and you shouldn't let others—your competitors, your customers, some set of rules you absorbed from society— determine your value. If you come to see that the price you currently feel you can charge is too low, that should tell you that you need to adjust. You need to find a different area of focus, acquire more skills, locate different customers. You might not control the price you can charge right now, but you can—and must—over the long term.

## RULE #4: FEWER PASSIONATE CUSTOMERS ARE BETTER THAN A LOT OF INDIFFERENT ONES.

**Value pricing requires selling to the right people.** Saying good-bye is the hardest part. When switching to the Passion Economy approach, it is counterintuitive, yet essential, to stop working with many of your existing customers. If you haven't applied the rules of the Passion Economy before, it is highly unlikely that most of your customers truly recognize your full value and are paying you the appropriate amount for it. There may be a few who do recognize your value and are paying the right amount; perhaps some others can be persuaded to switch to a passion-based relationship. But in almost all cases, the majority of clients are no longer appropriate and need to be gently handed over to some other professional. That is the only way to get to a point where the vast majority of your time is spent working on the things that add the most value for customers who most clearly recognize that value.

**Don't say good-bye too quickly.** You can never have too narrow a niche, but you can rush to your niche too quickly. It is possible that the best audience for your business is left-handed chefs with a hunger for the perfect knife with which to cut an onion or some other very specific group. It will take time to find enough members of that group and persuade them that you and only you are right for the job. It can be tempting to wake up one day, realize that your customers aren't the right fit, and tell them all to go away. But unless you have amassed a sizable war chest of excess cash, it is best to transition slowly and deliberately. Some firms create a new name and, for a while, essentially operate as two companies—a legacy firm for existing customers and a new one that works only with the targeted niche. At least once a year, go through your existing client base with your team. You should expect to find that about 10 percent of your clients are no longer appropriate for the firm. You can then gently explain that another firm will better serve them. Often, you will find that these clients cost you money. They are paying you, but when you add up all the time you spend servicing them—and not servicing more appropriate customers— you learn that some of your clients are hurting your business. When a customer doesn't value what you are selling, she typically requires an enormous amount of time and effort precisely because there is a gap between her expectations and what you offer. It's like taking a bunch of square pegs and having to saw them, sand them, and jiggle them to fit into a series of round holes.

The proper pace for eliminating customers depends on your financial condition, your transition plan, and other factors, including your comfort level with asking longtime clients to go away. Don't move so fast that you end up bankrupt, but don't move so slow that you get stuck spending your time serving people who don't understand or don't pay for your full value.

**The best customers, eventually, are the ones who seek you out.** When you have identified the proper niche and served clients in that niche well, you will eventually develop a reputation among your target customer base such that new clients reach out to you before you need to pursue them. The narrower your niche, the more likely you are to receive inbound interest rather than having to pursue an aggressive sales strategy.

**Your passion, pricing, value, and target customers are all different views of the same thing.** The essence of the Passion Economy is that a person's particular set of passions and skills becomes a product or service that is matched to the pressing needs of a particular kind of customer at a particular time. This interaction creates real value for the customer that translates into a price that is sustainable for both the seller and the buyer. In short, all of these things are so tightly linked that they are best seen as different aspects of the same core thing. None of it works if any one element is off.

### RULE #5: PASSION IS A STORY.

**Whatever you're selling, you're selling a story, and it better be a true one.** Value is not a physical thing: a lump of metal and plastic and glass. It is also not a period: the hours of effort that a professional puts in to achieve some task. Value is a subjective measurement of how some product or service makes a person's life better. It is a story, and like all good stories, it has characters and a plot and a feeling of completion, and maybe a bit of drama. This can be true for even the most prosaic of purchases. Say you are frustrated with your soap, and you go online and find a new one that is highly rated, and it comes in the mail, and you love it—that is a story. It has a hero—you—facing an obstacle, taking action, fearing failure, then triumphing. Sure, it's a story that nobody would sell to Hollywood as a movie. But it is more important than whatever combination of chemicals make up that bar of soap.

**Always tell the truth.** Forget morality for a moment; forget a desire to be a truthful person. Even if all you care about is profit at any cost, you still should never lie. The value-creation process requires an investment of effort and capital that generally pays off only over time. You need your customers to tell others about you. You need to hone your message. You can lie once to get a big deal, but you can't build on that lie, and you can't sustain that lie unless you lie all the time. You have to maintain the lie with every new interaction with every new customer. Your business, built on a lie, is less stable. The lie can be uncovered, and maintaining the lie requires extraneous effort that doesn't increase your core value. In short, lying is bad for business.

**You can and must tell your story, especially if you're bad at telling stories.** A truthful brand, built on passion and real value, tells a story even if the person who created it is shy and generally lousy at storytelling. I have often noted that awkward, earnest storytellers can be far more convincing than slick and polished ones. It can be worthwhile to hire professional marketers to help deliver the story and bring it to life in a way that lands for other people. But this won't work if the story is fake or made up by some outsider. The visuals, the marketing materials, the company's name are rooted in the essential truth of the passion and value of the product or service being sold.

**The story is told in every detail of your business.** When you have a passion business, you embed the vision into every aspect of the interaction with customers. This means that physical products are made of materials that reflect the passion and are designed in a way that supports the passion. Services are provided in ways that, similarly, express and reflect a company's core passion and value.

I recently hired a lawyer who told me that he would not charge me by the hour but would, instead, agree to a fixed fee for the work we were going to do together. He explained that charging by the hour contradicted his core values of serving his clients; it would create an incentive for him to spend more time even if it wasn't strictly necessary. Or, on the other hand, he might choose to rush some work to save me some money. He preferred not to think about time at all but, instead, to focus on providing me with the greatest service. I found this comforting.

### RULE #6: TECHNOLOGY SHOULD ALWAYS SUPPORT YOUR BUSINESS, NOT DRIVE IT.

Using the right technology can be a boon to you in this economy. Thanks to the Internet, it is easier than ever to find well-matched customers all around the world, to stay in contact with them, and to more quickly design the products they want. Great software can help you better manage your business—assisting with everything from inventory to design to up-to-date customer profiles. If you focus solely on being cutting-edge, though, you risk letting the technology take over what should be very robust relationships with your customers, employees, and colleagues. In this age of technological advances and automation, personal relationships in business are more crucial than ever.

**Do what technology and large industry cannot do—not the same thing, only slower.** To succeed in the Passion Economy, one should not condemn large-scale business and technology or dismiss them as inferior. Instead, the successful passion-based business owner recognizes the tremendous power of larger firms and their tools of automation and avoids competing directly. If your core customer cannot easily distinguish your products or services from those of a larger competitor, you need to shift and offer something else. As we will see later in this book, no human accountant can compete by promising to be faster and cheaper than TurboTax; a small, American-based pencil manufacturer cannot outdo its rivals by selling huge volume at rock-bottom prices.

Technology is changing quickly, of course, and with increased adoption of artificial intelligence, automation will likely reach far more industries more quickly than we can imagine. This means that a passion-based businessperson needs to pay close attention to the tools available to their much larger competitors, aware that a product or service that was safe from competition yesterday may not be so safe tomorrow.

**Technology-driven scale creates the space for businesses built on value and passion.** Businesses built on great scale, by necessity, cannot richly engage narrow audiences. Sure, they can use computer programs to create personalized recommendations or to let customers design their own style of shoe or shirt. But that is not the same as personally guiding a customer to some option he could never have imagined himself, offering a service, rooted in passion, that satisfies needs the customer doesn't know he has. It would be irrational for Amazon to employ a bunch of experts on historical dictionaries. But you can, if that's your passion, and you can use Amazon to reach the people who most value them.

**Technology tends toward bigness, so stay small.** A central feature of this economy is that technology-driven innovation scales to unimaginable size. Create Facebook or Twitter or a new cell phone and, soon enough, everyone on earth has access to them. Unless you happen to have billions of dollars and a genius for cutting-edge technological innovation, don't ever bother going big. There is safety in smallness. If you richly serve a small niche in a way that is hard to scale, no big company will ever think to go through the expense of identifying so small a market and serving your customers' rather particular needs.

### RULE #7: KNOW WHAT BUSINESS YOU'RE IN,
### AND IT'S PROBABLY NOT WHAT YOU THINK.

The core thing you are selling is the real value you can bring to a customer who craves your offering. Often, a value-delivery system is tied to a particular moment in history. Human beings have been eating bread for millennia, and we all value a fresh-baked loaf. It stops hunger, it provides the aesthetic experience of taste, and it offers a comfort deeply rooted in familial, cultural, and, sometimes, religious values. But the way bread is delivered has continually changed. If your passion is creating bread, you could open a bakery, mass-produce loaves and sell them through supermarkets, create a bread-making class, directly ship bread to customers, or offer home bread delivery. The value you create—that perfect loaf—is what shouldn't change. The way you deliver it is secondary. Too often people focus on that secondary aspect. They're in the bakery business, or they are a supermarket supplier. Don't be locked into the secondary value-capture end of your business. Focus, instead, on the core value you create and be quite experimental and creative about how to capture that value.

My field, journalism, is going through a painful transition. We know that people truly value the ability to learn about what's happening in the world and hear analyses of it. But many don't particularly want that news to come in traditional packages, like newspapers. Figuring out how to get news to the public and—this part is more difficult—make money from doing so has become a serious challenge for the field.

We are going through a massive transformation of nearly every business because of the forces of globalization and automation. The basic packaging of medicine, finance, law, education, retail, travel, and countless other fields is changing. This is painful and disruptive and also offers enormous opportunity. If you can focus on the core value you add and not the package it comes in, you can create new packages, new types of businesses that will profit in new ways.

The ability to book flights and trips online vastly disrupted the travel agency business. Travel agencies shuttered their doors in droves. However, we're now seeing new businesses where people are making their living by creating personalized travel experiences. There is such a saturation of booking websites, ratings websites, and travel blogs that travelers are looking, once again, to get help with planning a trip from individuals with real knowledge of the place they are going. The travel companies that employ these individuals may book flights, hotels, and car rentals, but that's not their business. What they are selling is knowledge. They intimately know the particulars of a certain area and can steer customers toward all the best options, usually in a range of price points. They invest in their clients' experiences in a way that giant travel websites and booking sites cannot. They are part of the Passion Economy.

**Change your value capture constantly. Change your value creation slowly.** In just the past decade, the ways products and services are sold have gone through multiple transformations. We went from physically purchasing things, even digital files, in physical stores, to getting so much online. We used to pay only with cash, check, or credit card; now there is an ever-increasing set of payment options, from Venmo to PayPal to Bitcoin to whatever has come out between when I'm typing this and you're reading it. Value capture is just a tool, and you should use whichever tool is quickest and easiest. Value creation, though, is the core of your business. Treasure it, tend it, change it only quite slowly and deliberately.

## RULE #8: NEVER BE IN THE COMMODITY BUSINESS, EVEN IF YOU SELL WHAT OTHER PEOPLE CONSIDER A COMMODITY.

A commodity is an undifferentiated product that is easily copied and replicated by others. Commodities are widgets. Generic soap is a commodity; so is the dry cleaner on your way to work and the barber down the block. Commodity businesses are price takers, meaning they get paid whatever the market price happens to be. The only way for them to be truly successful is with volume and an ability to produce more cheaply than anybody else. That's why commodity businesses tend to be dominated by huge, global corporations that use automation and outsourcing to cut their costs to the bone.

Passion businesses never sell commodities. By definition, a passion business differentiates itself from others so that it can charge a unique price that represents its unique value.

But here's the thing: there is no rigid line between commodity and passion. When the Apple iPod first came out it was dismissed, at least by some, as an overpriced commodity MP3 player. In any Sephora there are a ton of expensive shampoos and hand creams screaming "unique value" and charging a huge premium for it. But if you analyze the actual substance in any given container, it will most likely turn out to be nearly chemically identical to something selling at Walmart for $2.99 a bottle. Starbucks thrived because it was able to take a commodity product—coffee—and wrap it in an added-value experience of a pleasant shop and a lifestyle brand.

Workers in a twentieth-century business were, largely, commodities. They had a particular job with a title and job description that made clear that whoever happened to hold that position at any given time could be replaced by someone else who would, in an instant, have the same title and job description. It was too difficult for large firms to identify the unique capabilities and passions of each of its workers, so it was simpler to treat them as commodities. Today, it is far easier to identify the exact contribution of each worker. Online metrics and audience surveys can identify precisely how different workers perform, zeroing in on which ones are adding to the bottom line and which are offering minimal value.

Commodification is like gravity, always pulling at everyone, always trying to get each product and service and worker to fall to a common level. That is why Apple is constantly trying to launch new products and features, with Samsung and others continually nipping at its heels. In a value-added business, a passion business, you should always be asking yourself, Am I letting my business, or even myself as an employee, slip into the commodity trap? In the workplace, you can become a commodity by, say, working long hours without adding extra value to the job you are performing. Once you stop asking how you can set your business or products or even yourself apart from the commodity version, you have dropped out of the Passion Economy.

# CHAPTER 3

# BEHOLD THE DAIRY BRUSH

*How a long, bristled brush explains the*
*future of the American economy*

For some time now, on a shelf just above my desk, I have kept, for inspiration, a dairy-bottle cleaning brush. It's not especially beautiful. It is a foot and a half long, with a wooden handle and a thick mass of prickly white bristles surrounding the top two-thirds of its length. I've never used it to clean anything, but I glance at it from time to time to remind myself of the core lessons I have learned about how the economy has changed and how to thrive in this new world. It's a literal manifestation of the central lesson of this book. This is a nineteenth-century brush that is guiding a very twenty-first-century company.

The brush itself is a 9075P Braun Quart Bottle Brush that retails for $41.20, though I received it as a gift from Lance Cheney, the president of Braun Brush, a family-owned business situated on Long Island. Braun Brush, the "Makers of Specialty Brushes Since 1875," as its slogan declares, is rightly proud of its heritage. The company was founded by Lance's great-grandfather Emanuel Braun, who emigrated from Germany to New York City as a fourteen-year-old in 1865. Broke and alone, Emanuel roamed the streets looking for work. He was eager to apply himself to any trade that offered a decent wage.

Eventually, he found a gig cleaning milk bottles at a Brooklyn dairy.

It was, to be sure, stomach-churning work. Before the invention of homogenization and pasteurization, used bottles were returned to the dairy with a film of dried milk fat coating their insides. The soured milk and moldy fat produced a putrid smell, horrific even by the standards of nineteenth-century New York City streets. Braun's job was to make these grimy bottles look as good as new so that they could be refilled with fresh milk and sent out for delivery the next morning. Day after day, he squeezed a damp rag into the glass mouth and ran it around the inside of the bottle, wiping off as much residue as possible, until the glass glistened. When he fell short of his goal, which he did on many occasions, his boss would bark at him to start all over again. After all, no company wanted to ship milk in a filthy bottle.

Since Braun couldn't quit his job, he instead became fixated on finding a way to make it more tolerable. It's hard to imagine today, but in the 1870s brushes were cutting-edge technology. The hairbrush was patented in 1854, but it was considered a faulty, frustrating product. The bristles were not reliably spaced, and the primitive state of glue meant that they generally fell out. The daily practice of brushing one's hair frequently turned into an annoying ordeal that resulted in a blob of hair, skin cells, bristles, and glue, and maybe even a little blood. Other personal and industrial brushes suffered from similar, if less painful, problems.

Young Braun was an enthusiastic tinkerer, and he endeavored to figure out how to make the right sort of brush to solve his dairy glass problem. He began by forming a long, thin tool with a pinewood handle and horsehair bristles. He experimented with baleen—a durable substance found in the mouths of whales, which use it to filter water for tiny krill—but the baleen proved too expensive. He finally settled on Tampico imported from Mexico, an ideal compromise between function and cost.

Back then, brushes were normally made by drilling holes in the brush head, inserting the bristles, and filling in the space around the holes with a heaping amount of glue. This process required a wide head—one too wide, it turned out, to fit into the mouth of a glass bottle. This was a maddening problem for Braun: he had discovered both the proper type of wood and the correct bristle and yet he couldn't put the two together to clean the damn milk bottles. It was only after a few more years of experimentation in the basement of the house in which he lived and worked in Bushwick, Brooklyn, that he devised a clever work-around: he wound a long metal wire around particularly strong bristles and then secured the wire into grooves in a narrow wooden handle. The resulting brush was narrow enough to fit into a dairy bottle, yet strong enough to withstand thousands of washes. Eureka: Emanuel Braun had his brush!

In an instant, Braun had revolutionized the task of washing milk bottles. He could handle a few dozen in an hour, rather than a day, and the bottles would be much cleaner.

Braun's solution is a perfect example of the first rule of the Passion Economy: pursue intimacy at scale. Braun had an intimate solution to a narrow and specific problem that only someone who had spent all those hours trying to clean a milk bottle could have devised. He then became an expert in the various bristles and handle materials available. He understood the problem, and he had arrived at a solution with an expertise that few could match. The problem was that in his time Braun didn't have access to scale. There just weren't a lot of ways for an inventor in Brooklyn to let dairy operations around the country and the world know about his new product. But he did quit his bottle-cleaning job and start Braun Brush, which he spread the word about the only way he could: by foot. He walked to hundreds of dairies all over Brooklyn to demonstrate his invention. He got enough orders that he could afford to buy an old barn, which he converted into a simple brush factory. Every morning, he set off from his factory on foot to sell and deliver brushes all across Brooklyn. Every afternoon, he returned to make more brushes for the next day's deliveries.

Braun didn't stop with one dairy brush. Over time, he realized that there were countless problems for which a brush could offer a solution. In the dairy business alone, grooming brushes were needed for animals, and muck-out brushes were needed for stalls. He developed long, narrow brushes to clean water pipes. He made wide, soft brushes for smoothing the top of cheeses that were being produced on an industrial scale. Braun stayed away from hairbrushes, which would be perfected by Lyda Newman, a teenage African-American female inventor who received a patent in 1898, but he successfully branched into other food businesses, developing, for example, a gentle beaver-hair brush used to spread chocolate on candy. His proudest achievement, however, remained that very first dairy brush, an almost perfect product that has yet to be improved upon to this day and is still widely used.

Emanuel Braun's enthusiasm was perfectly suited to an economy largely built around local artisans. His son Albert merely elaborated on his father's success. Brushes, Albert realized, had infinite possibilities. Their three elements—a handle, a set of bristles, a binding agent—could be used to solve all sorts of problems. Indeed, Albert became a brush artist, and he often sketched out his product ideas in a massive leather-bound ledger book. Albert dreamed up all sorts of brushes: brushes for dairies, brushes for bakeries, brushes used to sort parts that came off factory assembly lines, and brushes for washing the wheels of carriages. When movies became a popular source of entertainment, he developed a special wide and not-too-sharp brush for cleaning movie screens. After watching some people play the newly popular game of tennis, Albert jotted down some notes and created what would become New York City's leading tennis court brush—extra wide, with two very long handles. He created fanciful products that cleaned expensive upholstery, buffed wooden armrests, and dusted the crevices in highly detailed decorative carvings.

Albert Braun never had a son of his own, so he passed his business on to his son-in-law, Max Cheney, in the early 1950s. By this time, the system of artistic experimentation no longer seemed to be working. The U.S. economy was becoming nationalized. President Eisenhower's interstate highway system would create an integrated trucking industry that then allowed a small brush manufacturer in New York to serve clients in Alabama, Colorado, and Oregon.

This appeared to be a huge boon to Braun Brush's business. All those clever solutions developed for clients in Brooklyn, Queens, and Long Island could now be sold to dairies and bakeries and firehouses all across the country. But adjusting to the new system meant that Max Cheney had to change gears. For two generations, Braun had focused on creating countless specific brushes customized to exact needs. Now Max had to figure out which brushes had the most practical applications, and then determine how to make as many of them as possible and distribute them all over the country. He decided to embrace commoditization.

Max stopped worrying about creating new brushes and instead categorized all of the brushes his father-in-law and grandfather-in-law had invented. He created special sections of the factory for dairy brushes, and others for bakery brushes, and still others for those used in the burgeoning car-wash industry (another beneficiary of the interstate highway system). Max ordered as many Yellow Pages phone books as he could—he wanted one for every town and city in the country. He had piles of hundreds of them and would hire teenagers from the neighborhood to spend their summers leafing through these books, writing down the names and phone numbers of every business in specific industries. He had ledgers filled with the phone number and address of just about every bakery in the country, every dairy, every movie theater, and every tennis court. He would call these companies, send specialized catalogs, appear at trade shows. He elevated the business by establishing hundreds of national accounts.

Max was fully a twentieth-century man. His metrics for success were nothing like Emanuel's. Max didn't relish the idea of creating lots of different brushes for lots of different purposes. It cost more money to shift production from one brush to another. It was faster and cheaper to make more of the same and find new markets in which to sell it. He wasn't having as much fun as his predecessors had—he had, after all, sacrificed creativity—but he enjoyed his nice, steady life.

This is the company that the current CEO, Lance Cheney, entered as a young man in the 1980s. Lance joined the company just after college and found it unbearably boring. Each day was the same. Lance, by his admission, was a truly awful employee who kept his job solely because his dad was far too forgiving. He came to work late and hungover many days because he loved spending his nights listening to music in clubs in Greenwich Village. He quit a few times to pursue some dream or another. Once, he went to school to be a sculptor; another time, he tried to start a band. He was, by his own admission, too lazy and unfocused to succeed at either effort. So he eventually came back to Dad, who always had work for him.

By the 1990s, Lance and his father had settled into a comfortable routine. Lance matured nicely, began coming to work on time, and helped his father with the business. For him, though, the job continued to be painfully dull. He would dutifully check the latest production numbers and make sure the salespeople were meeting their targets, but his only joy came from side projects he would pursue in his spare time, at the back of the factory floor. By then, he had become an expert about various types of bristles and brush handles, and he began to make boldly colored sculptures out of firm nylon bristles. Through a friend, he met Richard Artschwager, a famous painter and sculptor who'd developed an interest in working with brush bristles. Cheney became his technical consultant and fabricator and constructed seventy brush-based sculptures, including one that has shown at the Whitney Museum of American Art, a stunning yellow exclamation point made out of brush bristles. There wasn't a lot of money in this work, and Max thought Lance was wasting his time on it, but it was fun, so he kept it up.

Lance and Max developed a daily routine. They would meet for lunch, talk through the business, go over the numbers, and then chat about life. They were very close but had one ongoing disagreement. Every single day, Lance would tell his dad that the company should go back to its early roots and focus on creating new kinds of brushes, exciting ones that solved problems and used brush technology for art. His dad would laugh and then ignore him, and they'd return to other topics.

In the 1990s, Chinese manufacturers began shipping huge numbers of brushes to the United States. At first, they focused on the lowest end of the brush industry: cheap paintbrushes sold in big-box retailers. The Chinese brushes were inferior. The bristles fell off easily, streaking the paint and leaving a residue. Each year, though, the imported Chinese brushes got better, and their makers spread into more specialized areas. During his lunchtime talks with his dad, Lance warned that the Chinese would be coming for them soon. Max laughed this off, too. By 2002, however, Chinese factories had begun making exactly the kinds of brushes Braun produced. The Chinese-made brushes were much cheaper and, Lance had to admit, nearly as high-quality as Braun's. His warnings to his dad were increasingly desperate. He feared the business would one day collapse. His dad reassured him: *We're doing what we've been doing for a century. We'll be fine.*

Lance Cheney, when I met him, was athletic and young-looking for fifty-five, and he brought to mind a youthful Kris Kringle—Santa before he put on the weight, and before the beard fully grew in. Young Lance himself would have screamed if anybody, early on, had told him that he would end up doing what his father, grandfather, and great-grandfather had done. But one day in early 1988 he had come across an ad for a new computer from IBM called the System/36 model 5363. It was a transitional computer, bridging the gulf between room-sized mainframes and far smaller individual desktops. The 5363 could fit on a desk (though it took up almost all of the space) and was cheap enough that a company like Braun could reasonably afford one. And while its software paled in comparison to the user-friendly operating systems that would come later, model 5363 was designed to be used by people without advanced computer training.

Lance became fixated. He wanted one, and he needed his dad to approve the expense. Enlisting the help of a friend of a friend with a computer background, Lance prepared a spreadsheet for his father, showing that the computer would allow Braun Brush to better send targeted catalogs to every potential customer in the country. Eventually, Max relented and agreed to the purchase.

In the late 1980s, it took only several months to learn how to use a business computer properly (a decade earlier, such computers had required a full-time employee with years of training). Finally, the computer was up and running, and Lance realized he had no idea what, precisely, a computer could do for a brush manufacturer. But after reading through the manual a few times, Lance stumbled across some helpful information. This computer, he realized, could organize all of his dad's customer files. It would be far better than the system of ledgers, note cards, and typed pages that filled a wall of file cabinets. He spent months typing in the information, slowly learning how to build a functioning database.

That computer brought with it a fundamental shift in how the brush business worked. Before computerization, as Max's ledgers suggested, it had been incredibly difficult to find and organize information. But these new computers led to the creation of new database companies that could ship a box of floppy disks that contained the name of every business in any given industry. Quite quickly, Braun Brush found that longtime customers were being overwhelmed with better offers from other companies, which were selling the same types of brushes at ever-cheaper prices. Soon the problem was compounded by the sudden influx of cheap brushes coming from China.

Meanwhile, Lance and Max continued to eat lunch together every day. It was a simple ritual. Max liked the soup and a sandwich from the deli down the block; Lance preferred a big salad. They would sit down with a large stack of industry publications—*Brossapress*, *Brushware*, and the big one, *Broom, Brush & Mop*—and call out observations to each other. Generally, these points were deep in the weeds. "Continental Brush is getting out of the power-washer business," one might say, or "Deshler Broom just moved its factory to Mexico." Lance or Max might mention a new order for, say, three dozen brushes to clean out pizza ovens and talk briefly about how much to charge. Or they might go over a client's request for a new kind of bottle-cleaning brush. They never fought, never raised their voices at each other.

If you witnessed any one of those lunches, it would be hard to see that anything dramatic was happening. But, slowly, imperceptibly, over the course of the years between 1988 and 2002, Lance and Max developed wildly different views about Braun Brush and, more broadly, about the American economy in an age of technology and trade. Each man's views coincided with those of his generation.

For Max, who had grown up in postwar America, when the United States dominated nearly every global market with its goods, the key to a successful business was sales—volume.

Back then, most businesses had thrived by adhering to the commoditized economy: playing it safe and selling the same thing over and over again. Max wanted to sell as many brushes as possible to as many people as would buy them. His goal was never to let a sale fall through. He would lower prices, promise to deliver brushes more quickly—anything to get that sale. Lance flew to Germany for the big annual brush-industry conference, Interbrush, in Freiburg, and met with every major brush-making-machinery supplier. The Cheney men bought a new machine, the Zahoransky ET 120, the cutting edge in computer-driven brushmaking, which could create huge numbers of common brushes and then quickly be reset to make a few custom products. It cost $250,000, the single largest purchase in Braun's history, but it couldn't slow the company's decline as China and other low-wage countries grabbed more and more of the market share.

Lance often chafed at his father's willingness to do anything to get the product out the door. Lance was able to use that new computer to run reports that showed that entire lines of the business were not profitable, or that they could sell millions of certain types of brushes and remain stuck where they were, just above profitability. Max was the boss, though, and he got his way. Still, Lance couldn't help but point out every news item about yet another competitor going out of business because it couldn't compete with commodity brushes.

Eventually, as Lance tried to convince his father of the new economic realities, the lunches became more difficult. If Braun were the only company in the world that owned a brush-making machine, it could dominate the competition. But everybody was buying these machines, everybody was churning out more and more brushes, and the competition was only getting more intense. There were Chinese companies and much bigger American ones that would always offer more brushes and lower prices. It was clear that a low-cost, low-price, high-volume strategy would, eventually, destroy Braun. It was, Lance said, a miracle—and a sign of Max's incredible salesmanship—that the company was able to stay flat in this difficult time. The gravity of the new economic reality, however, could not be ignored. Lance had some victories. In 1997, he bought the domain brush.com and created the first major Internet brush sales site. But he wasn't able to fundamentally shift the business.

Max stayed at work, even as his health failed and his knees made it hard for him to walk the factory floor. He had developed cataracts that made it difficult to see, but he hid this (or thought he did) from the workers in the plant. Max's mind was sharp, and he remained an active leader of the company right up to the day he died, suddenly, of a heart attack.

It took a few weeks for Lance to mourn his father, sort through his papers, and get back to the factory full-time. Once he did, he immediately set to work. He gathered his sales staff and announced that, from that day on, they would not sell a single brush in direct competition with cheap imports from China. If a Chinese factory could make a reasonably similar brush, then Braun would get out of that line altogether. They were leaving the commodity business and moving into the highly specialized brush game. This way, they wouldn't be competing on price and volume. They could be competing, as his great-grandfather had, on the value they provided. Welcome to the Passion Economy.

Those inexpensive commodity brushes, the ones his father had put in those catalogs that had been mailed to all those businesses for years, made up the majority of Braun's sales. Specialty brushes, though, had huge profit margins. They were designed for customers with such specific needs that there would be no competition. The problem was that such customers were rare. Lance told the team that success would come not from the number of sales they made but from the quality of the sales. They should be thrilled by low-number sales. The lower the number, the less likely the Chinese brushmakers would be to compete for that same business. And if there were no competitors, Braun could price its brushes not according to the commodity competition but entirely in line with the value the brushes brought to the customers. If they wanted a particular brush—if they needed it—they would pay a premium for it. He also told his employees to relax. At the very least, Lance Cheney—former art student and drummer—knew this new approach was going to be a lot more fun.

Lance started the transition to a specialization brush company by jumping at a fluke opportunity. He got a call from a person who had just finished a routine inspection of a nuclear power plant. There were metal staples covering the floor of the coolant tank. This is, obviously, a huge risk; little metal pieces floating around in a nuclear power plant could cause unimaginable damage. The inspector realized that the staples came from his own brushes. He jammed a brush with stapled-on bristles against the fittings on the coolant tank pipes to wipe away crud. That jamming sometimes ripped away some bristles and staples.

Lance responded by copying the basic design that his great-grandfather had developed to clean milk bottles. He created a brush whose bristles were not separable from the core and were so thoroughly integrated that no bristle could ever escape. Even better, there were no staples used, so none could contaminate the coolant tank. He brought several of these brushes to the nuclear plant and, after extensive testing, proved that they were safe. Today, those brushes are used at nuclear generators all over the world. The company saves millions of dollars a year. Though the raw material for those brushes costs only twelve dollars or so, Lance sells them at a handsome profit. By pricing them so high, he can guarantee that he will continue to make them to the exacting specifications of the nuclear industry. This is precisely what Passion Economy businesspeople should aim for: a product whose price is determined by the value it provides the customer, not by the raw material that is used to make it.

If Max Cheney could see Braun Brush today, he would not recognize it. The firm still makes brushes, of course, but its profits don't come from the manufacturing of a physical product. Its profits come from the creativity, knowledge, and thinking that goes into those products.

Lance became a customized-brush specialist, called in on all sorts of serious, specialized projects. He is especially proud of a project he completed for NASA. When the Mars rovers *Spirit* and *Opportunity* were sent to Mars in 2004, they were programmed to drill into Martian rock to ascertain the rock's chemical makeup. The drill needed a clean surface, so NASA needed a brush that could remove dust from the rock. It had to be robust enough to survive the extremes of the Martian environment but light enough that it wouldn't add expensive precious weight to the spacecraft. From time to time, Lance says, he looks up into space and thinks about the fact that he made a brush that is up there.

Lance discovered something that he had suspected back in the days of begging his dad to change the company's strategy: it's possible to make a lot more money producing far fewer brushes when the brushes you make are truly solving a company's or an individual's most challenging problems. Lance often charges thousands of dollars for these brushes, and his customers gladly pay the bill because the brushes are saving them far more than that.

Lance now makes fifteen thousand different kinds of brushes with a staff of thirty brushmakers—or, more accurately, artisans. He sells various unique brushes that are tailor-made to the specific needs of a tiny customer base. Lance and his team have expertise in three things: handles, bristles, and glue. Just like his ancestors, he and his staff have become brush artists: they have deep expertise in fibers and the various ways of attaching fibers to a core to form a brush. Boar hair, for example, is particularly good at spreading oils. Nylon bristles are much better with acrylics. Badger hair has the perfect combination of suppleness and strength to remove the whitening, called "bloom," caused by cacao butter separating from the chocolate; it doesn't absorb any of the chocolate and also is soft enough not to leave lines. Horsehair is what you want for polishing wood; it's firm enough to scrape away detritus but, unlike nylon, won't cut into the wood. Lance knows about all of the various options for synthetic fibers and can explain the advantages of wooden handles, plastic handles, and metal handles. The real test of a brush expert, though, is glue. A glue needs to be perfect for the job: Will the brush be exposed to heat or cold? Will the fibers be yanked on or pushed from the side? Will the brush need to stand up to years of extreme abuse (as in the Mars rovers) or merely a few hours of a painting job?

Lance's joy is obvious when he's talking about the business. He loves every aspect of it. He loves the unique qualities of each kind of fiber, and he loves the fact that he knows those qualities so well. He loves inventing new brush solutions, and he loves finding customers who will delight in them. I doubt that brushes were his inevitable passion. His obvious passion is in creativity. He loves creatively solving problems, and he equally loves artistic creations. I would imagine—as would he—that he could have been happy in many other jobs and industries. He could have been a lifelong artist or a maker of specialty fabrics. But he was born into a brush family, he inherited a brush factory, and he figured out how to marry his core passions to the realities of his life.

Lance doesn't especially love technology. He prefers getting his hands dirty, thick with glue and loose bristles, as he fabricates some new brush. Unlike his forefathers, though, Lance can use existing technology to market these products to niche customers all around the world. He has launched a line of chocolate-polishing brushes for the prepared-dessert industry, an industrial croissant-buttering brush, and a heat-resistant brush that can clean hot deep fryers. The original milk-bottle cleaning brush (now with a plastic handle), by the way, is still a solid seller.

He also created a special brush that helps sort chips as they move through the massive machinery at the Frito-Lay plant in Texas. As with the nuclear power plant, Frito-Lay executives were quite worried that a poorly made brush could jeopardize their business. If even one loose bristle found its way into a bag of chips, it could lead to an expensive lawsuit and horrible publicity. Lance persuaded them that he could make a brush that was strong enough to never lose a single bristle, yet soft enough to never break a single chip.

In each case, Lance explains that his pricing is based not on the raw material—which often costs only pennies or a few dollars—but on the years of training, skill, and creativity that went into designing the brush. Furthermore, Lance does something that would have horrified his dad. He eliminates hundreds of brushes from the company's catalog each year. Often, these are exactly the brushes that have the highest sales volume but the lowest profit margin. If someone in China can make the same brush with roughly the same level of quality, Lance drops the line.

Many of Lance's customers wouldn't, themselves, use the word "passion" to describe their feelings about his brushes. Executives at Frito-Lay and the nuclear plant were simply making practical decisions about business challenges. Lance's passion, however, is infectious. He gets most of his custom work through word of mouth. People share his name with others who need a unique solution to their problems; they remember him because they were taken by his passionate engagement with the subject of specialty brushes.

In other cases, though, Lance is selling his passions more directly. Lance's proudest accomplishment is something few of us would think of as a brush at all. He kept up his side project of using brush bristles for art and developed a brand called Brush Tile, which uses brushmaking techniques to create tiles made out of fibers. By affixing different colored fibers, including optical fibers that can light up, horizontally to a vertical square anchor, Brush Tile creates remarkable, textured walls. Lance says he remembers sitting in the office one day and reading about Microsoft and Google, and how rich those companies had become. "I was thinking, How can I sell brushes to them?"

He realized that they seemed to be constantly building and renovating offices, trying to create a unique, graphically powerful image. Indeed, Brush Tile forms key walls in the headquarters of Oracle, Google, Microsoft, Amazon, and many other companies. When companies buy artistic tile for their entryways, they are willing to spend a lot more than when they are buying brushes to clean their floors.

In many ways, Lance has gone back to the company's roots, creating specialized brushes to solve narrow problems that no other company has addressed. He is also using the best of what his father and grandfather did: he is using the tools of twentieth-century scale. Lance isn't looking around Bushwick, Brooklyn, for problems within walking distance. He can reach companies all over the country and the world and learn of their most intractable and important problems. Because of this enormous reach, he can swat away the easy money of producing commodity brushes in bulk and instead zero in on the single most profitable—and exciting—brush-related problems. Braun Brush is now a fully modern, twenty-first-century company, a model for others; though, significantly, it is not a high-tech company.

I find the simplicity of Lance's business to be inspiring, a wonderful model of just how successful we can all be with a bit of modest expertise, curiosity, creative thinking, and the ability to listen to what other people want. Here is a man who knows these three things well and can think creatively about how best to combine them to solve an infinite array of complex problems. He has, in essence, turned the brush business into a solutions business. The thing he is selling is not a handle, a bristle, and glue; it is his—and his staff's—expertise in how to use those three things to solve problems. That is enough for him to have built a thriving business that supports him and forty employees. The business has been growing steadily since he made the transition from commodity brushmaker to solutions provider. The company has grown more in the past decade than it did over the entire twentieth century.

The wonderful thing about intimacy at scale is that when you have access to the entire world, you can find that your narrow area of interest and expertise can provide a solution to the most difficult problem for someone, somewhere. The more technology expands, the more artificial intelligence grows, the more robotic machinery improves, the better Lance will do. He will be able to find more and more problems and solve them more precisely and build the solutions more cheaply. He is not just future-proof; in fact, the very future that scares so many people will help him do what he does better and better. Every step forward in technology and global trade makes it easier for Lance to find problems and focus his attention on solving them. If automation and outsourcing continue to grow, that's only good news for his business.

After getting to know Lance, I researched the brush industry. There were a lot of companies like Braun in the United States: family-run firms that churned out a huge number of the same sort of brushes for years. I visited one of them, Kirschner Brush, in the South Bronx of New York City, less than an hour from Braun's headquarters.

My guide was Israel Kirschner, a tall, energetic man, sixty-nine years old, who seemed, frankly, as surprised as I was that his ancient family business was still operating in the Bronx. It's a mess of a place in a sagging factory building. There are old machines. "That could be a hundred years old," he said of a bristle-cleaning machine, and then he bragged, with a wink, about his latest purchase, bought sometime in the 1980s: a weird spinning contraption that puts glue on bristles. Around the machines are piled boxes, and little pieces of replacement parts and brush handles are haphazardly spread all over the dark, worn wooden floors. The place looks as if it hasn't been cleaned in decades, and Kirschner seems very much in on the joke.

No one could make a better case against the continued existence of Kirschner Brush than Israel Kirschner himself. His father started the company during the huge economic boom after World War II, and for decades the company made and sold rugged professional brushes for the toughest painting jobs. Most of Kirschner's customers were large construction firms and government agencies that needed brushes to paint bridges or the walls of massive buildings, and other major projects. A single bridge or large wall might require hundreds of brushes, and Kirschner provided them. Then, in the early 2000s, Chinese manufacturers started shipping these types of brushes to the United States in huge numbers. At first, Kirschner recalls, the brushes were cheaply made—the bristles fell off, the handles were rough plastic. His clients wouldn't consider buying junk that would smear paint and deposit loose bristles, all while hurting the hands of their workers. It didn't take long, though, for the Chinese factories to improve. Their quality level rose, and Kirschner found it increasingly difficult to justify his much more expensive brushes.

He handed me a one-inch boar-bristle brush with a wooden handle. Like all of his products, it's small and simple but quite elegant. For a moment, I thought he was an example of the Passion Economy. After all, he seemed just as passionate about his brushes as Lance is about his. Kirschner, however, doesn't follow the other rules. He doesn't match his brushes to those who most want them—he continues to sell them in bulk, largely to municipal governments who couldn't care less about the subtle beauty of a well-crafted brush. He doesn't listen to his customers to adjust his products to their needs. And he continues to make a product that others can do at greater scale.

He told me that, using his ancient machinery and a fair bit of labor, it costs him more than a dollar to make this brush, which means he has to sell it, wholesale, for two dollars, and a retail customer pays four dollars. A Chinese competitor was selling a nearly indistinguishable brush for thirty cents. The Chinese factories, of course, have access to cheaper labor, but they also have many newer and more efficient machines that make more brushes more quickly and with less waste than Kirschner can. To compete in the same industry, Kirschner would have to spend millions of dollars upgrading his equipment, building a new factory. Instead, he plugs along. Each year—each month—he makes less money than he did during the last one, and he knows that someday soon, he'll shut down. Kirschner stays in business because it's what he likes to do and because he still has some old customers around. I spoke to one of them, Michael Wolf, of Greco Brush, who says that he could switch to Chinese-made brushes and save a lot of money. But, he told me, "my father did business with his father back in the fifties. We're keeping it going, the two of us." Of course, every year, a few of those customers retire, die, or succumb to price pressure.

This is a familiar story for all sorts of American businesses. There was a way of making a solid living for decades, and then, quite suddenly, a combination of new technology and trade ripped that business apart. Our country is filled with Kirschners; these are people who spent their lives thriving under a system that suddenly disappeared, and they couldn't adjust.

I liked Israel Kirschner a great deal. He was funny and self-aware and seemed comfortable with the fact that he was simply too old to change and his kids weren't interested in taking over. A few years later, while writing this book, I was sad to hear that Kirschner died and his kids sold the business to a large company. There wasn't much to sell; the equipment wasn't worth anything, but they still had those remaining customers, and that had some value. Kirschner hadn't been able to shift to this new economic system, in which profit comes from solving new problems. It wasn't that Kirschner wasn't bright or knowledgeable—he probably knew as much, if not more, about bristles, handles, and glue as his competitor Lance. It was simpler than that. Kirschner could see that the economy had changed and that sticking with the things that had worked before was no longer effective. But he couldn't think of what to do instead.

Braun, with its milk-bottle-cleaning brush, has become my totem, my model of how to thrive in the twenty-first century. Modern technologies, especially computers and the Internet, allow people to match their particular passions and knowledge with the people who most need them. As we'll see, there are many ways to do this, and one's strategy needs to be adapted, because each industry, business, and person is unique. That is one of the core lessons of this book: for most of the twentieth century, the safest, most lucrative strategy was to be as much like others as possible. In the twenty-first century, the best strategy is to be fully yourself and to highlight your areas of difference from everyone else. That's where the money is.

Very few entrepreneurs can make money through sameness, by offering the same sort of product over and over again. Whether you are an accountant or a brushmaker, there is a pretty good chance that someone else—or, increasingly, some computer or robot—can provide an approximate version of your product for far less. As a result, many men and women have found themselves in the unenviable vortex of working longer hours, earning less, and living in a state of fear that their job may one day disappear. Most brushmakers have given up or, worse, been forced out of business. It's been a vicious cycle.

For most of the 1990s, Braun Brush was stuck at $1 million a year in sales. As I said, it has grown dramatically since. Lance Cheney's key to success isn't a secret. Making it in America now means not only stepping out of the commodity game—deciding not to make the bottom-level product that companies in lower-wage countries can produce for a fraction of the price—but also combining the best elements of the nineteenth century (artisanship and tinkering) with those of the twentieth (scale). Lance certainly shares his great-grandfather's wild creativity and problem-solving, and he had access to his father's organization and standardization. Because of computers, automated machinery, and global trade, Lance is now able to take all he inherited, all he learned, and all his ideas and spread his reach all over the world, thriving in the Passion Economy.

I particularly like the fact that Lance's best customers evaluate his passion in especially unimpassioned ways. He has to truly solve their problems in an enduring, measurable way if he is going to charge the premium prices that allow him to thrive. For many of his customers, his passion, his emotional drive, is translated into clear, logical terms. They can see how many more hours of uptime his products have given them, how much money they have saved or can earn because of his brush innovations. But even the most logical operational analysis can only conclude that these problems would not have been solved were it not for a passionate, frustrated artist who inherited a big factory and figured out a new way to think about brushes.

# CASE STUDY: KIRRIN FINCH

## *MARKET RESEARCH: FRIENDS INVITED*

Laura Moffat and Kelly Sanders got married in Vermont in 2014. Laura, who grew up in Scotland, and Kelly, who spent her childhood in New Jersey, shared a lifelong frustration. Even as little girls, they had realized that nothing they wore was quite right for them. They knew, for sure, that they hated dresses and anything too girly. But clothes for boys weren't perfect, either. They didn't want dinosaurs and rocket ships on everything. As women, they made do. Laura would buy men's work shirts; Kelly, who is petite, still shopped in the boys clothing department. Clothing designed for men and boys, however, does not fit most women's bodies well. Women typically are curvier, with larger bustlines and proportionally wider hips. Men's and boys' shirts are too tight on top and at the bottom. However, clothes designed to fit a woman's body inevitably came with feminine touches they both disliked.

Laura and Kelly were not especially obsessed with clothes. Laura worked in pharmaceuticals; Kelly was a schoolteacher. But when they decided to get married, their lives changed in more ways than the obvious ones. They both wanted to wear suits at the ceremony inspired by traditional menswear, and yet nothing they tried on fit well. Hating the idea of feeling uncomfortable on their wedding day, they commissioned a tailor to custom-make suits that had traditional male styling and would also fit their bodies. On their special day, they felt fantastic. It was more than just the pleasure of a well-fitted garment. They felt that, for the first time, their clothing fully matched their true identities.

The newlyweds took a nine-month honeymoon, an adventurous trip around the world. They spent much of that time talking about the feeling of a perfect garment, and they began to imagine a business that would give that same feeling to others. They knew there would be some sort of market. They had plenty of friends who were like them: gay and straight women who wanted to wear menswear-inspired clothes that truly fit a woman's body. There was, as well, a growing population of people who identified as nonbinary—meaning they did not see themselves as either female or male—who would also want menswear-inspired clothes that fit. Laura and Kelly knew there would be customers, but how many? Would this be a minor, niche product or could they build a substantial business?

Neither knew of Scott Stern, but they followed a path identical to the one he suggests. They would focus on the U.S. market, at first. Laura and Kelly could find no reliable data on their target customer, who they defined by the term "tomboy," a broad category that included lesbian and straight women as well as people who identify as nonbinary. The best data they could find covered the LGBTQ market, which would make up a significant portion of their target audience. It was tricky to calculate, since many straight women crave tomboy clothes, and many gay women and transgender and nonbinary people don't. Even more confounding, opinion surveys and the U.S. census do not yet have standardized tools to denote the full range of gender identities. Laura and Kelly estimated that roughly 5 percent of people identified as women in the census would be potential customers. A significant percentage of this group would be especially loyal to a company that was owned by members of the LGBTQ community and was so thoughtfully serving its needs.

They went on to analyze the purchasing power of their target audience and its population distribution. They concluded that more than a million women, largely—but not entirely—concentrated in major urban centers, would have the interest and disposable income to purchase their clothes.

These numbers are vague. But even if they are off by 50 percent, they are incredibly helpful at the early stage of company formation. Laura and Kelly knew that their company would start small. They had no intention of reaching millions of customers in the first few years, but understanding that the market was potentially that big allowed them to invest more time, money, and effort in a business that could grow large enough to be their life's work. These numbers also showed them that the market wasn't so massive that they would, one day, rival huge apparel companies like Levi's or J.Crew. This was good news. It meant their target market was probably too small to invite competition from those huge players, who could quickly shove them aside.

That initial gut-check potential-market estimate can require a few minutes of creative thinking and some Google searches. Those moments can save a budding entrepreneur years of wasted effort. Is your target market so narrow that it can't sustain a business? Is it so vast that a larger firm will push you to the sidelines? Or is it a Goldilocks market: big enough to make your business successful but small enough that you can dominate?

Next, Laura and Kelly did the opposite of big, broad, vague estimation: they went narrow. They had a few shirts manufactured and hosted a market research party. They reached out to friends and friends of friends to assemble a couple dozen likely customers. They contacted some lesbians who referred to themselves as androgynous or tomboys, nonbinary people, and straight women who liked how menswear looked but couldn't find any men's clothing that fit, and they invited them to their home to enjoy some food and drinks. The occasion was festive and fun. And Laura and Kelly learned that there were, indeed, people who passionately wanted the very thing Laura and Kelly were passionate about creating: menswear-inspired clothes for a female or nonbinary body.

They also began to delve into the details. What about the shirts most appealed to their target customers? What did they think of the button size, the chosen fabrics, the cut of the collars? They asked about pricing and whether customers would buy shirts online or only in a store, where they could sample the clothes.

Without needing to hire an expensive market research company, Laura and Kelly rapidly learned that their core hypothesis seemed correct, and they were able to invest in their first few hundred shirts confidently. Those sold quickly, so they decided to double their order and then doubled it again and then again. When those also flew out the door, Laura and Kelly understood that they had a real business.

By then, they had enough actual customers and ongoing revenue that they could justify more targeted market research. Now the company, which they named Kirrin Finch, is thriving. It offers dozens of shirts, pants, blazers, hats, and accessories for its target market. Laura and Kelly have begun to focus on scaling up production so Kirrin Finch clothing is at a more accessible price point for all of their target consumers.

# CHAPTER 4

# ACCOUNTING FOR THE BRAVE

*By turning a traditional model upside down,
a bored money cruncher learns that he can thrive
by figuring out his true product and its true price*

Jason Blumer resembles the cartoon character Tintin, complete with bright red hair that sticks straight up above his forehead and a look of constant, eyes-wide-open astonishment at everything he sees. The only differences are that Blumer has a more bulbous nose, wears glasses, and speaks in a thick southern drawl. Blumer embraces his cartoon-like features, always wearing brightly colored, perfectly round plastic eyeglasses and punctuating his commentary with exclamations like "Whoa," "Cool beans," and "That is crazy!"

Blumer changes lives. I was able to catalog more than three hundred businesses in the United States and Canada that are far more successful because of Blumer. I spoke with dozens of small business owners who told me that they are richer, happier, and more deeply fulfilled because of what Blumer has taught them. One man, who runs a website design company in Dallas, told me that Blumer is the single most important person in his life. "Oh, except for my wife," he added. "And my kids. Although some days, Blumer is right up there." The two men have met once. The man also told me that his monthly check for Blumer's services is his single-biggest expense and the only one he is truly happy to pay.

Jason Blumer is an accountant. An accountant who transforms people and their businesses. Which is to say, he is nothing like the image that comes to mind when one hears the word "accountant." First of all, he wears flip-flops, jeans, and T-shirts to nearly every meeting. He doesn't own a suit and threw out all of his ties years ago. He says the word "dude" in almost every sentence. While he does talk about typical accountant details like tax structures and profit and loss statements, he quickly tells clients that he finds that stuff even more boring than they do and that he's pretty lousy at thinking it through. He would much rather ask his clients to explain how they define happiness and success and to precisely describe the unique combination of skills and interests they possess.

A typical Blumer client is a creative small business owner—a graphic designer, public relations consultant, the head of a digital agency who is good at what she does, works extremely hard, yet doesn't make enough money to sustain herself. This is quite common. Creative owners of small companies often lack the business background to understand how to engineer a successful strategy. They take whatever clients come their way, work as hard as they can, and hope to get ahead. Blumer asks them a lot of questions. He asks them what makes them happiest, what they think they can do uniquely that few others can. He challenges them to carefully define the value they bring to their customers. Over many months, Blumer—sometimes gently, sometimes more forcefully—helps these businesspeople relaunch themselves, so that they can work fewer hours yet provide far more value to their clients and make far more money.

Blumer can point to hundreds of success stories, but the best one he tells is his own. Blumer was not a natural business visionary. Quite the opposite. He knows all the mistakes people make and how hard it is to change, because he made all those mistakes and it took him a very long time to fix them.

Life shifted for Blumer one chilly fall morning in 2003. He awoke shortly after six a.m. and commenced the first routine of his routine-filled day. He walked quietly to the shower so as not to wake up his two young daughters. He scanned his closet for one of the identical blue suits that his wife had purchased on his behalf. As he glanced in the bathroom mirror, folding his tie around his neck, Blumer was reminded, yet again, of how little he resembled the young man he once had been, the one with the long hair and jeans and ratty Converses—the guy who dreamed of being an artist and, more important, achieving heavy metal glory.

Blumer grew up just outside Greenville, South Carolina. His father was an accountant at a series of small, local businesses, but Jason doesn't remember him talking about work or accounting. His dad was most energized when discussing his long hikes in the Appalachian foothills just north of town, something he tried to do every weekend. Jason was an uninspired student and ended up at North Greenville University, a small Christian college. He doesn't remember much about his classes. His focus was his band, Silence So Loud, a Christian heavy metal band.

For a brief moment in the late 1980s and early 1990s, Christian metal was hot. Bands like Stryper, Bloodgood, Barren Cross, Whitecross, and Leviticus were making a good living playing at Christian colleges and music venues in the Bible Belt and far beyond. There was so much hunger for this kind of hard-rocking yet Christian music that even a small—and, he'll admit now, pretty lousy—local band that knew how to distort its guitar licks and screams into a microphone could get some regular gigs.

Blumer, then, had the standard-issue hair-sprayed mane as

he played all over upstate South Carolina and even traveled to nearby states. There was a solid week where a misunderstood message from a relative who knew somebody in the music industry led the bandmates to believe they were on the brink of major stardom. Then, as most college bands do, they broke up, with a bit of acrimony. Shockingly quickly, Jason cut his hair, finished his accounting degree at Wofford College—he had chosen the major because it was his dad's job and he had no other idea what to study—and met and married his wife, Jennifer. Soon she was pregnant, and he was looking for work as an accountant.

He took a job at the first firm that hired him and learned that he would make money based on how many hours he worked and how many clients he maintained. He was a mediocre accountant—it took him six tries to pass the CPA exam—but he was soon bringing in $60,000 a year, which is a very good living in upstate South Carolina. He was able to buy a small but lovely home for his growing family (his second daughter was soon on the way).

If you'd asked him then if he liked his job, he would have looked at you strangely. It hadn't occurred to him to even consider that question. Jobs, he thought, aren't things people like; they're things people do so they can support their family and, if they're lucky, fund some nice hobbies on the side. If you had pressed, he would have confessed that he truly hated wearing a suit and tie and that he found the work boring, and even a bit depressing, although he wouldn't have known what to do about it.

Then came a fateful assignment in the fall of 2003, at a factory in a small town about ninety minutes from Greenville. The factory was ancient* and had been purchased by a larger national company, which had hired Blumer to perform a thor-

* Identifying details about this business have been changed at Blumer's request to preserve confidentiality.

ough audit of its books. The project grew to become massive; it would eventually require Blumer to make the ninety-minute drive each morning and evening for more than two months.

Those drives became intense periods of self-reflection for Jason. The factory was in a rural town, far from the bigger cities around Greenville or the interstate highways. To get there, Jason drove through a chain of small towns that were dying. Upstate South Carolina's economy had been completely dependent on textiles. For nearly a century, the area produced thread and T-shirts and socks and other fabric-related products. Textile mills were wonderful for the local economy. They provided such steady work for so many people that it was common for parents to tell their children not to finish high school—they'd end up working in the textile mill whether they had a degree or not, so why not get there early, make some extra money, and build their seniority at sixteen, rather than eighteen.

Also, no part of the United States was more devastated by technological advances and trade with China than North and South Carolina's textile industry. Almost overnight, some machines could automatically turn cotton into thread and that thread into fabric, without any human intervention. A joke made the rounds about how a modern textile factory has two employees: a man and a dog. The man is there to feed the dog, and the dog is there to keep the man away from the machines. There were some jobs the machines didn't destroy—mostly cutting and sewing work to turn fabric into clothes. But those jobs disappeared thanks to cheaper labor, first to Mexico and Central America and then, soon enough, to China. Between 1995 and 2003, it was as if a plague had swept through upstate South Carolina, taking away all the ambitious working-age people (of course, they were moving to other places with better opportunities) and leaving behind the old and infirm.

Driving through these struggling towns, Blumer found himself wondering what would become of him. Many of his clients were textile firms or other companies that supported them. Would there be much work left? When you look at it, he thought, accounting is not all that different from textiles. Increasingly sophisticated accounting software allowed millions of customers to do their own taxes. Offshore accountants, in Europe and Asia, offered reliable and inexpensive competition via the Internet.

Blumer knew that this particular job he'd been assigned to was safe. That was because the company he was auditing was such a mess that it would be a long, long time before a computer could replace a human being, riffling through sloppy piles of paper. On his very first day, the ancient treasurer of the company had told him that they would have to visit several parts of the factory to accumulate the required information. She then led Blumer on a tour of what seemed like every office and closet in the building: the records room, in the basement, with its boxes belching up deposit receipts; the box in the foreman's office with receipts for every bit of machinery purchased; a room on the first floor where two older women entered every sale into an ancient ledger book. Blumer realized then that he would need to re-create the cash flow of the business, matching every dollar coming in with every penny going out, with only the sketchiest of clues to go on. The job would require untold hours of tedium. It would take weeks. It might take months.

The worst part, Blumer understood, was that this job was the best he could hope for. A heinously boring assignment that was immune from competition from computers or offshore accountants far away was going to be the main part of his work from then on. Like pretty much every other midlevel CPA at a midsized firm, Blumer had come to be evaluated not by his talent but, rather, by one single, draconian metric: the number of hours he billed—or, as it was known in the business, the utilization rate. At some long-ago juncture, it seemed, someone had determined that accountants needed exactly 30 percent of their workday to eat lunch, go to the bathroom, and attend meetings. This meant that the other 70 percent should be devoted to the noble calling of billable work. For decades, a 70 percent utilization rate was the baseline requirement of any young accountant who dreamed of earning a raise or making partner. When slumps hit, those below 70 percent were usually the first to go.

Blumer had become his company's expert on computer technology, eagerly studying every new accounting software program that became popular. This provided great value to the firm. Accounting was becoming increasingly automated, and it was helpful to have someone on the staff choosing the right digital tools and training other accountants in how to use them. But in the brutal logic of the field, his time spent learning about computer technology had zero value because it was not billable to a specific client. His utilization rate had regularly begun falling below 70 percent, more than once hitting 60 percent. Accountants who hit 55 percent were often let go quickly, and Blumer was afraid that this was where he was headed. Which was why, he knew, the massive, sloppy auditing job should have been a dream come true: weeks of full days. He would eat a quick sandwich and head right back to work, getting his utilization rate above 90 percent one month.

Instead, he was miserable. The work was unpleasant but, worse, it was useless. It truly didn't matter. Even if he performed the most extensive, brilliant audit, his customers, the people at the company headquarters who had bought the factory, wouldn't care. When one company buys another one, its higher-ups often order such an audit so that they can show that they've done all the appropriate due diligence. But it was clear that this factory would be shut down, everyone who worked there would be laid off, and the only thing of value would be its client list, which was why the factory had been bought in the first place. Blumer's audit would go into a file drawer somewhere in headquarters and perhaps never even be looked at.

So much of what Jason was doing was just like that audit. It was perfunctory. It brought no delight to anybody. The very best cases were those in which he helped a client save some money on taxes, which did bring that person some amount of satisfaction. That wasn't enough for Jason. It's one thing to be happy to owe the government less money; it's something else entirely to be truly thrilled by a creative piece of accountancy.

It is dangerous for an accountant to ask the question, What good does my work do? Nonetheless, the thought crept into Jason's head during his commute, which was normally filled with gripe-fueled fantasies. Perhaps, he'd think, in some alternate universe there was a way for him to delight clients, do creative work, and never again have to hear about utilization rates. Then he'd remember, with a jolt, that he lived in a world where mortgages have to be paid, work has to get done, and that work isn't fun.

Slowly, over those drives, his daydreams became more concrete. He began to picture what his ideal job might look like. He started to form a plan. It seemed a little risky, and he needed to talk to his wife first, but he wondered if the greatest risk would be *not* to take the leap he was contemplating.

Accounting's transformation into a safe, boring job is something of a tragedy. Accounting, after all, was once among the most innovative professions the world's economies had ever seen. During the fifteenth century, Venice was the center of the cultural and economic world. The republic's wealth came, in large part, from its legendary Arsenale, the most formidable military manufacturing complex on the planet. By controlling the seas, Venice controlled commerce as well. Venetian merchants never had to worry much about their businesses. Most businesses were small enough that a merchant could keep track of his inventory in his head, along with the aid of some unreliable scratches on paper. It was easier this way, too. Before the adoption of Arabic numerals (which were invented, in fact, in India), merchants had to add and subtract using Roman numerals. If you have 357 bushels of wheat and each one brings in

29 ducats, you would have to multiply CCCLVII by XXIX. Unsurprisingly, few bothered.

Consequently, few Venetian business owners could answer the two most fundamental questions in economics: How much did they make and how much did they owe? Since they couldn't fundamentally answer the question of their solvency, they were left particularly vulnerable when the economies of France and Spain, among other emerging naval powers, began to compete in their markets and eat into their profits.

Accounting saved the day. In 1494, the Venetian friar Luca Bartolomeo de Pacioli first laid out the details of double-entry bookkeeping—matching credits and debits, painstakingly following the provenance and destination of every transaction. While it might have seemed like a simple solution, accounting was the Internet of its century. The innovation allowed merchants to know their business more accurately, to understand their top customers and products better, to figure out what to order and what to avoid, to decipher which corners could be cut and which could not, and to handle far more volume. It provided the financial baseline that allowed businesses to grow larger, competition to become fiercer, and commerce to change more rapidly.

Most conversations about the Industrial Revolution focus on machine innovations, but our modern economy owes as much to accounting as it does to engineering. The Industrial Revolution was made possible by huge mechanical advances—steam power, railroads, the telegraph—but also by the financial advances that powered them. Francis Cabot Lowell, for example, opened the world's first integrated textile mill—the first truly modern factory—in Waltham, Massachusetts, in 1813. His Boston Manufacturing Company was able to turn raw cotton into finished cloth under one roof. Lowell's engineering breakthrough—a belt-and-pulley system that carried power from one water wheel to several machines—took a year to perfect. But the real challenge, the one that occupied him for a decade, was figuring out how to balance the books of a multi-stage manufacturing process.

Previously, manufacturing had been simpler, often a one-step process. One business spun cotton into yarn; another wove that yarn into cloth. Accounting reflected this simplicity. Business owners merely needed to make sure that their finished goods sold for more than the cost of their raw materials. But Lowell, whose company bought raw cotton, spun it, knitted it, wove it, cut the cloth for final sale, and paid the workers who performed these tasks, needed to know what each step cost him and whether it was, itself, profitable. He could sell finished cloth for far more than the raw cotton and still lose money by overpaying for one of the many steps in his integrated process.

Further, he needed to know which parts were more or less efficient and which sorts of investments—whether it was new machinery or more workers—would pay off in the long run and which would lose money. Since he had several investors (another brand-new innovation) and owed a fair bit of money to the bank, he needed to be able to divide his earnings in a variety of different ways to ensure his company's solvency. It took years to develop the Waltham system, which allowed Lowell to monitor the precise profitability of each step of his factory from his mansion in Boston, half a day's horse ride away. By the early 1820s, the Boston Manufacturing Company's owners had opened several much larger plants all over New England, transforming the area's economy and pushing the United States into the Industrial Age. It would never have happened without accounting.

Accounting kept driving American economic growth for the rest of the century. The rapid growth of railroads brought even greater financial challenges. Managers needed to monitor a business that was spread out over a massive geographical area. At the same time, the telegraph meant companies had to keep track, in real time, of far more information than any business-person had ever had access to. By the early twentieth century, a new invention—the multidivisional company—had brought about a whole new set of profound challenges, as managers needed to learn how to allocate resources across several different businesses. At each step, invaluably, accountants developed new techniques that solved new challenges.

The American century, in many ways, was the accounting century. A profession that had barely existed a few decades before had become one of the most reliable occupations in the country. As business became more competitive, every company needed accountants to oversee costs and revenue and make sure the firm was staying above water. When the government passed laws requiring every public company to monitor its books carefully, in addition to the internal staff accountants, companies also needed to employ outside accountants to perform audits.

When personal taxation became the law in 1913, regular Americans began hiring accountants to make sure they filed their tax returns properly. There was a steady increase in schools that taught accounting and in the number of trained accountants, but these gains never quite kept up with demand— and as a result, accounting all but guaranteed lifetime employment for anybody who learned the craft.

This transformed what had been a bold field of creative visionaries in the nineteenth century into a job that too often became synonymous with "boring and predictable." The phrase "creative accounting" adopted a seamy, illicit air. We don't want our accountants creative or passionate; we want them bored and boring, sitting at their desks, making sure all the numbers add up just right.

Then came computers, the Internet, and global trade. It turns out that a job whose greatest value comes from performing routine tasks is exactly the sort of job that can be done by computers or by workers in other countries who will work for less. Most accountants realized this and reacted. Many of the big accounting firms shifted to consulting, charging clients not just for counting their money but for helping them make more of it. Local accountants struggled to hold on to business by lowering prices, promising to find more lucrative tax breaks, and searching out other ways of competing against machines and overseas competition. It became a desperate effort to stay ahead of the game.

Blumer realized that the sudden increase in competition had removed the floor from the field—accounting was no longer a job with a guaranteed decent salary. He also understood that it had removed the ceiling, too. Blumer now saw that he could have computers and other people do all the things he hated most about his work—the counting, the auditing, the tax filing—so that he could focus on his dream of finding ways to be truly creative and even inspire his customers, bringing them value they would happily pay for.

When his endless auditing job ended, Blumer told his wife he had a dream. He half-expected her to tell him that he didn't just have a dream, he also had two children, a mortgage, and responsibilities. She didn't. She told him to pursue that dream, even if it meant some economic hard times—which, indeed, it did. Blumer quit his $60,000-a-year job and joined his father's all-but-moribund accounting firm. "Firm" is probably too grand a word to describe that business. It was a desk in a bedroom on the second floor of his father's house and a handful of clients, most of whom had been with his father for decades and were fairly elderly and slow to realize that computers could save them money.

In the movie of Jason Blumer's life—if anyone would ever make a movie about an accountant who didn't solve crimes—this would be the period that looked the darkest. Somehow, in his quest to fulfill his dreams, he had taken a massive step backward. He was still spending his days working on tax returns and the occasional audit, but now his customers were paying less and were precisely the sorts of people most likely to eventually drop him in favor of software.

For Jason, though, this was a magical period. The accounting work was simple. Filling out tax returns for retirees was far easier than the months-long audit for a dying factory. And with a shorter workweek, he could spend some time exploring his new ideas. He found books and podcasts and blogs that helped him think through his gut sense about how an accounting firm could bring a valued new service to its customers. I picture his process as something like the movie *Ocean's Eleven:* Blumer was assembling a team of brilliant minds, each one focused on a particular aspect of the problem at hand. Though, of course, in this case, the team never actually gathers together, and the problem at hand is not stealing hundreds of millions from a casino but figuring out how to be more satisfied, and valuable, as an accountant.

Blumer's first major discovery was Ron Baker, a vision-ary accountant obsessed with one issue: accountants shouldn't charge by the hour. Baker is a thickset man from Northern California, a proud "conservatarian," which he defines as a con-servative with libertarian economic leanings. He is fifteen years older than Jason and, in the 1980s, had been a staff accountant at KPMG, a massive firm, doing work much like Jason had: audits and tax filings for companies. During that time, he noted that in a typical engagement with a client, he and the other KPMG accountants would usually have several insights within the first few minutes of reviewing the customer's books. Because they had so much expertise, Baker and his team could see, in an instant, if the company was maintaining its books poorly.

Often, especially in older companies, financial records are kept according to rules set up decades earlier and rarely reviewed. Most people might assume that financial records are organized in some standard way, perhaps according to princi-ples encoded in law. There are, indeed, rules and laws govern-ing financial records, but these leave enormous discretion to each company to customize the methods it uses. Even though financial records look like rote recordings of objective facts, they are, in fact, living documents designed to answer specific questions. A fast-growing, brand-new company might engineer its books to focus on how quickly and costly it is to acquire new customers. An older firm in a mature market might want to highlight how best to lower the costs of producing its products, since it would be less likely to acquire large numbers of new customers and can raise profits only by lowering costs.

Too often, Baker discovered, companies were doing neither of these things. Someone, long ago, had come up with a system, and the finance team was applying that system without realizing that it no longer answered most of the firm's current questions. Baker could often see this at a glance and immediately present a company's executives with new ideas about how they could use their financial reports to identify and solve some of their most intractable problems.

Because of Baker's training and expertise, he was able to present ideas that could bring millions of dollars of profit to a company. Often, the initial idea took him less than a day to come up with. There were a few cases where the most valuable insight took only seconds because the failings of a company's records were so obvious. Baker, however, wouldn't be paid for that insight. Like nearly all accountants, he was paid by the hour. This was ridiculous, he thought. A typical engagement with a client might take three hundred hours, billed—this was the 1980s—at one hundred dollars per hour. But those hours were not equal. The first chunk of one to ten hours was worth far more than one hundred dollars—providing millions of dollars of real value to the customer—while the subsequent 290 hours were worth far less. Baker spent most of that time checking figures to make sure they were entered correctly, work that a first-year associate or, soon, a computer could do just as well. Baker hated that part of the process. He also hated the idea that he wasn't getting paid enough. What if all he did was provide that first essential insight, charge what it was worth, and then let someone else do the boring scut work? Baker decided that the way to solve this was to quit charging by the hour. Full stop.

Accountants should charge customers based on the value they bring to them—that was Baker's breakthrough. This would allow accountants with truly valuable insights to spend all of their time just providing those insights, thereby making more money. It would change the entire profession. Young accountants would learn that the best way to make a decent living was to find out how they could add value, not just perform a rote function. This change would have the happy additional benefit of allowing accountants to eagerly embrace computer technology and outsourced accounting services. It's far better to let someone or something do the boring, less-valuable stuff, freeing up a skilled professional's time for the potentially exciting work.

Baker started to imagine what America might look like if accountants were, thus, freed. They would provide more and better insights. It would become economically logical for accountants to spend more of their time developing knowledge and skills to benefit their clients. Why spend years developing the expertise to provide great insight if you'll be paid just as much for an hour doing things a calculator could do?

Baker loves to point out something else about hourly billing: it creates a complete disconnect between service provider and customer. Nobody has ever said, Boy, I'd love three hours of an accountant's time. They want an accounting problem solved and don't care how long it takes to do it. They want to pay the right amount. When the price is determined by value, Baker argued, the accountant and the customer have more well-aligned incentives. The accountant is incentivized to provide better value, not to extend a job as long as possible.

Hourly billing also helps turn accounting into a more commoditized service, as if each accountant does exactly the same thing in each hour of work and two accountants can be mathematically compared through their prices. Accountants, however, are quite differentiated. Some, like Jason, are remarkably good at quickly finding sharp insights that can transform a business. Others are better at carefully handling the slower work of making sure accounts are properly managed.

Baker became obsessed. The word "obsessed" is overused, often inaccurately. Not here. Baker quit his job, started a think tank—the VeraSage Institute—and devoted his life to convincing accountants to stop charging by the hour. He created a "Declaration of Independence," a part tongue-in-cheek, part earnest explanation of his beliefs, written in a purposefully overwrought style:

> We hold these Truths to be self-evident, that all Value is Subjective, the Customer is sole arbiter of the Value which we in the Professions create . . .
>
> Time Accounting has foisted onto the professions the implicit assertion that Time x Rate = Value. This Equation is emphatically false, and is in need of being rejected as without Reason. The Notion that Time is Money is hereby directly rejected.
>
> Time Accounting misaligns the interests of the Professional and the Customer whom it is pledged to Serve.
>
> Time Accounting has focused the Professions solely on hours, not Value, thereby keeping the Professional Mired in Mediocrity at the expense of Entrepreneurial Excellence in the pursuit of opportunities.
>
> Time Accounting places the voluntary transaction risk entirely on the Customer, in direct defiance of the Customer's interests the Professions have pledged to Serve.
>
> Time Accounting fosters a production mentality, not an Entrepreneurial Spirit, thereby hindering the

Professions in their attempt to innovate and contribute to the dynamism of the Free Market.

(It goes on: https://verasage.com/DofI/)

Baker travels the world giving speeches to groups of accountants and, now, other professionals who charge by the hour; he holds an annual conference; hosts a podcast; and has spread his message to anybody who will listen. By his estimate, he's converted approximately 10 to 15 percent of the accounting profession to his way of thinking. And nobody is a more enthusiastic adherent than Jason Blumer.

The next member of the Blumer intellectual team was Tim Williams. Tim is quite different from Baker. Baker is big and loud; heavyset and rumpled. Williams is tall and thin, dresses impeccably, and moves with elegant precision. Baker believes that hourly billing is not only a bad way to run a business, he believes it is actually Marxist and un-American (from his declaration: "Time Accounting is a descendant of the thoroughly discredited Marxian Labor Theory of Value"). Williams, by contrast, is a left-leaning Democrat who believes that his ideas will create a more equitable society. For all their differences, Williams and Baker have become good friends and colleagues. Williams is a member of Baker's VeraSage Institute, and they find that their ideas meld into a cohesive whole.

Williams was an advertising executive, working at several of the world's largest firms and a few smaller ones. He also had his conversion in the 1990s, one that can be seen as a parallel insight to Baker's. Advertising was going through major changes. With increasing global trade, major companies—Coca-Cola, Boeing, and others—began to see their best opportunities for growth in other countries. These companies wanted to be able to hire one huge agency that could oversee their advertising and marketing efforts everywhere. This led to massive consolidation as large agencies bought smaller ones. Today, a handful of multibillion-dollar, multinational agency holding companies—most notably WPP, Omnicom, Publicis, Interpublic, Havas, and Dentsu—control nearly all of the large accounts. Williams started his practice by focusing on the smaller agencies that remained. There are more than thirteen thousand advertising and marketing firms in the country, all of whom are battling over the business that has not been gobbled up by the big players.

Many smaller advertising agencies determined that the best way to compete with the big ones would be to offer all the things the massive firms did. The phrase "full-service agency" became commonplace, referring to an agency that can do anything for any company. These agencies would work with any client who called and provide any service that firm wanted: design a new logo, sure; come up with a television campaign, no problem; push a new product in grocery stores, okeydokey. Williams had been a partner in an agency that unwittingly followed this strategy. While the firm received national accolades for its creative work, it faced the same challenges as other small agencies in attracting big national accounts. When an agency promotes itself as exactly like the big guys only smaller, it has already ceded the battle. The only competitive advantages it can offer are lower prices and more time focused on the client. It is not a profitable strategy to say that you will take fewer dollars for more work. On the flip side, it's not a winning strategy to say that you will offer the same thing as your competitors, just less of it. As Williams himself observed, small firms were so desperate for work, they would often say or do whatever they could to get the next account.

Over a couple of decades, Williams built a wildly different strategy. It was based, in essence, on saying no, often. Williams, who is now a consultant helping firms adapt his ideas, explains that the key for a small agency is not to be anything like those big companies. Small firms shouldn't be full-service; they should do just a few things for just a few types of clients and do them better than anybody else possibly could. To illustrate this principle, Williams introduced me to a firm he's consulted for, Wray Ward, in Charlotte, North Carolina. It had been a typical regional market agency, working for whichever business happened to be around. Its account executives would plan a big campaign for a bank while also drawing up a nearby furniture manufacturer's latest magazine ads and then turn their focus to the marketing needs of a large energy producer in town.

Working with Williams, Wray Ward's president, Jennifer Appleby, learned that this strategy was a dead end. Every year, more of her local clients were shifting to global firms based in New York that offered all sorts of benefits, including better bulk discounts on media buying and a wider suite of services. Williams began running a series of intense internal discussions at Wray Ward, pushing her colleagues to identify not what made them able to compete directly with the big guys but what made them entirely different. It took a long time, but Williams, Appleby, and her staff realized that there was one kind of client they truly loved working with; furthermore, they seemed to bring a special touch to those campaigns. They really understood furniture and home furnishings. North Carolina is America's furniture capital, with thousands of large and small firms there making beds and chairs and upholstery fabric. Wray Ward worked with many of these companies, and, as Williams pointed out, no advertising agency focused exclusively on their needs.

Appleby and her staff began to study the field. They learned far more than they already had about where and how furniture and home furnishings were sold. They subscribed to several services that gave them in-depth portraits of the furniture-buying public. They immersed themselves in the science of weaves and dyes and woodworking and metal furniture. It took a couple of years of intense study, but soon they were ready. Wray Ward's directors did not get rid of their existing clients—not always the best idea, as I've said—but they decided to accept new clients only in their chosen field. They were able to go to those customers with a depth and breadth of knowledge and expertise that no other firm could match. The huge companies were just too big to invest the necessary time and effort to learn the ins and outs of this one industry.

Williams showed Wray Ward's directors that their narrower focus on a specific type of client allowed them to charge far more for their work. They were not just offering a smaller version of the same thing others were providing but, instead, were coming to the table with a depth of specialized knowledge, insight, and data that nobody else could match. Wray Ward could, essentially, become a central partner in a furniture company's business strategy. Their marketing campaigns would be more appropriately targeted and more cost-effective. Wray Ward staff can explain to a client that, yes, they charge far more than the competition, but when Wray Ward is the agency, the client no longer has to pay for its expensive subscriptions to customer data providers; the client doesn't have to monitor competitors' marketing and advertising campaigns. Many clients find they don't have to spend as much time understanding the latest trends in furniture design.

Williams can point to dozens of similarly transformed agencies—a firm in Oregon that focuses on winemakers; a marketing company in St. Louis that will only work with mid-sized hospitals; a company in Arizona that caters to businesses focused on senior citizens.

In a sense, Williams's call for more narrow positioning serves the same goal as Baker's insistence on abandoning hourly billing. Both men advocate homing in on the true value that a specialized professional can bring to targeted clients. Hourly billing and full-service advertising are both rooted in simply following the external rules of a profession rather than zeroing in on what the actual service being provided is worth. Neither Baker's nor Williams's ideas seem, at first glance, all that modern. One could ask, then: Why are they becoming increasingly popular in the twenty-first century and why did so few people think of them in the twentieth? The answer is that they are more possible now because of modern technology and global trade. The latter has led big firms to get ever bigger to reach global audiences. As large accounting and advertising and other professional service firms have grown, they have, necessarily, left a space for smaller, more nimble firms to become more intimate with their customers. That intimacy has real value. Ask any client of the big firms how they are treated. They will say that they are courted aggressively at first and then are all but ignored. No one client—unless it's a truly massive firm—can hold the attention of a huge multinational professional service provider for long. At the same time, the Internet and other computer technologies allow a small company to work with clients anywhere on earth. Small outfits can provide intimacy at scale, which is a lot different from production at scale.

It would be years before Blumer would meet these heroes— Tim Williams, Ron Baker, and several others. Jason spent this time reading books, following intense debates on social media, and studying how to apply the ideas he came across. Finally, in 2010, he was ready. By then, his father had retired, and he owned the family firm outright. He instituted some new rules. He would not charge by the hour. He wouldn't even record how many hours he worked on any particular client's account. Also, he would get rid of nearly all of his customers. Following Williams's advice, he had realized that he most enjoyed working with creative service providers: website designers, ad agencies, marketing companies, and others who followed a specific pattern. He liked people who were extremely creative and good at their jobs but confused and lost when it came to business strategy. He would retain only those clients who fit the new paradigm.

Ron Baker often repeats a certain phrase: "Price justifies

cost, not the other way around." At first, this didn't make sense to Jason. Costs are external things—it costs so much money to have an office and to pay mortgage and utility bills. This is even more so for companies that make a product. How can a price determine the cost of anything from a Snickers bar to an aircraft carrier? Aren't these little more than raw materials—each of which cost something—that are assembled and manipulated into a final good?

Jason came to realize, though, that this idea of Baker's was profound. He sat down and analyzed how much time it would take him to serve his clients properly. He no longer wanted to do their taxes and audits and handle their payroll. He wanted to intimately know his clients and carefully guide them to business success. He concluded that he could not support hundreds of clients, as he and most CPAs normally do. He could not handle more than forty. If he had only forty clients, he would have no choice but to charge them more. He would also have to spend many hours each week deepening his knowledge so that he could properly guide these clients. That meant that he would never rise above that 70 percent utilization rate that most firms required. He'd be lucky if he spent 50 percent of the hours in his workday doing direct client work. He realized that this was not a plan to charge clients for his leisure time. They would benefit if he became more expert. He would immediately translate that knowledge to their businesses. He came up with a per-client fee that was much, much higher than the prevailing rates.

This forced him to realize something else: he would need to be extremely selective about the clients he took on. Only those who wanted what he had to offer would pay the bill, reliably, over time. That was okay, he thought, because he was planning to have an entirely remote-based business. He would not meet any of his clients in person but would do almost all the work over video chat, e-mail, secure servers, and the telephone. He also hired two other accountants to take over the boring work he didn't want to do anymore; they would also be free to work from their homes.

Blumer wrote a letter to all of his existing clients explaining the new business model and offering to recommend other firms who were going to continue to operate the old way—hourly billing for mostly rote work. Suddenly, he had no clients at all. He began a podcast and a social media campaign to publicize his strategy. The response was enormous. Within three months, he had thirty clients (you'll meet one of them in the next chapter). In one year, he tripled his income.

Today, Blumer is a celebrity in the accounting world. He has to turn clients away, since more people want to hire him than he can take on. Each year, he asks three or four existing clients to go elsewhere, because he no longer thinks they are a good fit. It's something few accountants can imagine doing. His own firm has become such a model that Blumer started a second business advising other accountants how to be more like him.

I have come to see Blumer as the iconic representation of the ideas in this book. He has been able to take precisely the forces that were upending his field and turn them to his advantage. In a more prosaic way, he was able to transform how price is determined. This is one of the most important elements of our new economy. We no longer have to think of everything from candy bars to hours of accounting services as identical units, charged in identical ways; far too many people accept whatever price is standard. We can focus on the actual value created by a specific relationship and charge appropriately for it.

The key lesson that Blumer teaches is that people spend far too little time analyzing what they are selling and how much they are charging. These are the two most important and, if done right, fun parts of a business or a career. Ask yourself: What are the set of things I know how to do and who would benefit the most from those things? How much, in real dollar terms, would they benefit? How can I frame what I do so that those people clearly see that benefit and agree to a price based on value, not on old traditions that might no longer make any sense?

Blumer himself demonstrates that this is not an immediate and easy process. It takes some internal soul-searching and a lot of experimentation. Blumer says he is still finding his way, trying to introduce at least one or two radical experiments each year. However, with help from people like Blumer and his guides, your own process can be sped up.

When I picture Blumer in my mind, I see him smiling, maybe reacting with a laughing whoop to something I've said or a goofy joke he's made. He has an easy, happy presence. I find it impossible to conjure an image of the man he was before he transformed his life—a frustrated, distracted accountant in an ill-fitting suit, miserably going through the motions of filling out tax forms, then returning home exhausted, barely able to enjoy time with his kids. I truly can't call that person to mind because Jason is now one of the most buoyant people I've ever met.

Jason's home life is far better, too. He has more time to spend with his children. As his wife explained to me, his satisfaction in his work allows him to be a more present, engaged dad and husband—though she's quick to point out that he's always been a good dad, even when he was the most miserable at work. It's at work that the transformation of Jason's life is clearest. I have seen Jason in action many times. I attended his Deeper Weekend, a retreat for about a hundred accountants who want to learn how to be, well, like Jason. It is thrilling to watch him stand before this group, walking them through the process of selecting a core niche and identifying the unique value they can provide. He is an electric speaker whose presentations are dense with practical steps, like teaching them how to price their services based on the value they provide. For all the pragmatism, the main message in any Blumer talk is Blumer himself. This is what he was meant to do: guide his clients and other accountants through the process he discovered on his own.

I asked Jason once if he truly is happier now. He looked at me as if I had paid no attention at all to any word he had ever said. "Dude," he said, laughing. "Dude. I am happier every minute of every day."

# CHAPTER 5

# IN VINO VERITAS

*How a bottle of wine and a farmer's dirty hands*
*explain the mechanics of pricing based on value*

Jason Blumer doesn't drink much, and when he does, he drinks bourbon. I asked him once what he thought about wine, and he said he doesn't know much about it other than that he likes it white and cold and not too expensive. Which is why it felt odd to drive around the Sonoma grape-growing region of northern California, knowing that, without realizing it, Jason had helped transform the lives of several of the most interesting and exceptional winemakers here and in nearby Napa. I was driving with Meghan Phillips, a brilliant wine marketer and self-described lousy businessperson whose company had nearly collapsed a few years ago. Desperate, she had hired Jason.

It is striking how quickly the urban parts of San Francisco fade away. Driving north, across the Golden Gate Bridge, it feels as if there will be nothing but concrete and cars for hours. Suddenly, though, the cityscapes disappear, and you are in a rural area of large farms, small hills, and single-story buildings. There are, essentially, three distinct wine businesses overlapping the same geographical area. The most famous is wine tourism, in which visitors—from discerning wine aficionados to bus tours of drunken revelers—travel around to tasting rooms and sample various vineyards' wares. This is the public face of the wine industry, the one available to everybody and the one that most tourists encounter.

There is also an invitation-only version of wine country tourism. This one features a seemingly endless calendar of parties for wealthy vineyard owners, celebrities, food and wine writers, and others who can help shape the public perception of a wine. Every night, exclusive dinner parties are arranged, often at the grand vacation homes of Silicon Valley veterans who have bought themselves a vineyard, and every week has its own roster of grander wine unveilings, charity dinners, and other events for which only a tuxedo or cocktail dress is appropriate attire.

Another, third world exists physically alongside these two more public manifestations of the industry but is, in many ways, disconnected from them. This is the world of the actual folks who grow grapes, pick them, and oversee the complex, laborious process of turning them into wine. These are people with callused hands, dirty boots, and jeans, and an approach to wine that is, at once, more pragmatic and more deeply reverential than the glitzier presentation most people see.

This is the world Meghan Phillips grew up in. Her parents weren't in the wine industry. Her father was a regional manager for a major supermarket chain, her mother a school counselor. But wine permeated her life. Her best friends were the children of grape growers and winemakers. At Sonoma State University, she majored in business with a concentration in wine marketing. Meghan, who is pretty and tall with bright blond hair and striking eyes, is in constant motion. She tends to enter a room with exuberant greetings and quickly shoots off a series of questions and observations. Some big personalities can be overwhelmingly self-obsessed, talking rapid-fire about themselves. That's not Meghan. She is interested in the others in the room.

Her tone is light, often laughing, so it's easy to believe that she's engaging in idle chitchat.

Over time, though, it's clear that she is probing with purpose and will quickly uncover some hidden truths about a person. I saw this in action more than once and was fooled each time. My first Meghan experience came when she picked me up at the Airbnb home I was renting in Sonoma with my wife and young son. Meghan came in, loud and laughing, carrying a big bag. As I got ready, she crouched down and asked my six-year-old son a few questions. A week later, I received an e-mail from Meghan telling me that her daughter, inspired by my son, had studied up on my son's favorite dinosaur. My son never met her daughter, and I had not realized how quickly Meghan had excavated his all-consuming dinosaur obsession and, at the same time, had thoughtfully perceived that engaging my son was the surest way to earn my goodwill. This did not feel manipulative but seemed like a natural outgrowth of her warmth and intuition. However, it was hard not to note that it also served her strategic interests of cementing our relationship.

Meghan says that Jason Blumer transformed her life. He didn't turn her into someone new. Instead, he helped her learn how to structure her business around her most authentic self. She came to Jason, as many of his clients do, in a specific sort of crisis, one brought on by sudden and enormous success.

While still in college, Meghan had worked at Viansa, a fast-growing wine brand in her hometown of Sonoma. Marketing wine requires a unique set of talents, and Meghan proved to have them naturally. To sell wine, marketers need to balance accessibility with mystery. According to countless wine marketing surveys, the single greatest barrier to sales is that many Americans are intimidated by wine and lack confidence in their ability to differentiate good from bad. Many wine marketers spend much of their time identifying the best ways to cut through consumer anxiety by making their wines seem fun and accessible. There is a risk, though, in going too far. Wines like Viansa's, which retail for $22 to more than $100, also need to convey a sense of magic, some special something worth the high price tag. Finding that right spot between welcoming and magical—which changes, depending on price and target market—is the essential challenge of wine marketing.

At the same time, wine marketers need to understand the bewildering set of regulations that govern their products' distribution and sale. When Prohibition was lifted, in 1933, alcohol remained a highly regulated product, falling under the jurisdiction of the entity that would later become the Bureau of Alcohol, Tobacco, and Firearms, as well as a bewildering set of state laws. Some states are extremely strict—Utah allows only government-owned stores to sell alcohol—while others, including Arizona, Colorado, and California, impose few restrictions. This patchwork of confounding laws has a huge impact on how wine is marketed. For example, most states allow wine to be sold in supermarkets, while in others, wine sales are permitted only in liquor stores. Shopping in supermarkets is entirely different from shopping in liquor stores. Supermarket shoppers are more likely to be women, often with children along, and quite sensitive to price and value. Wine is often an impulse indulgence, selected quickly, perhaps with a tinge of guilt or a spark of rebelliousness. Shoppers in liquor and wine stores, on the other hand, are more likely to be male and alone and eager to spend some time contemplating the purchase and even discussing it with a knowledgeable clerk.

It became clear, early in Meghan's career, that she seemed all but designed in a laboratory to be great at wine marketing. Meghan said that people who grow up around wine come to think of it in a way few others do: as an agricultural product, much like oranges or lettuce or almonds, made up of nutrients from the soil, sunshine, and water. Growing up in Sonoma, she could see that some farmers tended their crops obsessively while others sought to maximize profits at any cost. The same was true for those who bought grapes and turned them into wine. Fine wines were not some mystery that came from genius; they were the wines produced through hard work by passionate winemakers who bought grapes grown on the right kind of land and obsessively tended the fermentation process. Seeing wine in this way made it at once accessible and magical. Meghan can taste a great bottle of wine and experience the personality and hard work of the winemaker. To her, a good bottle of wine is both magical and accessible; there is no contradiction.

There was another key aspect of Meghan's childhood that made her a born wine marketer. Her father was not just a manager of grocery stores. He was something of a philosopher of the supermarket. For him, a grocery store was not merely a large space with shelves; it was more like a living beast, with a circulatory system, a beating heart, and a symbiotic relationship with those who stepped inside to shop. He told young Meghan about how, on each visit, most shoppers come in and take the same route to the same shelves to buy the same products. A smart marketer hopes to shake these shoppers out of their routine so they will try a new product.

Meghan's father was particularly obsessed with endcaps, the large displays at the ends of supermarket aisles. I had often wondered why endcaps regularly contain products that are not in the aisle to which they are adjacent. There might be a large display of chips and salsa at the end of an aisle that sells beverages, for example. Meghan had learned from her father that endcaps are designed to prompt shoppers to make instantaneous, subconscious decisions. If they are on their way to buy beer and see chips, they might buy the chips because they go well with beer. Even more, a cleverly designed endcap might slow a shopper long enough for her to peer down an aisle she normally doesn't visit. "My dad always talked about the perimeter and the inside of a supermarket," Meghan said. The inner part is where people head when they know what they want and are going to get it. The perimeter is more of a free-for-all, where shoppers are open to new suggestions. "People browse the perimeter and need to be coaxed into the aisles."

This insight helped her design one of her most successful campaigns. She created a retail marketing campaign for one of the largest wine conglomerates in the world, which owns dozens of wine brands. Meghan worked on one of its sub-brands, which was designed to appeal to single women in their twenties and early thirties who wanted a light, refreshing, easy-to-drink wine for nights they spent with their girlfriends. Meghan's first project was promoting the sub-brand's whites. The goal was to contrast this new wine with dark, red, serious, and romantic wines that might be consumed during a date. This wine was to be effortless, a light but enjoyable drink for a fun night. The target customer was likely turned off by all the competing brands and varietals in the wine section of a supermarket.

"Once you're in the wine aisle, it's a nightmare," Meghan recalled. "It's completely saturated. So I remembered my dad, and I thought, Oh my God, shop the perimeter." She realized that young women were walking all around the perimeter of supermarkets; she merely had to find where they went. She helped create a special display that would sit in the floral department. "We put tons of flowers everywhere, lights. That's how you cross-departmentalize wine. Get it out of the wine aisle." It was a huge success.

Soon Meghan was hearing from countless wine industry executives asking her for guidance. She decided that there was enough demand that she could start her own marketing firm. "It was extremely scary," she recalls. "I don't even know what I was thinking. I was pregnant with my first child, and my husband was still in law school. It was, objectively, a really bad decision. We had no financial security, no health insurance. Also, we started the agency in 2008, in the middle of the financial crisis." Thus was the Honey Agency born.

To her shock, she soon had more business than she could handle. The company quadrupled in size in its first year and then quadrupled again its second year. "It was insane," she remembers, laughing. She did no marketing for herself, simply answered the calls that flooded in. She took on major wine brands selling cheap, popular wines to a global audience; a bunch of local restaurants; a host of small mom-and-pop companies. She agreed to work with any client who asked her to.

The money was pouring in, but it was pouring out even faster. She had to hire so many people—designers, account managers, production people—to handle all the work. She had no system to ensure that they were spending their time correctly. She took on more assignments than any normal person could handle. "I was working all night," she remembers. "I had a newborn baby. I would be up at night, nursing and working. I couldn't sleep. It was bad."

Desperate to pay her bills, Meghan took on every single customer who called her, which meant a huge number of clients who had nothing to do with her passion for wine. When she looks back at those days, she recalls a particular client, a furniture manufacturer, who phoned one day asking for a new logo. Meghan and her partner met with him, an intense, short, wiry man who talked in an endless torrent. He explained that his business was suffering. He sold retail, direct to consumers, and he also sold wholesale to other retailers—two wildly different types of selling. Consumers pay more for each piece of furniture, but they also require a lot more time and hand-holding. He had more luck with his wholesale customers, with whom he could talk about the technical qualities of his furniture, but then he'd feel they were stealing business away from his retail side. Somehow, he had concluded that the solution was a new logo. He hated his logo, and he thought a really good one would communicate everything essential to all of his customers. Hmm . . . Meghan sat there in a state of shock.

*A logo*, she thought, *is the last thing he needs*. Before they could even conceive of a logo, she understood, he would need to make some hard decisions about his business. He should pick either retail or wholesale or, at a minimum, have a much better understanding of how to balance the two. Then, once he'd identified his target client, he needed to hone his message, understanding what it is he'd be offering. Meghan thought that, for the right sort of customer, his intense, technical monologues would be extraordinarily effective. He was obnoxious and self-centered, sure, but he did seem to know what he was talking about. She imagined an entire marketing strategy built around the know-it-all furniture expert. It would turn off a lot of people, but the ones who responded would become his most loyal customers.

Only once they had sorted all that out could they begin to think of what kind of logo would support the new campaign. But she didn't say that. She wanted the job; she felt she needed the job, so she simply said, "Sure, I'll make you a new logo."

The job was awful. He called constantly. He rejected nearly all of her recommendations. This was no solution to her problem. Meghan had a dozen clients like that furniture maker, people who were looking to her for a quick fix to a problem that required far more work. She felt trapped, and the only answer she could come up with was to work harder and faster and more. She took on as many clients as she could. This meant straying further away from wine clients and toward people like the furniture salesman.

For all her expertise in marketing wine, Meghan was, by her admission, a pretty lousy and ignorant businessperson. She set an hourly billing rate for clients and salaries for her employees based on what others were doing. Then she let her workers loose, allowing her to jump on whichever crisis was screaming loudest. Her accountant, at a local firm serving small businesses, was, she says, "horrible. He didn't understand the creative industry. He didn't understand my questions." She kept asking him to help her figure out why she was taking in so much revenue but keeping so small a profit. In response, he would explain how to file payroll forms and when her taxes were due.

Meghan began searching Google for accountants who understood the creative industry and found Jason Blumer's podcast and Twitter feed. Here was a man who had answers for all of her questions. He talked about how to bill properly, how to identify the right kinds of clients, and how to get rid of the ones who end up costing more than they're worth. He often said things that surprised her because they had little to do, at least directly, with the things accountants usually discuss, like profit and loss or money in general. He spoke a great deal about the need to grow slowly and sustainably, about ways of building cohesive teams, and how to best collaborate with other firms.

Jason had a few obsessions he returned to in every episode: never bill by the hour, make sure to get rid of clients who bother you, continually refine your core values and principles, and, above all, define your niche, establishing a focus so clear that your most likely clients automatically think of you when they need creative services.

Meghan was listening to Jason's podcast, reading his tweets, for several months, imagining how great it would be to have someone like him who she could talk to. It took her quite some time before she realized that she could call him. Finally, she looked at his website and, right away, realized that the lessons would begin before she even spoke to him. No phone number or e-mail address is provided on the site. Instead, potential clients have to fill out a form that seems designed to scare most casual visitors away (which, of course, is exactly what it was designed to do).

Blumer asks visitors to fill in their contact details and then attest to the fact that they are prepared to work, intensely, with him, and that they recognize that doing so will require a serious investment of money and time. Even after agreeing to these terms, clients still need to go through a rigorous intake process to ensure that they are a good match for the services he provides. ("I slow things way down," Jason told me. "If someone is in a big rush, it's a sign, right away, that they aren't going to be a good fit.") Oddly enough, one of Jason's requirements for clients interested in hiring him to be their accountant is that they not have a lot of complex accounting needs. It says so right on the website: "We find our best customers . . . do not have a lot of past tax, accounting or compliance issues to 'fix.'" This is because Blumer wants to make clear, even before the beginning of a relationship, that his firm focuses on advising creative companies about how to sensibly grow their business, not on solving the kinds of problems that drove Blumer to despise accounting in his previous work.

While many people seeking an accountant might balk at one who makes it clear that he's not particularly interested in traditional accounting, Meghan felt the opposite—she was energized by the intake form. "I was like, *Oh. He's teaching us already. That's what we're supposed to do: weed out bad clients. He is doing that to us right now.*" After she filled out the form and had an initial call with Jason, the two agreed that they were a great fit. Soon Jason flew to California to spend a few days with Meghan and her co-founder, Rebecca Plumb. They spent three days together in a retreat, going over the business. "We were underground in this concrete warehouse basement," Meghan says. It was a space a friend of hers owned and allowed her to use. "It was like a bunker. No windows. Uninspiring. It was like a jail." She notes that it was, oddly enough, the perfect place to meet. "The space was saying the same thing that Jason was: Get your shit together. You are in the depths of despair. If you don't get it together, you'll end up in an emotional bunker."

Jason was able to enliven the space. He is so exciting in these small group settings, which Meghan—like nearly everybody else I spoke with who has been through them—calls "therapy sessions." Blumer has a gentle, easy, inquisitive approach. He asks questions and makes observations that, from someone else, could come across as vicious and mean. From Jason, though, they seem loving. He told Meghan she was a "crazy train," she remembers, laughing and agreeing. "He said all my staff jumped on board my crazy train. I drove it and never looked up to see where we were going. He explained that everything needed to slow down."

Jason spent the first several hours asking Meghan and Rebecca what they wanted, both in business and in their lives. It was obvious that they didn't want to work so intensely for so many hours of the day, and that they didn't want to work for so many clients they didn't connect with or felt they were not truly helping. They walked Jason through all of their clients and explained the work they were doing for each of them. At one point, he laughed. He said that much of what they were doing was costing them money, and was certainly not helping them build a better business.

Meghan and Rebecca looked at two longtime clients, a large, local beauty school and a company that made high-end coffees for the wholesale trade. They observed that they had done some important work for both years earlier. They had helped each company find its core value proposition—alternative, authentic beauty in one case and clean coffee with no additives and no attitude in the other—and helped each develop a marketing plan, logo, and website that embodied that core. But they had to admit that they hadn't done much of value for either one recently. Meghan sent out an e-mail blast for the beauty school every week, a listing of upcoming specials and marketing messages that reached few people and had little impact on the business.

When Jason asked why they kept these clients, Meghan said it was simple: the clients paid them $500 a month each. It wasn't a lot, but every little bit helped. Jason pointed out that now that he was their accountant, they had to accept a rule: any client who is invoiced for $500 should be cut off. It cost Meghan and Rebecca more in effort and distraction than it was bringing in. "I had been up at three in the morning writing those blasts," Meghan remembered. "I didn't know how to get off that cash-flow chase."

Meghan and Rebecca then talked about that furniture maker, the one who'd hired them to make a logo. They explained that it was a nightmare working with him. Jason, with his ability to be at once almost painfully direct and encouraging, said, "The dude does not need a new logo! He needs a total review of his entire business. He needs to retool everything. Why are you just doing what he tells you he needs when you know he doesn't need it!" He pointed out that Meghan's gut instinct, which she'd had in the first few minutes of meeting the client, was the actual value she had to offer. Those insights would have been worth millions to that client. Instead, she'd kept quiet because she hadn't wanted to jeopardize the chance to design his stupid logo, for which she would be paid by the hour and which would provide him no value at all.

What if instead, Jason suggested, she sold that gut instinct and the immense value it brought? What if she told clients that she wouldn't just do whatever they wanted, that she would work with them only if they were willing to do the hard work of understanding their business and why it needed a marketing and advertising change? Meghan pointed out that the furniture guy would have yelled at her and walked out the door; before she finished saying this, Jason was smiling, and then Meghan and Rebecca were smiling, too. That was just the point. They should have wanted him to walk out the door. They needed to communicate what kind of firm they were so well that he would never have called them in the first place. His business cost them money by taking up so much of their energy and time for wasted work.

Both Meghan and Rebecca remember crying, frequently, in these meetings with Jason. "It was so emotional," Meghan remembers. "I was putting so much into my business, and I didn't have any balance, I didn't have time with my new baby and my husband. I thought it was all to make the business stronger. But Jason made me realize I was working way too much and sacrificing my family and it wasn't even good for my business." By working with any client who called, doing any project those clients requested, and having no time to review which clients were truly profitable and which weren't, Meghan was losing money. Jason was shocked to learn that Rebecca and Meghan had stopped paying themselves. "We put every bit of profit back into the business," Meghan explained. "We paid our workers. We invested in new equipment. We weren't making anything for all that work."

Jason said it was time for a radical shift in the Honey Agency's business. They would need to rebuild the business from the ground up. Most important, they would need to find their heart, their core, that set of offerings they could provide to customers that nobody else could quite match.

This was surprisingly easy. The Honey Agency was at its best when it was working with a specific type of customer: winemakers who had passion and deep knowledge but found it challenging to convey the richness of their products to potential customers.

Jason emphasized that creative agencies, like Honey, are at their best when they have identified a specific type of customer for whom they can do their best work. He said that the narrower the niche, the better. For example, he cautioned Meghan and Rebecca not to identify their niche as winemakers, or even winemakers in northern California. This niche, however narrow, was still far too broad for a company like Honey. Jason pointed to the way Meghan and Rebecca discussed their work for the big wine company.

That account was the kind that marketing companies dream of. They were working for one of the largest wine companies in the world, helping it launch a major new brand. The client was able to spend millions of dollars and to implement marketing plans at a massive scale. Why in the world would Jason suggest turning that business down in favor of tiny winemakers with a fraction of the budget or the reach?

The reason, Jason explained, was both emotional and pragmatic. It was easy to see that Meghan and Rebecca lit up when they talked about these smaller winemakers. They were energized and excited by the challenges they faced working with them. That was in dramatic contrast to how they felt about their large corporate client. Yes, it was a wine company, but its approach was not the expression of a particular person's passions about a specific set of grapes and winemaking style. Instead, it was a wine developed by a marketing department that had identified an untapped market of young women. Most of the wines that shoppers might come across seemed quite serious, with their French or Italian names or descriptions of obscure grape varietals. These women, the marketers believed, wanted something that communicated "refreshing, fun, light, and easy to drink."

The actual physical wine itself was almost an afterthought to the marketing message. It was engineered, not created out of passion. The grapes were sourced from all over the world and fermented in massive tanks. Typically, fine wines are aged, sometimes over many years, so that they can develop complex flavors, often a mix of characteristics that, in the best cases, come together to create a unique experience. That was not at all what the corporate makers wanted. They were looking for a simple, repeatable recipe that would provide a consistent taste. These wines were more like soft drinks or beer, mass-produced for quick consumption.

Meghan and Rebecca and their team found it profoundly challenging to work with such a client. There was no deep story they were hoping to reveal. They weren't trying to find a subtle combination of accessibility and magic, revealing the personality and passion of the winemaker. They were tasked with conveying a clear, straightforward marketing message that offered no ambiguity, no nuance, no room for discovery. These wines are fun and light. Full stop.

Even worse, for them, working with a large brand meant that they were not able to help craft the essential marketing message. That was done by the marketers at headquarters. Meghan and her team were given a set of instructions: take these marketing points and figure out how to apply them in supermarkets. They did a brilliant job. Meghan was able to reach back to her childhood training about supermarkets and build a marketing plan that would bring the wines out of the wine aisle and place them in colorful displays in the floral section of a grocery store. It presented the wine to its target audience of young women in a context far removed from the saturated aisles of intimidating wines. Even with this successful campaign, Meghan and Rebecca had to seek the approval of those headquarters-based wine marketers for every decision, every color, the shape of the endcap displays, every supermarket they would approach to host their marketing plan. Coordination with the massive marketing department and the many other outside agencies helping with promotion took hours of calls and e-mails each week.

Jason pointed out that Meghan and Rebecca were spending much of their time doing wasteful scut work that didn't add value. Being on hold or waiting for a conference call or sending a dozen e-mails to make sure a client approved of a plan was not valuable. Working with clients on projects—that furniture maker's logo—that didn't solve any problems was not valuable, either. It's extremely hard to build a healthy business out of a bunch of actions that don't add value.

Jason further explained that the Honey Agency could provide real value to a client when its owners solved a client's problem in an elegant and appropriately priced way. This, in turn, adds value to the Honey Agency. Each time Honey produces a marketing plan that gets results for its clients, the agency is practicing and learning how to produce effective plans for all future clients. Every time the agency's workers sit in on a frustrating conference call or create an unneeded logo, they are not improving their ability to serve future clients. An agency, like any company that provides a service, is made up of people who know how to serve others. This knowledge comes from education, natural talent, and, perhaps more than anything, practice. By being more selective with its clients and the projects it takes on, the Honey Agency could ensure that its staff would spend its time practicing and developing the right set of skills.

Meghan and Rebecca spent three full days in that grim basement with Jason. They emerged energized. They quickly called several clients and told them they were no longer the right agency for them. They wouldn't be doing ineffective e-mail blasts or logos for furniture companies that weren't ready for the actual hard work of crafting a true strategy. The most difficult decision, one they made because Jason insisted, was to double the rates they were charging clients. In this regard, they were like many people who have worked with Jason. But that's what forces a creative agency to learn how to fully convey to their clients the value they are adding. In Honey's case, this meant the agency could no longer work for large wine brands that don't recognize its unique value. The arrangement was too much like commodity work, the kind of thing almost any moderately capable agency could handle. The brand's higher-ups would never agree to pay double the rate when they could easily take that business elsewhere. They didn't need Honey's specific expertise; they needed a cheap, adequate agency.

The same went for the furniture maker seeking a new logo. If a company doesn't understand strategic marketing and isn't ready to invest much money, it, too, will seek the lowest-cost provider. The very act of charging considerably more ensures that the kinds of customers who won't truly value Honey's offerings won't hire them.

Meghan was excited but saw the risk. Jason was telling her

to get rid of many of her clients and then—inevitably—shock the other ones with a sudden, massive price increase. "Jason told me, 'You might crash and destroy the company that way, but you're going to crash the crazy train if you keep doing things the way you're doing them now. So you might as well try something new. It might work.'"

Meghan and Rebecca began to imagine what it might look like to do their work the way they wanted to. They soon realized that it would, ideally, involve six steps. (Meghan now refers to it as "the Hex Method," after the hexagonal structure within a honeycomb.) Step one: the Honey Agency team would do an enormous amount of research into the client, including talking to staff members, customers, trusted friends, business partners, and others. That would allow them to be fully informed when they did step two: a free-form exploration with the company's owners about what it stood for, what they loved, and what they wanted for their lives and their business. Then would come step three: the Honey Agency team would craft a brand vision that spoke to who the owners wanted to be, given the information they had unearthed about how its key partners perceived the company.

Next came step four, often simultaneously the most fun and the most fraught: Meghan and her team would sit down with the clients and go through the vision for the brand. "We want them to be emotional," she told me. "If they aren't laughing at times, getting mad at times, even crying, then we haven't gone deep enough." Once all the emotions come out, and a brand vision is established, they're ready for step five: designing and launching it into the world. Finally, there was step six: maintaining the brand vision and adjusting to changing market forces.

When Meghan and Rebecca finished crafting this plan, they realized that it did something remarkable. It transformed what the company was selling from a specific product—a logo, a website—to a process. The result would be a logo or a website or whatever else was required, but by selling the process, they were able to charge money for the hardest and most valuable work she did.

Once they had crafted the way they would present themselves, Blumer guided them through the ways he thought about pricing. Once you know what you are providing and the value it gives to customers, you can then price it according to that value. This typically means, Blumer said, that prices double or more, because there is a chronic underpricing problem in this country. Small businesspeople rarely have the confidence to charge for the value they bring their customers. As with so much to do with pricing, people think about it backward. You have a product, you get a customer, and then you see how much money that customer will give you, and that's the price. No, Jason insisted. You have a price, and then you find customers who understand that it is worthwhile to pay that price for the benefits they hope to receive: benefits based on very specialized knowledge.

Jason explained that Meghan could use price to convey even more information. He recommended adopting a strategy he employs. Price the core service at a level that allows a company to take on only as many customers as it can while still providing that great service. Jason believes that the price should be a bit shocking—a couple of notches higher than the prospective customer was prepared for. You want him to have an uncomfortable moment where he truly has to ask himself if this is worth the investment. (Oh, and always use the word "investment" to signal that this is not money the client is losing but money he is spending so that he can make more money later.) If the price is low enough that the prospective client can easily agree to it, he will, most likely, not be prepared to do the hard work that the engagement requires. Also, create a lesser offering at a lower price point—one that doesn't provide as much hand-holding or give as much support once a marketing campaign is launched.

Finally, create a superior offering, one that furnishes even more intensive consultation and support at a much higher cost.

This triple pricing strategy does many important things at once. It communicates the value of what the agency is offering—the price goes up and down based not on what deliverables you provide but on how much thinking you do to create those deliverables. It also frames negotiations. If someone wants to pay less, that's fine, but they get less. If someone wants more, great, but they have to pay more.

One of the hardest parts of transforming the business came when Meghan realized that many of her long-standing clients simply wouldn't fit in at the new Honey Agency. At first, it was painful. "My biggest problem is that I am a bleeding heart," Meghan said. "I had such a hard time telling people who were my first clients that I couldn't work with them anymore. I had a very hard time breaking up with them. But I would explain that they could get their needs met far better elsewhere."

The next step was even harder. "I remember writing that first proposal," Meghan says of crafting a post-Jason pitch to design a website. Before Jason, they had been charging $15,000 for this work. "No more. We decided to charge fifty thousand, more than three times as much. And that was an uncomfortable jump. I remember thinking, *I'm going to press Send on this e-mail, and I will be sending something I have never, ever sent before.*"

Some clients turned Meghan and Rebecca down, and others demanded to know more about why the Honey Agency was worth so much. This forced Meghan to "hustle," she says. She had to become a better salesperson, explaining precisely why her firm could, now, deliver three times as much value. She soon realized that she had *always* been hustling. That's what small firm owners do. "The hustle before Jason was ungraceful, unrewarding"—nailing down clients she didn't want to work with, pricing products she didn't want to create and that the client didn't need. "The hustle, now, was fun. It felt good."

It worked. Right away. "It was amazing," Meghan recalls. Within weeks, the Honey Agency signed up a few new clients who were right in their niche and willing to pay far more. Meghan, Rebecca, and their staff were working far fewer hours but accomplishing far more of real value. Meghan notes, "Because we were charging more, we were able to hire better people, better designers, so the campaigns became better." Since each client was paying more, it made sense to spend much more time researching their business and meeting with them. "We were uncovering more of what they needed, and so we were giving them more value," Meghan says. "And since we were with them more, knew their business more, we were able to show them how much value we were giving them. We could demonstrate that our campaigns were bringing in way more money than we were charging."

Over the coming months, Jason showed them some surprising results. The Honey Agency's revenue had fallen by 28 percent since they got rid of so many clients and stopped working so hard. But their profit had soared. The actual metric that matters—how much money Honey could use to pay its staff and build wealth for its owners—was growing dramatically. This was happening even as the agency became more like a normal, functioning business, with Meghan and Rebecca working normal nine-to-five hours, taking breaks for lunch, and even setting aside time in the day to research their target industry. "I had forgotten what it's like to read up on wine," Meghan says. "I was able to read all the magazines, learn what's going on in the industry. And that helped all my clients."

Since they had fewer clients, they were able to spend far more time with each one. And since they were charging more, the clients expected more from the Honey Agency. This was what Meghan wanted. She wanted clients who expected her to be a real partner in crafting their strategy and their public face.

"I started to learn so much about the industry, because I was spending so much time talking to these people, understanding what is happening."

The post-Jason shift had a different impact on Rebecca. She had been operating chiefly on autopilot, desperately trying to finish each day's tasks. She hadn't stopped to note how miserable she was. "I was in denial," she now says. "I am amazed at how strong my denial was." If you had asked her, before Jason, she would have said that she loved owning an agency and wanted nothing else in her life. Meghan was the public face of the company, handling sales and client relations and helping clients hone their strategy. Rebecca worked behind the scenes, managing a team of designers who created the logos and websites and other graphic materials that would support a marketing campaign. In the post-Jason period, when she began to have time to think and pay attention to her thoughts, she realized that she did not like owning an agency. Rebecca had been drawn to the field because she loved being hands on, working closely with a team of other designers on creative projects. When she became a co-owner of the Honey Agency, though, her job was not to do the artwork, it was to make sure that others were doing it. "I missed being creative," she says. "That was where my happiness was."

Eventually, Rebecca told Meghan that she wanted to sell her stake in the company and do something else. It was painful, as all breakups are, but both women knew it was the right thing to do. Jason saw this as a successful outcome. The goal of his coaching is to ensure that people are identifying the value they can uniquely create and charging the right amount for it. For some, like Meghan, that is fairly clear, and Jason's work is to help cut out all the costly distractions. For others, like Rebecca, the solution is to stop, fully, what you are doing and focus on something else. Jason wanted to have a life he enjoyed more, and he wanted the same for those he counseled.

It took Rebecca a few months, but she realized that her true passion was not in graphic design for marketing campaigns. She loved interior design, creating lovely spaces for people. She took some courses and soon opened her interior design firm, Studio Plumb, which allows her to work, creatively and intimately, with homeowners. She told me it's going wonderfully well. She's able to "make money doing what I love in a business that I'm better suited for."

Today, Meghan can quickly size up a potential new client and determine if it is one that would make sense for the Honey Agency to take on. "To do our best work, we need to hit a lot of variables," she told me. "The Honey Agency needs depth. We are best at revealing the story behind a company's food and wine products. We can't do that if there is no story. We need food- and winemakers who are passionate, who are seeking to make something meaningful for their customers, who get up in the morning eager to make great things. If they are seeking something meaningful, we can make their marketing campaign meaningful and memorable. We also need them to be ready to do something big, to begin to think strategically and to do the work of figuring out their market, their audience, and how best to reach them. And they have to trust us. If they trust us, we can do bold work."

Meghan has become, for me, a reminder that trust and great work require a relationship. We can't all do great work and fully speak our minds with just anybody. By focusing on those customers who most value what we do, along with sometimes painfully turning down those who don't, we can stack the decks in favor of trust and great execution. Having the right clients isn't enough, on its own. You also have to know how to do the work. But if you have the wrong clients, none of the other stuff matters as much.

# CHAPTER 6

# KNOW YOUR STORY

*No matter what it is you provide, the greatest value lies in the knowledge, passion, and skill with which you provide it*

I saw Meghan in action when she invited me to come along on a meeting with a new client, the Serres family, which owns Serres Ranch. Jean "Toots" Serres came to California from France in the late 1800s and acquired a farm that already had a rich history of California wine growing. Civil War hero Major General Joseph "Fighting Joe" Hooker planted crops here decades before the Serreses owned the property. Meghan was meeting with Toots's great-great-grandchildren, who, like every generation of the family over the past century, had been born and raised on this land and were now managing it. Serres Ranch is famous among winemakers. Its two hundred acres provide some of the most highly coveted grapes for some of the country's leading wines.

Most American wines are not estate-bottled. That is to say, they are not made on one estate. Estate-bottled wines are produced on-site by grapes grown on that site. In many of the classic wine-growing regions of France and Italy, the farmer overseeing the grape-growing operation is also the winemaker, managing the many steps needed to turn those grapes into wine. In the United States, there is a clear separation. For the most part, some businesses grow grapes, and others buy grapes and turn them into wines. Most wines are produced in co-packing facilities—specialty winemaking factories that produce dozens or hundreds of different wines.

The Serres family had always been focused on grape growing, not winemaking. (At least, they didn't make wine for sale to the public. The Serreses make some remarkable homemade wines for themselves and their friends. I know—I got to drink a lot of them.) They are grape growers, which means a winemaker contracts with them to grow, say, merlot grapes, and gives them specific instructions about how they want those grapes tended and harvested. One winemaker might ask them to prune the vines to minimize the number of grapes in each bunch to concentrate flavor. Others might want the opposite: many grapes, even if each one has less character. Perhaps the single most important decision is when to pick the grapes. In harvest season, farmers obsessively check the sugar content of grapes so that they can pick at the exact moment of optimal sweetness. Fermentation is the process of turning sugar into alcohol, so the sweeter a grape, the stronger in alcohol the resultant wine will be. (Though a winemaker can also choose to extend or shorten the fermentation process to increase or decrease sweetness and strength.)

The Serres children got to know this land, literally, from birth, sitting in the fields as their parents worked. The latest generation—John, thirty-six; Taylor, twenty-eight; and Buck, thirty-three—grew up with their dad, John (all first-born Serres men are named John or Jean), providing a continuing class on grapes and land and all the variables that can contribute to or destroy the quality of a wine. By the time they were in middle school, all of the Serres kids could identify, from experience, the areas on the farm that produced the most succulent grapes. They were able to see how the areas on slopes, especially ones with volcanic soil, produced the most promising grapes. They even knew why—the volcanic soil hampered the ability of the grapevines' roots to find nutrients, and the slope of the hill meant that there were fewer nutrients per square foot of earth. Surprisingly, the harder a grapevine root has to work to find nutrients, the more robust its fruit will be, leading to more complex flavors that create a more interesting and higher-value wine.

There is a unique relationship between a vineyard owner and her grape-buying customers. The owner knows the land and its grapes with deep intimacy. The grape-buying customers have strong views about what they want those grapes to turn into. So together the owner and the customers make key decisions about what to grow, where to grow it, when to plant it, how to tend the vines, and when to pick the fruit. The Serres family members had long talked among themselves about how to maximize the qualities of their land. There are those seven acres of sloping volcanic soil, off to the northeast (well, only five of those seven acres are great), and cabernet grapes seem to respond especially enthusiastically there.

The rocks in that soil encourage the vines' roots to go deep, which means they are consuming more of the soil's unique nutrients. The Serreses' customers used seemingly irrelevant metrics to judge the grapes. They often wanted grapes of a specific size and sugar content—which are important but less essential—and by promoting size through overwatering, they caused the grapes to lose much of the unique characteristic of this magical soil.

It was with this backdrop that Meghan and I, along with her creative director, Ashley Rodseth, and her account director, Maggie Giordanego, drove onto the Serres estate looking for the farm building. It was surprisingly hard to find. The estate is massive, with grapevines stretching in all directions. Off in the distance, just below some hills, we could see a group of ranch-style houses and single-story buildings. An optical illusion created by the many long lines of vines and the immensity of the land made it hard to judge how far away the buildings were.

We eventually found the long, low, red farmhouse and, in

an old wooden barn behind it, a large conference room. Giant animal heads adorned the walls—a moose, an impressive stone sheep, a deer. John Serres, a huge man with a bushy red beard and wearing a bright yellow plaid shirt, sat behind a desk. He is the oldest of the current generation of Serreses and has a quiet solidity, rarely speaking and then only in short phrases, in a deep voice. His younger brother, Buck, is his physical opposite: wiry and clean-shaven, bending himself around a chair, always moving, with a constant nervous energy. Buck was covered in mud, from his boots and army pants to his baseball cap and out onto his well-worn hands. Taylor Serres, twenty-eight, is the youngest child and, clearly, in charge. She is pretty and no-nonsense, with long hair in a ponytail. She speaks for the family and does so in complete, well-thought-through paragraphs. She talked about why the family had selected Meghan to be their marketing consultant and their plans for the day.

Taylor said that a few things were clear. They want to create their own wine, one that will embody the very best this land can produce. They want to pick the best spot—those five slope-side acres of volcanic soil—and plant only the types of grapes that will perform best there. They will tend to those grapes obsessively, treating them with the maximum of care. They are prepared to wait until the vines are producing the very best grapes possible, even if that means waiting a decade or longer for the perfect growing season. Then they want to dazzle the world with a masterpiece, the best possible bottle of wine they are capable of in that location—with a bold price point of around $150. Taylor wants to shock the market with the price and the quality and force people to recognize that Serres Ranch can produce remarkable grapes. She's clear about the fact that while she wants the wine to be profitable, she isn't trying to shift the family business away from wholesale grape producing. Rather, she wants this new wine to show the winemaking community just how fabulous Serres Ranch's growing land is, so that winemakers will pay more for their grapes and, frankly, defer more to the Serres family about growing and harvesting decisions.

Taylor then explained that she has a second strategy. She is willing to wait for years to make that perfect wine, but she'd like to get another, less expensive wine out as soon as possible. This will serve several purposes. It will signal that the family is shifting toward wine production, so that the industry will be receptive to their showstopper in a decade. It will also help them practice winemaking, so that they'll get better at it. Taylor knows that she wants the two wines to convey the deep knowledge and passion she and her family share. But she has no idea what the wine will be called, what the bottle will look like, how much she will charge for the cheaper wine, or how and where she will sell the wines. I realized, sitting there, this was what I had been eager to see for years. This was what Jason had taught himself and then taught Meghan: How do you zero in on the specific value that you are uniquely creating and, then, how do you convey that to your potential customers?

As we sat there, talking, for several hours, it became unquestionably obvious that the Serres family is as authentic as a winemaking family can be. Their knowledge and experience and life-consuming desire to produce the best possible wine were clear. I felt somehow annoyed that I would have to wait a decade or two to try that amazing high-end wine I knew they would create. I have never spent anything close to $150 on a bottle of wine, but I would have bought several of them right then and there if they were available. The Serres family wouldn't allow themselves to offer a wine that wasn't special, and the more time I spent with them, the more certain I was of that. Ah, but there lies the problem. Their potential customers would not get to spend any time with them. To the wine-buying public, this would be another wildly expensive bottle of wine on a shelf.

The Serres siblings, like most people who are excellent at and passionate about something difficult, have a hard time identifying what, exactly, makes them special. For them, it's a combination of countless things. They grew up on this land, raised by people who grew up on this land, who were raised by people who grew up on this land. They know every inch of this ground and every vine that has been planted. They know the countless variables that go into a perfect grape—the sun and the water and the temperature and the makeup of the soil. They know the wine industry, since they are constantly talking with their customers, who are among the leading California winemaking grape buyers. They know which varietals and which fermentation techniques are becoming more popular, which are disappearing, and which have real potential that has yet to be uncovered. They also know that indescribable gut feeling that true experts have: they can walk up to a vine in early fall and understand that the grapes are ready to harvest, even if they can't fully document why they know that. Eventually their wine will need a name, a logo, and a marketing plan designed to get the crucial essence across to a potential buyer in a hurry, and that's where Meghan and her team come in.

"The initial discovery is going to take four to six weeks," Meghan explained to the Serreses. She would be sending a lengthy questionnaire about the family and its business to each person here, as well as to a carefully selected group of outsiders who know the Serres family well, including employees, customers, neighbors, and friends. "It's a lot of legwork for you guys," Meghan warned, explaining that the survey will lead to a series of in-person conversations in which Meghan will guide the family toward ever more precisely refining the essence of their brand identity.

Meghan told them that she'd like to start by asking each member of the family what they thought that essence might be. John, the eldest, suggested that they might call their wine French Heritage. "If we're going for that top price point, I think people associate French with quality," he explained, pointing out that their great-great-grandfather came from France.

"I don't think of myself as French," younger brother Buck said.

"Me neither," Taylor added.

"*I* don't," John admitted.

"I think of myself as American," Taylor said. "And as a farmer. But we can go with French Heritage if that gives us prestige."

Meghan asked if they use a particularly French style of winemaking or if being French is a big part of their identity. All three of the siblings shook their heads. Meghan doesn't have to say the obvious: French Heritage will not be the name of this wine. It's a false note, a reach for something that isn't authentic.

Taylor brought up the history of the land. Joe Hooker bought the estate in 1854. He was an officer of the U.S. army who had fought—with little distinction—in the Mexican-American War and then settled in California. He is said to have planted the very first European grapevines in the country, though he wasn't much of a winemaker or a farmer. His home was famous for its wild parties, and he was known as a drunk and a philanderer. At the beginning of the Civil War, Hooker was appointed a brigadier general in the Union army, commanding the force that most directly confronted General Robert E. Lee. Hooker's headquarters was, like his home in Sonoma, famous for its revelries, complete with women and alcohol. Hooker suffered a humiliating defeat in the Battle of Chancellorsville. When he retired from the military, he retreated to his estate. It was then owned by the Watriss family, who hired Toots to work the land. In the early 1900s, Franklin Watriss died without an heir and left the property to the Serres family.

The Serres siblings thought it might be fun to name their wine Fighting Joe and have an old-time picture of a man holding up his fists. Buck said they could play on another theme: people have long believed that Fighting Joe's house, which still sits on the edge of their farm, is haunted. "It is," Buck said. "I've heard piano playing. And there's no piano there."

Once again, Meghan asked how important the story of Fighting Joe was to them. They acknowledged that though it was a fun story to tell, it had very little to do with them. Meghan also pointed out that Fighting Joe didn't really sound like the name of the kind of superior wine the family planned to make.

John said, "Yeah, that doesn't scream quality."

"It doesn't scream one hundred and fifty dollars," Taylor added.

"*I* don't scream one hundred fifty dollars," Buck said with a laugh. "There's nothing one hundred and fifty dollars about me."

Meghan put an end to the Fighting Joe name, adding, "I want to be careful we don't remove too much of you." She didn't like the idea of focusing on someone else, someone not from this family. "I want the wine to show that your hands have been in this soil for generations."

The siblings' father, also named John, entered the room. He's a large man, like his oldest son, and was wearing jeans, a blue work shirt, and a worn-out cowboy hat. He had so much mud on him that he looked as if he were wearing a costume, playing the part of the hardworking farmer. When he reached out to shake hands, I saw that his were thickly callused and his thumb was missing. He listened to the conversation in silence for a minute and then said, "We can make great wine. We've done it plenty." So many award-winning wines have been made from grapes from this farm. "We can step up the quality level even higher," he noted. "We want a flagship wine, a quality wine. Without doing the chichi, yadda yadda fancy stuff."

I was struck by the fact that, though the people in the room had been talking for only about thirty minutes, they were already identifying some of the core elements for this new wine's messaging. It would be authentic to this family, to their specific set of traditions and passions and hard work and knowledge. But I found myself quietly wondering if all this was necessary. If they wanted to move a lot of very costly wine, shouldn't they look outward, not inward? Shouldn't they figure out what marketing messages are best at selling expensive wines? And, anyway, was their authentic self all that valuable? These were a bunch of farmers covered in dirt. They had none of the fancy, cosmopolitan flair I associated with elite wines. That, I thought, is actually a great selling point; many people are intimidated by or dismissive of the fanciness of wine. I felt confident that many people who met the Serres family would instantly be drawn by their pragmatic, hands-in-the-earth, dirt-on-overalls approach to wine. But that's precisely the challenge: most potential wine consumers will never meet the Serres family.

Meghan seemed to anticipate my thoughts, perhaps sensing that the family was wondering the same thing. She asked how much wine they planned to sell.

"We're not going to start with twenty tons," Taylor said. "We're thinking more like four tons." The wine industry has a variety of ways of measuring output. A ton of grapes typically produces a little more than two barrels of wine. Each barrel can fill about three hundred bottles, or twenty-five cases. So four tons of grapes would be two hundred cases, an extremely small run.

Meghan explained that a run that tiny would not sell like other mass-produced wine, which sells millions of cases a year and needs to appeal to so many customers that its marketing message has to be simple and quick. The people buying those wines, which cost ten dollars or so, are not going to spend time finding out the true essence of the brand's identity. They'll typically buy a bottle on a whim, drink it, and think little of it. The Serres family's target buyers are entirely different. They are people who crave a deep experience with the wine they buy. They will spend a great deal of time learning about the winemakers and understanding their philosophy. Part of the joy of buying a $150 estate wine is the ability to know its story and share it with friends while drinking. It is essential that the wine's marketing plan be rooted in the truth, because its target customer will find out the truth. If they marketed theirs as a fancy, even pretentious French wine, customers would be disturbed to meet the Serreses and see that they are very American, very good at growing grapes and making wine, but the opposite of fancy, pretentious, and French. Consumers would reject that inauthenticity—and the wine. The wine press and the critics who rate wines would feel similarly. An authentic message, though, one that reveals the family's truths, would strengthen the relationship between consumer and brand.

As I thought about it, I realized that I might be their perfect customer. I like wine, but I am turned off by the pretentious trappings. I also feel condescended to by much of the language of wine. These careful farmers, though, were convincing me that their wine would be the result of genuine deep knowledge of vine, grape, and soil. They would make a series of decisions, informed by decades in the sun, about how to make these grapes as great as they could be. It was clear that they would not sell something mediocre and try to pass it off as magnificent. If I ever saw Serres Ranch wine on a shelf selling for $150, I could be confident that it was worth that price.

But how could they tell that story to people who would never meet them, never see their apparent commitment to the craft? The answer to this question turned out to be so important, so revelatory about how to thrive in this economy, that I will explore it extensively later on. As it turns out, wine is, to my surprise, the perfect product with which to understand the Passion Economy. It has, for centuries, done the very things we all must do now: communicate work that we are passionate about to the proper global audience, thereby monetizing it. To an extent, we must all be like winemakers now.

I called Meghan a few weeks after our meeting with the Serreses. She had moved through step four of her six-part Hex Method. There weren't tears at the brand-positioning meeting, but there were some raised voices, some hearty laughs, and a solution that made everyone deeply happy: Serres Ranch wine would have, as its core image, tilled rows and an SR brand that looks as if it came right off a cow's rear end. The word "French" will not appear.

# CASE STUDY: CONBODY

*POSITIONING MEANS DOING THINGS*
*SOME PEOPLE WOULDN'T LIKE*

Coss Marte has had two successful businesses, though he's proud of only one. When he was eighteen, he was a remarkable innovator but in a terrible industry. Coss's mother came to the United States from the Dominican Republic with little money and no prospects. She got an apartment in a public housing project on Manhattan's Lower East Side. Growing up there, Coss witnessed the expansion and devastation of the crack epidemic. Every corner in his neighborhood was occupied by drug dealers. Many of the grown-ups around him became addicts, robbing homes, mugging passersby, doing anything they could to pay for their habit.

Like many young people in his neighborhood, Coss ran errands for the dealers for a little pocket change and a nod of praise. By the time he was eighteen, Coss himself was dealing. He was a born entrepreneur, constantly seeing opportunities that others missed. In the late 1990s, Coss noted two simultaneous trends. Middle-class white people—hipsters and yuppies—were moving into his neighborhood, and cell phones were becoming ubiquitous. Coss figured that at least some of those people would want drugs but would be too scared to come to the projects. He printed thousands of business cards offering to deliver drugs to whomever texted an order. He bought a suit and practiced speaking like a professional. He then went to the bars the wealthy new residents frequented and handed out his cards. Soon business was so good that he had to hire some employees. He started a training program so he could teach former street-corner hustlers how to dress professionally and how to shake hands and speak with clarity and reassurance. Within a few years, Coss was earning $2 million a year. Perhaps unsurprisingly, the police became interested in his drug business. Coss was arrested and sentenced to nearly a decade in prison.

When he was arrested, Coss was obese. A routine physical revealed that, at twenty-three, he was facing an elevated risk of diabetes and serious heart disease. With little else to do, Coss devoted his time behind bars to physical fitness. However, he did not like going to the jail weight-lifting room because it required extra scrutiny and the possibility of conflict. An older cellmate taught him some rigorous exercises he could practice in his cell. Coss learned more techniques from other veteran convicts and developed several of his own. He was soon in remarkably good shape. Toward the end of his sentence, Coss experienced a religious transformation when reading the Bible. He felt guilt about all the lives he had ruined through drugs, and he became determined to follow a better path after his release.

After six years, Coss went back home to his mother's apartment across from the projects. He knew that the old life could be seductive and he didn't want to fall back into drug dealing, but it was hard to find work. His case had received a lot of media attention, so any employer Googling his name would learn about his drug-dealing past. He decided to go into business for himself; however, he had no money, no resources, no contacts, no possible investors. He would wake up before dawn, head to a nearby park, and work out, using the techniques he had learned in prison. He didn't need weights or fancy equipment. He used his own body weight and whatever was at hand. An old iron bar became his chin-up tool; a log allowed him to do dips. He would call out to other early morning exercisers and tell them that he could train them. He soon had a small group of regulars he would guide through a tough but effective prison-inspired workout. Coss's passion for these workouts was clear and infectious. Word spread, and more clients signed up.

Coss now has a gym and a profitable business. He calls it Conbody, and it offers a no-frills workout based on the exercises he learned in prison. He exclusively employs other ex-convicts (who must survive a difficult recruitment and weeding-out process). In addition to the lure of Coss's own passion, Coss has attracted clients because he solved two problems that often stymie people (especially New Yorkers) when it comes to working out at home: lack of space and lack of equipment. He has developed a subscription-based app that offers video tutorials for at-home workouts that require no equipment and no more space than a prison cell.

Coss offers so many powerful Passion Economy lessons. He was able to take the single most negative aspect of his life—his criminal conviction—and turn it into his core value. Many people, no doubt, have little interest in going to a gym owned and staffed by ex-convicts. That is precisely the point of passion positioning. New York, like most cities, is filled with gyms that offer the same promises: we'll help you lose weight, gain muscle, and stick to your plan. When a value proposition is so universal and unobjectionable, it is impossible to stand out from the crowd. To be effective, a Passion Economy business can't sell itself using universally accepted values. For any business to attract some group of passionate followers, it must contain elements that some people will love and others will dismiss, or even find off-putting. This is not to say that a business shouldn't also offer universally embraced services. Coss, too, helps clients lose weight, gain muscle, and stick to their plan. But he does so in a unique way. He has a fanatically loyal customer base. Far more than half are women, and all of his customers find his no-nonsense, no-frills approach appealing. He also says that many clients tell him that they like the experience of doing some social good while working out. They are helping Coss and the other ex-convicts become rehabilitated.

The magical tool that allowed Coss to take his greatest liability and transform it into his unique strength is storytelling. He tells his story well, and his gym—with its spare, prison-like aesthetic—reinforces that story. His staff members add to the overall tale with their own stories. We all have stories. Perhaps some aren't quite as dramatic as Coss's. But there is some audience that will find each person's story meaningful. If Coss can do it, everyone can.

# CHAPTER 7

# THE AMISH LESSON

*How the Amish learned to find the true value of technology*

Pioneer Equipment's factory sits alongside a backcountry road in the farmland of Dalton, Ohio, a ninety-minute drive from Cleveland, due south. The workday begins just before six a.m. as the first horse-drawn buggies arrive. It's pitch-black outside. All the homes on this road, like the buggies, belong to Amish families, and so there are no electrical lights.

As I stood in the darkness, I could barely make out neighboring farmers, holding small lanterns, walking to their barns to milk their cows and feed their horses. It took some time for Pioneer's employees arriving in buggies to unharness their horses, guide them to the large barn, give them a bit of feed and, maybe, a carrot. If not for the large truck-loading bay alongside the factory, a visitor might think he had been transported back to the nineteenth century.

By six-fifteen, the factory is coming to life. Pioneer makes horse-drawn farm equipment—a full range of tillers, plows, cultivators, harrows, and other necessities for Amish farmers and non-Amish hobbyist homesteaders who farm with horses and mules. These are big steel objects, typically about half the size of a pickup truck, with a variety of spiny parts poking out, designed to cut into earth, plant seeds, pull weeds, harvest crops, and perform a whole host of other tasks essential to running a farm. To make these pieces of equipment, Pioneer's employees—a few dozen Amish men, with the obligatory long beards, straw hats, suspenders, and drop-front trousers—operate enormous machines that cut steel bars to size and weld them together. (The Amish are able to use pneumatic power tools connected to generators.) A handful of young, unmarried Amish women work in the office; they wear white head coverings and long, modest dresses. There is a near-constant cacophony of screeching metal saws and clanging stamping machines and bright sparks shooting off welders' stations like tiny fast-motion fireworks. Although a careful eye would note that this is not the nineteenth century, this factory is clean, safe, and remarkably efficient.

I came here because Pioneer Equipment is the ideal place to illustrate a crucial point about the twenty-first-century economy: success in this economy requires staying on the cutting edge of your field's technology, even for people and companies who use little technology themselves. Unlike just about every other factory in the United States, Pioneer's machinery is not run by a computer; nor do its workers use designs crafted with engineering software. The company doesn't have a website; few people here even know what Twitter is, and few have ever been on Facebook. Few have ridden in an airplane or owned a car or a smartphone. Though, hidden from the casual viewer is proof that this is, in all the ways that matter, a fully modern company that is thoroughly defined by the twenty-first century.

Despite its appearances, Pioneer, led by the remarkable Wengerd family, is one of the most innovative firms I've visited. The Wengerds develop several new, exciting products every year. (Pioneer's John Wengerd referred to their elegant Pioneer Homesteader farming implement as "the iPhone of farm equipment." He's never owned an iPhone, but a non-Amish friend lets him play with his from time to time.) The Wengerds are also remarkably customer-focused, going out of their way to understand the ever-changing needs of the people who buy their products. Ultimately, it doesn't matter that they run their business, for the most part, with pen and paper, only the occasional phone call, and a lot of in-person visits. (There are computers in the building, used for accounting, basic e-mail, and—in one set-aside unit—some computer-aided design.) The lessons I learned by observing their business can apply to any of us.

Pioneer was founded in 1975 by Wayne Wengerd, who speaks with the soft, deliberate voice of someone who carefully thinks through everything he is going to say before he says it. The word "founded," however, seems a bit grand for what Wayne was doing back then, which looked a lot more like a strange hobby. In the mid-1970s, when he was in his early twenties, Wayne, a natural mechanic, took over a corner of his father's barn, and after his chores were done, he would tinker with farm equipment. Eventually the tinkering developed into a small business, repairing old plows and tillers and other gear for his Amish neighbors. At first, he did it because it was fun; he liked figuring out how farm gear worked. Soon, though, he learned that there was a huge need for exactly the services he provided. Amish farmers had an equipment crisis.

Wayne has a mix of passions that in any earlier era of Amish life would have been entirely incompatible with one another. He truly loves the Amish church. The Amish religion is a medieval offshoot of Anabaptism, a movement that holds that only adults should be baptized because babies cannot make a true decision to accept Jesus as their Lord. In the 1500s and 1600s, in the mountain villages around the corner where Switzerland, Germany, and France intersect, the Amish and their Mennonite forebears were persecuted, and often killed, for a belief that was seen, then, as heretical. The bulk of the Amish moved to the United States in the 1700s and 1800s. The Amish came to believe that the surest way to lead a good Christian life (at least for them) is to humble oneself before one's church and community. Amish settlements are broken up into church districts. Each district holds about thirty families, who meet every other Sunday for services, which are held in the homes of church members. An Amish family cannot live more than a horse-buggy ride away from other members of their church district; living farther away would require them to drive to church, which is forbidden. The Amish wear the same clothes as one another, live in similar houses, and generally avoid any showiness that would make one person seem superior to others.

Wayne loves being Amish and takes his commitment to his church very seriously. He wants his children, their children, their grandchildren and great-grandchildren, to maintain the Amish way of life. Wayne loves other things, too. He loves tinkering away at mechanical things, like plows and other farm equipment. He loves traveling and meeting people from distant Amish and non-Amish communities. (Wayne and some of his children visited me once in New York City, for an amazing whirlwind trip of discovery. He was made giddy by all he learned and everyone he met, though he was also very happy to go back home afterward.)

Wayne also has a passion for business. He isn't driven to accumulate wealth. His business is extremely successful, but Wayne continues to live modestly. For him, a business is like a huge, fascinating puzzle. There is a long-term strategy that needs to be identified, questioned, reformulated. That strategy also needs to be broken down into the daily work of operations. It is a puzzle that is never solved, since new challenges and opportunities always come up. Wayne's passions have been passed on to his children. Spending time with the Wengerds is a delight because they all seem so happily engaged in their work, their families, and their community. Their passions are so palpable and entwined into their Amish life that it is odd to think that their business might have been seen as something like heresy to many of their ancestors.

For most of Amish history, the vast majority of Amish people farmed. Farming is a profession tailor-made for Amish values. It requires an entire family to work together and to stay close to their land. Farmers in any area are, generally, subject to the same weather and the same economic forces, so the Amish could remain fairly uniform in their levels of success and could face common challenges together. If Wayne had been born a few decades earlier, he could not have combined his passion for the Amish way of life with his passions for business, mechanical tinkering, and travel. Back then, if he had wanted to remain Amish, he almost certainly would have been a farmer. If he had wanted to start a business and to travel and to learn about machinery, he would have had to leave the Amish community.

This was not just true of the Amish. Before roughly 1900, most people who'd ever lived were farmers and had few options other than to spend their days working as hard as they could, alongside family members, to produce enough calories to survive. As America became urbanized and industrialized during the fast-growing widget economy of the twentieth century, non-Amish people left the farm. At first, this was good for the Amish, who remained farmers. They could acquire more land, and they could always get horse-drawn farm equipment. Before World War II, the majority of American farming was performed by horse-drawn equipment, meaning there was little difference between Amish and non-Amish farmers, and several large manufacturers produced a steady stream of reliable animal-powered farm gear. As the production and use of tractors skyrocketed among the non-Amish in the middle of the century, non-Amish farmers tossed away their old, perfectly good non-motorized gear. This was wonderful for the Amish. For more than a generation, Amish farmers didn't have to spend much on equipment because there was so much around that could be had, essentially, for free.

By the 1970s, though, this boom time for animal-powered farm equipment was ending. Little new animal-powered farm equipment had been manufactured in the past decades, and all that once-free gear was beginning to rust, rot, and fall apart.

At first, Wayne learned that he could make a solid living just repairing the old products. Soon, however, it became clear that repair wasn't enough. Someone was going to have to start making new farm equipment for horse-drawn farming. The big companies, like John Deere, were certainly not going to waste any time at this fringe business. It might as well be Wayne. His many passions could come together. After all, creating a business focused on horse-drawn farm equipment would help the larger community, not weaken it, by allowing other Amish to continue to farm.

Wayne didn't realize it at the time, but in becoming a businessman, he was part of a revolution that was transforming the Amish. Over the past century, the main Amish communities in the farmlands of Pennsylvania, Ohio, Indiana, and Illinois were within fifty or so miles of big cities, such as Philadelphia and Cleveland. Before widespread freeway systems, those fifty miles posed an unthinkable commute for anybody who worked in the cities. But more freeways, combined with a movement to the exurbs in the 1970s through the 1990s, meant that farmland was getting gobbled up by developers. People were willing to put up with a bit of a commute in exchange for larger, cheaper homes than the ones available closer to the cities. That new demand pushed farmland prices higher and higher.

At the same time, the Amish were going through a baby boom. The Amish population doubled between 1970 and 1990 and then doubled again by 2010. Retention—the number of Amish children who choose to remain Amish as adults—also grew, to more than 90 percent. This seems to be a side effect of the widening gap between Amish and non-Amish life. Before World War II, an Amish person with an eighth-grade education and a plow driven by a mule wasn't all that distinguishable from many of his non-Amish neighbors. This made it fairly easy for Amish children to leave their community and still make a decent living. Today, of course, America is far more urban, and our economy rewards education and engagement with technology. A young Amish person considering leaving the church is confronted with a much larger gap.

There was another factor keeping the Amish within the community: there were a lot more ways to make a living. No longer did every Amish parent expect every Amish kid to farm. They couldn't, because the math was clear: Amish families are typically quite large, and with land prices rising, many young Amish couldn't afford to go into farming. Others realized that they didn't particularly want to farm and preferred the idea of opening craft-based businesses, like home building, landscape management, carpentry, and such.

Amish life is, by tradition and definition, communal. An Amish person needs to live in a community with other Amish people, or else they are not Amish. The Amish are not against technology, in and of itself. They are just against technology that could destroy the community. That is why they do not drive cars or regularly ride in airplanes—because doing so would allow Amish people to live far apart from one another. They do not invite computers and phones into their homes because they would disrupt family time. Many do not allow motorized tractors because farming should encourage families to work together, building a sustainable but modest business. Motorized tractors, automatic feeding machinery, automatic milking systems, and the like encourage massive growth and the kind of efficiency that allows one farmer to handle hundreds of acres alone, with no chores for the children. Modernity has added a certain elasticity to these rules: many Amish regularly ride in cars as passengers and use mobile phones for business purposes (and, especially among the young, for socializing). There are several companies—some Amish-owned—that sell computers that have been altered to prevent the display of images or any connection to the Internet. (At an Amish trade show, I saw booths for several of these companies, each one highlighting just how little their computers are able to do.)

Many Amish have started communities in still-rural areas in upstate New York, Wisconsin, Wyoming, and Kentucky (Amish people now live in twenty-six states and in the province of Ontario, in Canada) so that they can focus primarily on farming, and many have chosen to do what Wayne did: they have gone into business. Like Pioneer, some of these businesses have become quite large (at least by Amish standards), employing dozens of Amish people in stable work that pays more than farming ever could.

Today, the Wengerds tell me, fewer than 10 percent of Amish people make their primary living from farming. The culture, however, continues to hold farming as central to Amish life, and many Amish in business also work to grow enough produce to feed their families. For those who have started "daughter" communities in rural areas so that they can farm full-time, the profit margins are slim, and innovative equipment is essential.

It's odd, these days, to imagine that there is much innovation left to be done in plowing technology, one of the oldest in the world. The first known plowing of a field occurred in Kalibangan, the capital city of the ancient Indus Valley civilization in the far north of what is today India. About a century ago, archaeologists discovered a preserved field from 2800 B.C.E. that looked an awful lot like modern farmed fields. There were still the remains of grooves in the soil from some sort of plow, laid out in a grid structure. The plow itself has never been found. Plows have been pushed by people or driven by beasts of burden—oxen, bulls, eventually horses and mules. A plow's basic shape and function were, essentially, settled by three thousand years ago. Plows from then look pretty much like plows now. A plow should be angled between 120 and 180 degrees, steeper for thick soil. It should be curved in such a way that the earth is pulled up and folded over in a clean, straight line. Those are the basics.

The major innovations have come from the materials that make the plow, which have become increasingly stronger, allowing for much faster plowing, especially of rocky soil. The biggest breakthrough came with the dawn of the Iron Age (about 1200 B.C.E.), and then several breakthroughs followed around 1100 C.E. when farming became more technologically advanced in northern Europe. The challenges farmers faced there would be familiar to farmers today. There was rocky soil and farmland that was far less fertile than the riverside farms of the ancient Near East and the Indus Valley. As metalworkers developed stronger steels, plows became better at digging through hard soil. Rocks were still a major problem, though; they could stop a plow in its tracks with a force that could hurtle a farmer through the air. In the early 1900s, a new plow design helped plows run over rocks when they hit them, but it wasn't foolproof, and some rocks were still damaging plows so badly that they became instantly unusable.

Given the breadth of farming's history, it's stunning how much innovation Wayne Wengerd, and now his children, have been able to bring to non-motorized farming equipment. It isn't because they and their employees are brilliant, heavily educated engineers. Like all Amish people, they stopped school after the eighth grade. The innovation comes from something much simpler: they ask a ton of questions and pay rapt attention to the answers.

By the 2000s, Wayne had a family of twelve children—fairly common among the Amish. And most of his children work at the company. From their first day on the job, Wayne taught his kids to listen carefully to what customers have to say. Every single time a customer—either a farmer who uses the equipment or a distributor who sells it—mentions something he doesn't like on a piece of Pioneer equipment, someone writes it down and puts it in a folder. The same goes for features customers would like to see incorporated in the equipment. It's a simple system. Sometimes this occurs via a phone call. Sometimes it happens in person at one of the many Amish farmers' gatherings they attend or at the annual Horse Progress Days, the premier horse agriculture show in the United States, which the Wengerds help host. The customers' and distributors' comments get jotted on scraps of paper or a napkin, stuffed in a wallet, and then dumped in the folder back in the office. A few times a year, Wayne and the boys have a meeting. They take out all the slips of paper with all the complaints and suggestions and they have a long conversation about which they should address, which they should keep on hold, and which don't make any sense.

Perhaps the Wengerds' greatest customer-driven success was their solution to the rocky soil problem in Camden, Michigan. Camden is one of the last ideal Amish communities. Most of the two hundred Amish families there make their living as full-time farmers. That wasn't always the case. For a while, young Amish residents of Camden were following the Amish trend of leaving farming behind to work in a factory or construction. Over the past fifteen years, they have returned to farming for one reason: pumpkins.

Camden sits a few miles down the road from Premier Melon, one of the country's largest watermelon distributors. Josh Bailey is not Amish. He would hardly be mistaken for an Amish man, since he loves his pickup truck so much and he's perpetually on his cell phone. He had never met Amish people before he completely transformed Camden's community.

Bailey started Premier Melons in 2004, after growing up in a farming family in southern Michigan and selling watermelons for his uncle's business, a business he became convinced he could do a better job of running. That led to him founding Premier Melons, and its success quickly proved him right. Because watermelons are big, heavy, round, and prone to breaking, they are a tricky product to distribute around the country. Toss a bunch in a box, put it in a truck, and there's a decent chance several of them will crack open. If the truck has to go a long distance, those broken melons will rot, the rot will spread, and the whole shipment will be ruined. Bailey had a few brilliant ideas. He developed a special cushioned container into which he could cram lots of melons without risking damage. He also created a network of farmers all over the United States and South America so that he could always have a steady supply of watermelons as close as possible to his various clients. His business exploded when he became the primary supplier of watermelons to Walmart, Kroger, and other major nationwide retailers.

Then Bailey had another idea. He had become so good at moving watermelons, he thought, *Why not get into the pumpkin business?* Pumpkins are also big and heavy and round. He knew the farmland around his part of Michigan would be perfect for pumpkins, though it wasn't all that great for much else. Talking to a seed salesperson, he learned about the Amish community in Camden, including what hard workers they are and that they were desperate for a crop that could support their way of life. Camden farmers, pumpkins, Bailey: it was the perfect combination. Today, if you buy a pumpkin from a big-box retailer, there is a decent chance that Amish people in Camden grew it and sold to that retailer by way of Josh Bailey.

The pumpkin business transformed the lives of the Camden Amish. They had been abandoning farming because they had always primarily been dairy farmers and low milk prices had made it extremely difficult for them to make a living— especially because they needed to milk by hand instead of using the automatic milking machines that non-Amish dairy farmers had adopted. So dairy was out. Pumpkins, on the other hand, have proven remarkably lucrative for Amish farmers. That is, if they can get past one very, very big problem: rocks in the soil.

A horse-drawn plow is a fairly simple vehicle. A shaft connects the horses' harnesses to what resembles in some ways a reverse tricycle, with two wheels in front and the wedge-shaped plow acting as the third wheel in the back. In place of handle-bars, some levers adjust the height and direction of the plow. A seat perches above the plow, metal but contoured for comfort; the farmer sits there, holding the horses' reins. A strong horse can get some good speed going as the plow cuts through the ground, ripping out the dead roots of the previous year's crops as well as any weeds that have grown, and unearthing the more fertile soil beneath to prepare it for new seeds. But if the horses are going pretty fast and that plow hits a rock, the entire plow body can hurtle upward, flinging the farmer into the air. "We call them hard potatoes," Henry Graber, one of the first Cam-den farmers to grow pumpkins, told me laughingly. "We have quite a few rocks here." He described how you know you've hit a rock: You'll be on your plow, hitched up to six workhorses, moving forward, enjoying the day, and all of a sudden, you're lying in the dirt somewhere.

"It can throw you right off the plow," Henry told me. "Or you can go up and come right down on the metal. My boy, when he was about fifteen, he got thrown and come down on his head. He laid there, knocked out for a while. A sixty-year-old was plowing here a month ago, and he hit a rock just right, and it threw him off. He comes down hard on the ground. He broke his back. Had to go to Ann Arbor Hospital, made surgery for him."

For the Amish farmers of Camden, it was truly miserable. They finally had land to farm, but their kids were telling their parents that they didn't want to farm rocky soil—they didn't want to get maimed or killed plowing the pumpkin fields. As it turns out, Henry Graber had a sideline as a local dealer for Pioneer Equipment, and he started urging the Wengerds, every chance he could, to please, please come up with some solution for those miserable rocks.

At first, the rocky soil problem was on the Wengerds' "no sense at all" list. They didn't know how to begin to address the problem, and even if they could, they figured it was an issue for only a couple of communities. But Henry Graber kept calling, many times each year, and buttonholing the Wengerds at every gathering at which he saw them. They started with an informal survey, calling Amish farmers and their distributors in a few remote settlements around the country. They soon found that there were many people in new settlements in the northern part of the country—particularly in New York, Wyoming, and other places where farming had been disappearing before the Amish moved in—where folks were running their plows into those "hard potatoes" and getting tossed clean off. The Wengerds quickly saw that if they *could* find a solution to Henry Graber's problem, they would be able to sell a couple hundred rock-resistant plows each year. Since plows typically cost around $6,000 each, this would be a solid investment of their time.

But how could Pioneer make a plow frame that could withstand an encounter with a rock? Pioneer's existing plows—among the strongest horse-drawn farming equipment ever made—could become bent after hitting a rock. The rock wouldn't destroy the plow, but it would twist it just enough that the machine would never work quite right again. It would wobble or list to one side, making it difficult for horses to pull and rendering clean plow lines impossible. Uneven lines meant too much of the farmland was underused.

As it happened, youngest brother Eddie Wengerd, who managed the factory floor, had learned of major advances in a kind of steel used for cars and airplanes—high-strength, low-alloy steel. Because carmakers—for legal and marketing reasons—had committed to dramatically lowering gas mileage, they had needed to find ways to lessen the weight of cars without reducing their strength. This had led to a major research effort, involving universities, steel companies, chemistry labs, and others seeking high-strength, low-weight steel.

Of course, nobody involved in that effort was thinking about Amish pumpkin farmers and their rocky soil. Still, the solutions those steel companies came up with meant that Pioneer would be able to build a steel plow strong enough to move right through rocky soil but flexible enough that it would not be permanently damaged when it hit a big rock.


Whenever Pioneer considers a new product, one of the brothers will break it down into parts and then research each part to find out if other manufacturers are already making a product that works well. Even though they do not use the Internet, Pioneer has a large network of suppliers of raw metal, wheels, welding equipment, and the like. By asking these vendors, Pioneer can stay on top of trends and learn about potential partners on a new product. The next great breakthrough came when the Wengerds found out that one of their suppliers, a Norwegian company, Kverneland, made a plow component specifically designed for rocky soil. It consisted of the plow bottom—the part that looks like the bottom of a ship and digs into the earth—as well as a plow rest. The Kverneland plow rest had a spring mechanism that allowed the plow bottom to swing upward independently, without transferring the force to the plow itself (on which the farmer sat). Made with strong but flexible metal and attached to a spring, the Kverneland plow bottom could move through rocky soil with no danger to the farmer.

It's no coincidence that Kverneland is a European company. In the United States, plow research had largely ended by World War II, when American farmers began using heavy-duty tractors, along with chemicals, to fertilize and weed their fields. Because plowing is, essentially, a mechanical way to kill weeds and turn over soil to get nutrients into the earth, chemical use on American fields rendered plowing mostly redundant. European farms, though, tend to be much smaller than American ones, and European rules about chemical use are much stricter. As a result, plowing technology continued to be researched by a handful of firms in Europe, led by Kverneland. Kverneland's researchers have developed hardening technologies that have allowed them to make new types of steel even tougher. The result is a plow that can cut through the earth much like a razor.

But Kverneland doesn't make plows for horse-drawn farming; it makes high-end plows for people who farm with tractors. Kverneland's plows would need to be modified to work with horses. From a purely financial standpoint, it wouldn't make a lot of sense for Kverneland to spend the time and effort jerry-rigging its plows for a few Amish farmers. Kverneland sells five thousand plows each year to farmers all over the world. For a multinational like Kverneland, Pioneer would hardly be worth the time.

The Wengerd brothers, however, figured it was worth a try. David called Kverneland and was soon talking to Dominik Haselhorst, a senior executive who is in charge of plows (as well as harrows and cultivators). Haselhorst had just taken over Kverneland's two major factories in Norway and was responsible for sales in dozens of countries around the world. Kverneland focuses its sales efforts in Europe, Africa, Canada and parts of Asia where plowing is still common. It does relatively little in the United States. Still, Haselhorst was immediately curious about this call from an Amish company in Ohio. He had heard of the Amish and had found them fascinating. Almost immediately, he saw that working with the Amish could give Kverneland a strong marketing message to all its customers. Part of Kverneland's strategy is to create plows that are engineered to slice through the earth with a minimum of pulling force; farmers who buy Kverneland plows are looking for small, fuel-efficient tractors rather than the giant ones necessary on industrial-sized farms. If the Amish began using Kverneland plows with horses, Haselhorst thought, other potential customers would recognize how efficient they must be when pulled by a tractor.

After some research, Haselhorst realized that he merely

needed his factory to add a different attachment for the plow bottom to adapt it to Pioneer's needs. He also needed to make sure the plows' bodies were black; Kverneland's typical bright red paint would be seen as too showy by some conservative Amish. Soon there was a steady stream of Kverneland plow components on ships heading across the Atlantic, their cargo to be delivered first to Pioneer and then to Amish farmers all over the country and to non-Amish horse-farming enthusiasts in North America, and even Europe.

I have spent an almost absurd amount of time learning the ins and outs of Amish farming techniques, the pumpkin business, and the global plow industry because I see in all of that a series of crucial and highly optimistic lessons about how to understand our modern economy. We hear so often that technology is replacing people, that those who don't understand technology are doomed to fall out of the workforce, and there is merit to these arguments. However, the story of Pioneer's success makes clear that you can innovate even without having access to, or knowledge of, every new technology or marketing tool.

The lesson here is not that we should reject technology or that we should embrace all of it. It is that we should remember that any form of technology is a tool to solve problems. It is solving problems and satisfying customers that makes a company successful. Technology without solutions is always going to lose out to solutions without technology.

Another lesson is that we can all access many of the most important technologies without needing to become experts or even know that much about them. None of the Wengerds know the metallurgical principles that make high-strength, low-alloy steel so strong and flexible. They have access to experts who can provide solutions for them, so they can focus on the solutions they know how to provide to their customers.

A perfect example, one that applies to anybody with a business making physical goods, is the revolution in logistics and shipping that has occurred over the past forty years. It has been very hard for Pioneer to find cheap and reliable shipping. The company produces large, bulky products that need to be transported to local Amish communities spread widely in remote, rural corners all over North America. For most of the past forty years, shipping has been moving toward uniformity: uniform-sized pallets that fit in uniform-sized shipping containers and are transported by uniform-sized trucks and railcars to uniform-sized warehouses and then on to their final destination. It is this uniformity that has allowed first Walmart and then Amazon to upend retail in America. For well over a century, the seemingly simple challenge of getting things from a seller to a buyer has defined so much of what we consider the basic architecture of American life. It led to the railroads and the location of cities alongside them, the growth of department stores and mail-order catalogs, the construction of interstate highways and ports and the massive ships, filled with containers, that fuel global trade.

These many solutions to the problem of getting goods from seller to buyer have been really beneficial for big businesses and not so great for smaller ones. Whether it's Montgomery Ward shipping dry goods and other products all over the western United States in the late 1800s or Nike and Apple producing goods in China and then selling them in nearly every city on earth, it has been a huge advantage to be huge. That way you can fill up a railcar or a container ship with your products and use a national or global network of warehouses, trucks, airplanes, and the rest to move your goods around the world. In contrast, the small business owner has had only a small number of expensive options available: mostly FedEx, the post office, and the unbearable confusion of global shipping, involving mind-numbing amounts of customs forms and tariff rate sheets in which the small player is always charged the most for the worst service.

It turns out that the advantages big companies have over small ones in logistics are the result of something quite surprising: one of the most challenging math problems, a problem that many believe can never be fully solved. Mathematicians call it the Traveling Salesman Problem, and they talk about it so much that they often refer to it as "TSP." The problem is this: A salesperson has to visit a bunch of clients spread around several cities. What route will allow her to visit these clients the most quickly? It seems like a fairly trivial, pragmatic problem, one that could be solved with a map, a ruler, and, perhaps, some string. Computers, surely, could dispatch this problem in a fraction of a second.

Well, no. It turns out that once you get beyond around twenty stops, it becomes impossible to find a route that is, without question, the optimal path. If there are twelve stops, there are 19,958,400 possible routes. If it's twenty stops, that number becomes two quintillion (a billion times a billion). At forty stops, the possible number of routes is a quindecillion, or a one followed by forty-eight zeros. The numbers keep rising to absurd amounts. Big companies, like Walmart, UPS, Nike, and Amazon, are making millions of stops every day, all over the world, using planes, ships, trains, and trucks, and before long they will be deploying drones. If nobody can figure out the fastest, cheapest way to make forty stops, then the million stops UPS makes every day are completely beyond the possibility of optimizing ideally. It is this math that led to the creation of our existing distribution system.

One of the purposes of warehouses and fixed rail, ship, plane, and truck routes is to simplify the problem by reducing the number of possible stops. Each year, these companies search out ways to improve their routes (knowing they will never perfect them) and always find enormous savings. UPS, for example, has saved millions of gallons of fuel by *slightly* improving its routes, and the company expects to continue to save more money each year by steadily refining those calculations.

Let's forget, for a moment, the massive challenges of these huge multinational corporations and look at Pioneer Equipment. Pioneer has seventy-three agents, each of whom is in a different Amish community, spread all over North America and largely in remote rural areas. Pioneer's shipping challenges are greater, though, because its shipping needs vary so greatly from day to day. On a Monday, for instance, the Wengerds might need to ship some relatively compact Homesteader plows; Tuesday they'll have to send out a bunch of massive, irregularly shaped plows. Many days they are sending both and shipping them to locations far apart from each other. For most of the twentieth century, such a shipping challenge was so low on the list of priorities and so difficult to address that companies like Pioneer had to spend a small fortune shipping their goods and were guaranteed the worst levels of service. This was no small issue. It meant that there were not a lot of small companies manufacturing big, bulky items that required complex shipping. Instead, there was consolidation into a handful of huge manufacturers, like John Deere and Caterpillar. The Traveling Salesman Problem is not the only reason massive companies did so well in the twentieth century. There are many economies of scale that helped them grow and crush their smaller competition. But logistics, distribution, and supply chain were major contributors to twentieth-century bigness.

None of the Wengerds know about the Traveling Salesman Problem. All they know is that, in the past few years, they have had far more and far better shipping options. They have been able to partner with logistics companies that can guarantee prompt, cheap shipment of even the bulkiest of goods to their clients, no matter how remote they happen to be.

A couple of hours drive southwest of the Wengerds, in Columbus, is Chris Elliott, a consulting manager who helps companies improve their logistics operations. He remembers that even as recently as 2004, logistics was a guessing game. Truck dispatchers would use paper maps, their experience, and their gut instincts to tell drivers where to go. Then came GPS, which replaced the paper maps but didn't help all that much with route planning. Today, Chris explains, advanced computer software, using complex mathematical models and artificial intelligence, can explore enough of the route options to dramatically improve the ability to get goods from one location to dozens or even hundreds of points. For Pioneer, this means the Wengerds can ship every day for far lower rates than they could have years ago. It is one more great technological advance that they know little about but that transforms their business.

I think of the Wengerds often when I hear people say that they are afraid that modern technology, especially artificial intelligence and robotics, will destroy businesses and take away jobs, that only a tiny elite of wealthy technogeniuses will be able to thrive. The Wengerds have built a business based on solving real problems for a group of people they understand with great intimacy. By focusing on their target audiences' core challenges and solving them, the Wengerds can see all these technological advances as wonderful tools to further their business, not threats.

The Wengerds can support a fairly large business—employing dozens of people, producing thousands of tractors each year—by serving a tiny subset of one of the most obscure subgroups in the United States. There are fewer than half a million Amish people in the world, and according to the folks at Pioneer, less than 10 percent of them are farmers. Fewer than half of those farmers buy Pioneer equipment. Their target audience is some twenty-five thousand people spread, thinly, in some of the remotest corners of the country, people who don't use smartphones or websites and so are extremely hard to communicate with.

At first, I thought the Wengerds succeeded because their target audience is so tiny and obscure that nobody else would ever think to sell to them. But that's not true. There are six Amish farm-equipment makers and several non-Amish companies that refurbish PTO-driven farm machinery for use with horses. It seemed almost impossible for several companies to thrive with so tiny a customer base, until I realized that those twenty-five thousand Amish farmers each operate a business that has, at minimum, $500,000 in capital. That means the collective machinery of Amish farmers is worth more than $12 billion. That's more than enough money to comfortably support the dozen large businesses serving them, especially when modern technology reduces the cost of the raw materials and transportation and allows that money to be spent in a targeted way on real productivity-enhancing machinery.

The Wengerds illustrate several rules. Some are reinforcements of those principles we learned earlier: focus on your core customer; don't provide things that others can do more cheaply; ask for, and respond to, customer feedback. Simply put: technology can be your friend if you are focusing, solely, on solving your core customers' challenges.

In this book, I use the word "passion" in its modern, colloquial sense, as an intense enthusiasm. I like that the word connotes a strong, almost overwhelmingly positive emotion, one that can drive a person's entire life. But the Wengerds make me recall that the word "passion" has a far more complex history. It comes from the Latin *passionem*, which means "suffering." It came to be associated with one specific case of suffering: Jesus's suffering on the Cross (thus the phrase "the Passion of Christ"). As words do, "passion" evolved. By the Middle Ages it had come to mean the suffering of any religious martyr; then it came to refer to any sort of suffering at all. By around five hundred years ago, "passion" meant any strong feeling, good or bad, experienced by anybody. According to the *Oxford English Dictionary*, the word had taken on the meaning I attribute to it by the 1620s: "An intense desire or enthusiasm for something; the zealous pursuit of an aim."

I like that, for Wayne and his family, the word "passion" applies in a fuller sense. Yes, he has the modern sort of passion. He loves business, he loves tinkering, he loves working with his family. But the ancient meaning is important, too. For Wayne, a devout Amish Christian, must never allow himself to forget the suffering of Jesus and the salvation that suffering provided. There is no contradiction here. The very idea of Amish faith is to imbue every moment of one's workaday life with a conscious awareness of Jesus and God.

I happen to be an unobservant Jew and spend little time thinking about God or spiritual things. But I have found that the closer I adhere to a Passion Economy approach to my work, the more meaningful my work becomes. I see this in so many of the people described in this book. Some are explicitly religious, and their work passion and spiritual passion reinforce each other. Some are atheists or agnostic. Still, every person in this book finds that their business brings them something far richer and more existentially satisfying than just a paycheck. For some, that means they are more connected to God and their faith; for others, it means they feel a greater sense of psychological and emotional well-being. Perhaps these are just different ways of understanding the same phenomenon. We are better off when we do things we love.

# CHAPTER 8

# THE NORTH CAROLINA FACTORY THAT LET

# CHINA DO THE CHEAP STUFF

*Know your end user*

One morning in the early 2000s, Allen Gant, Jr., was sitting in his well-adorned office, bouncing his left knee, tapping his fingers, and trying to stop himself from picturing the apocalypse. In the small North Carolina manufacturing town of Burlington, he had grown accustomed to seeing plenty of bankruptcy sales, the spinning machines, looms, and acres of thread all boxed up and shipped to some new factory in Mexico, China, Bangladesh, or another country where workers would make textiles for a small fraction of their U.S. counterparts' wages. Now Gant envisioned it happening to his own company, and he envisioned it happening soon.

It wasn't supposed to be this way. For nearly his entire life, Gant had been the picture of southern gentility. Every day, he put on pressed chinos, a starched button-down shirt, a bright cardigan, and a blazer with a fluffed pocket square. He smiled broadly and greeted each employee by name as he entered the large, bright offices of Glen Raven textiles, the company his family had owned for well over a century. On the way to his office, Gant walked by oil portraits of the three other men who had run this firm: his granddaddy, the Bossman, who founded Glen Raven not long after the Civil War; his uncle, the Major, who built it into a giant national textile power; and his daddy, who raised Allen to be a courtly gentleman with an easy confidence. Gant's very office was a reminder of the good fortune that had made Glen Raven a perennial force in the nearly trillion-dollar textile business. It was nestled between the Haw River, which gave power to the first Glen Raven mills, and the railroad tracks, which carried the company's yarns and fabrics and ladies' hosiery from tiny old Burlington to New York, Chicago, and points west. Now, Gant feared, it was all about to be over.

Like all behemoths, Glen Raven began modestly. In the 1850s, the Bossman moved to a remote pocket of North Carolina as part of a stream of hungry young men, with no pedigree, seeking to make their fortune on the frontier. They came to the Piedmont region—the middle of the state, between the coast and the Appalachian Mountains—because there was an emerging economic boom and anybody willing to work a hard day could profit from it. The textile plants were moving south.

Burlington seemed as if it were designed precisely for textile production. Its hills were steep enough so that the Haw's descent could create enormous raw power. Yet they weren't too steep to preclude the creation of large factories. The city was close to Raleigh, a major trade port, and it was surrounded by thousands of poor farmers who were looking to earn a little more money in a job that was more dependable than toiling on the land. At first, there was no local wealth to fund these new mills. All the money came from the textile families of New York and New England, who were heading south to avoid the rising wages and early stages of unionization that would shrink the profits of their northern mills. Eventually, though, some of the locals learned enough and saved enough to go into business on their own. In 1880, after years of learning the trade, the Bossman created his own mill on the Haw. In 1901, he renamed it Glen Raven.

If Burlington were the ideal location for Glen Raven to

make its textiles, the United States in the twentieth century was the perfect place to sell them. Glen Raven was a prototypical American company for the American century. In 1900, most Americans lived in rural areas, where mothers often sewed their family's clothes. The typical person had two outfits: work or school clothes and their Sunday best. Often these were handed down and patched for years.

The rise of the textile industry in the South was an extraordinary boon to these families. Soon enough, the average cost of a yard of cloth kept falling, which meant families could buy more clothing, which meant the mills could employ more workers, who could buy even more clothing. Now that average American had many outfits. Entire categories were invented—sportswear, casual wear, loungewear, beach wear, formal wear—and the aspiring American had to have clothing from all of them. The huge spike in buying led to an explosion of stores and other businesses, most of which needed textiles for things like awnings and uniforms. Glen Raven and the textile industry, as a whole, became a microcosm of an unprecedented virtuous cycle that laid the basis for the American Dream. When businesses grew, they paid their workers more, and those workers bought more, allowing the businesses to grow even faster. This cycle meant that each generation became far richer than its parents'.

Innovation, or the idea of constantly creating new products and services, has become an important buzzword of our modern economy. After all, companies such as Apple are continually trying to find their new breakthrough product before a competitor beats them to it. But during the twentieth century, innovation was generally avoided. Glen Raven—like all great American businesses of the twentieth century, as I pointed out earlier—made its fortune by manufacturing the same product, over and over again, for years and years, often tweaking the production process to make it cheaper and more efficient. The economic logic of the twentieth century is summed up by the idea of the "experience curve": as a company made something over and over again—working out the kinks, streamlining production, eradicating any extra costs, developing an experienced workforce—the cost of each unit went down in direct proportion to the number of units it made. The goal of any ambitious executive was gaining market share. The more units a company could sell, the lower its costs would be. That, in turn, would allow it to invest in ever-faster machinery, which would drive costs down more. The key to success was not coming up with new things to sell; it was in the efficiency of the operation that was used to make a standard product. The victors in key market areas were not those with the most original products but the companies with the best systems for manufacturing standardized goods. Kellogg's cereal beat Post; a Hershey's bar beat Charleston Chew; General Motors devoured David Dunbar Buick's company. In each case, and thousands of others, it wasn't the superior product or the greatest innovation that won. It was the company with the most efficient system for mass-producing the same products cheaply.

In the twentieth century, risk in the marketplace was often eschewed. To become efficient, factories were run according to strict rules in which everybody knew their place and followed a clear set of instructions. New products and ideas were as likely to screw up a company as they were to benefit it. If workers constantly needed to learn new ways of working, if machines had to be constantly retooled, that crucial efficiency would be lost and a company would lose market share, which meant it would lose profit.

Glen Raven had generally stayed away from introducing new ideas. One exception was early on, when the Bossman developed a system to make sturdy canvas embedded with a durable dye. It was the perfect fabric for store awnings, and demand was enormous; the country was becoming urban, stores were opening on nearly every city block, and every one of those stores needed an awning. Another advance can be credited to one of the Bossman's sons, who people called the Major and who was among the first to see the value of man-made fibers, such as rayon, which were cheaper and more durable than cotton. And in 1953, the Bossman was on a work trip with his wife when he noticed her increasing frustration while adjusting her stockings and garters. In a flash, he imagined a combination of panties and stockings that would require no garters. He called them Panti-Legs. It took six years to perfect the product. They came at the perfect time, just when women were entering the workforce and needed a comfortable leg covering that could be worn all day without constant adjustment.

When Glen Raven did offer new products, they were more akin to superficial tweaks, such as awnings in new colors or Panti-Legs in slightly different fabrics. It was the textile version of General Motors creating many different models of automobile, each catering to a different market, from a small set of standardized cages. Or Frito-Lay, which uses the same "platform"—in this case, a potato chip—to create varieties such as "salt and vinegar" or "barbecue." No matter what large manufacturing companies made during the twentieth century, they all competed the same way. Competition was often friendly, since there seemed to be enough business for every major player to enjoy their slice. This was particularly true in the textile industry. Every few years, one company or another would get an edge—a new machine, a new process, a tweak on an old product—but pretty soon everybody else would catch up. In the end, the textile industry was small enough that everybody knew one another, kept track of one another, and met a few times a year to talk about the business over bourbon, cigars, and poker.

In the early 1990s, however, this old order began to change. Allen Gant, Jr., started to hear from customers about cheap acrylic yarns coming out of Mexico. They told him the Mexican exporters were offering hundred-pound bundles of acrylic yarn for less than ten dollars, almost half what Glen Raven charged. This allowed American companies to produce fabric out of that yarn that would cost much less, leading to garments available in stores at deep discounts.

Gant was anxious at first. But when a client sent him some of the Mexican product, he was instantly reassured. The Mexican yarns were terrible. This was a common first reaction to cheap imported goods (as we saw earlier, with the brush industry): they were subpar, so American manufacturers dismissed them as no threat. The Mexican acrylic yarns were uneven; they bulged in some places and were far too thin in others, which meant they would clog up knitting machines. Customers who did decide to risk switching to Mexican manufacturers for the price break found themselves returning to Glen Raven after too many orders didn't show up on time or never arrived at all.

By the late 1990s, however, the Mexican companies were producing much higher quality yarn and delivering the product more consistently and reliably. Customers now started to talk about even cheaper yarns coming from China—seven dollars for a one-hundred-pound bundle!—but those had quality problems, too. So Gant did the only thing that his years in the business dictated: he doubled down on the experience curve to ramp up production. He borrowed $12 million and refitted his spinning factory with a brand-new line of acrylic yarn-spinning machines. The volume would allow Glen Raven to sell yarn for six cents less a pound. Within a year, though, Chinese mills began shipping yarn for ten cents less a pound.

In response, Gant tripled down. He bought more new machines, encouraged his engineers to squeeze waste out of every process, and begged his suppliers to lower the cost on their raw materials. Eventually, he saw that the virtuous cycle of the twentieth century had given way to a vicious one. By the early 2000s, Gant realized that China had essentially copycatted what the Bossman had done a century earlier—they had leveraged their massive population of ambitious and poor former farmers into a growing labor force that undercut the biggest textile companies, including many of Gant's neighbors. Gant wasn't sure what Glen Raven could do to compete with that. He couldn't cut costs any further. The things Glen Raven knew how to do, it seemed, were simply no longer valuable.

This led to the bleak morning in Gant's office, when he sat jiggling his leg and contemplating the possibly inevitable demise of his family's business. It led to a sense of despair and dread. Then it led to some serious and very important thinking. For decades, the company had succeeded by following the core logic of the twentieth century: finding huge markets in which it could sell massive quantities of the same thing and make its profit on volume. Now, he realized, the new economy was showing him that he needed to upend that model and find much smaller markets where there wasn't competition and where Glen Raven could make its profit by charging a premium. He was having the sorts of thoughts that Scott Stern—the MIT professor—wished his father, the purveyor of cheap Nike knockoffs, would have had. Gant saw that the high-volume, low-cost business was gone and was not coming back to Burlington. Perhaps he could shift to the opposite strategy: selling a smaller number of products but charging far more for them. To do this, he would have to transform the company into something other than the ultimate widget firm that made the same thing as quickly and cheaply as possible. He would have to teach his staff how to become a company that learned, that adapted, that experimented, and, sometimes, failed. The obvious products, the ones that have clear and known value, are quickly widgetized. To make Passion Economy products, Glen Raven would have to go beyond the obvious, the known. He wasn't sure, however, that he or his staff would be able to make the shift.

Gant got up from his desk and walked into a room filled with his senior managers. He explained that for generations in his particular standardized commodity business, no one had posed the simple question of what the customer wanted. Glen Raven had no contact with the people who ultimately paid for its products. The company was one piece of a supply chain. Glen Raven made acrylic yarn, which it sold to other companies, which would, in turn, make sweaters or pantsuits and then sell those to a wholesaler, who would sell them to a retailer, who would sell to the final customer. Now, he said, it was time to find out what the ultimate customer wanted and what they were willing to pay a premium for, and only then would Glen Raven decide what to make. Put another way, they would no longer make commodities—products virtually identical to those made by competitors with profits reliant on their ability to compete on price. Instead, they would make only products for which there was no competition. They would identify customer needs that were not being met. Moreover, the risk aversion of the past was finished—they would try and fail until they got it right.

Gant explained his new realization. In the twenty-first century, American companies couldn't make money by having the cheapest, fastest, most efficient operations. Emerging economies, with their cheap labor forces, now ruled that business. The real money for a company like Glen Raven was not in making things but, rather, in coming up with the idea for the things in the first place. He told his staff to scour the world for ideas of new products they could make, new ways of producing textiles that would satisfy some need that nobody else had uncovered. It might even mean finding needs the consumers didn't yet know they had.

"Glen Raven is dead," he said. "We're a new company now. So what do we do?"

One of Gant's top deputies, Harold Hill, was sitting in the back, wearing a lavish suit. Hill, who had grown up in the Piedmont, had never lost his appreciation for its fine cotton. He had once worked on Wall Street and had returned to the area. He raised his hand.

"I think I have an idea," he said.

Harold Hill's roots were in the textile business. His father, a textile factory foreman, had worked hard and earned a decent salary during the last stretch of the industry's heyday. While that salary helped his son eventually attend college and business school, Harold never quite felt comfortable on Wall Street. He didn't envision a career handling distressed debt or working in mergers and acquisitions. As he told his friends, he wanted a manly job. So Hill, who has the body of a tight end, returned to North Carolina to rejoin the textile business on the management side.

His job at Glen Raven, however, wasn't exactly what he had bargained for. He ran an operation known as the Park Avenue Plant, which provided custom dyeing and finishing services to apparel manufacturers. (A children's pajama manufacturer might ask for a flame-retardant chemical to be impregnated into its fabrics, for instance, or a sweat sock maker might order some odor-fighting chemicals.) The basic work was the same, no matter which substance was applied: huge tubes of fabric were spooled into a long, flat dish that contained the appropriate chemical. The fabric would then spend a specified amount of time sloshing through the chemical before eventually being drawn into a very long heater—essentially, a giant electric oven—that sealed the molecules in. It was a steady business but not a very profitable one. It also seemed, like many of Glen Raven's other lines, on the verge of commodification. Several other companies in the United States had similar equipment and could easily pump out a comparable product. Hill's business could succeed only if he could dye and finish fabrics slightly less expensively than his neighbors did. He could. But he knew that it was merely a matter of time before a company in China or Honduras entered the market, matched his level of expertise, and beat his price. At that point, his business would be screwed.

While running the moribund plant, Hill had perceived a central problem with Glen Raven's overall business. The company had thrived for just over a century by playing a pivotal role on the supply chain from raw material to finished fabric product. Now it could no longer be a middleman. Cheaper commodity producers were devouring that business. Instead, he concluded, Glen Raven had to find a way to connect with its customers directly, and that required a design focus. He and his team scoured textile industry publications, research reports, and government data for ideas about what corners of the textile business still existed in America.

There were various niche markets, but the most appealing was the car business. The automobile industry, he learned, was spending hundreds of millions of dollars on textiles made in the States. While cars are, of course, built mostly of metal, there is actually a lot of fabric in the cabin and the trunk. After a bit of research, Hill realized that much of the fabric was used on something that the auto industry calls the "headliner," or the inside of a car's ceiling. While it's only a nine-foot-square patch, so many cars are produced each year that the headliner business alone easily adds up to many tens of millions of dollars. The vast majority of that money was going to one company, BASF, which had dominated for thirty years. BASF had designed a special nylon fabric that met all the government regulations—it was fire-resistant and wouldn't emit any noxious fumes—and it came in specially designed modules for nearly every car made in the United States.

Hill's research, which began in the mid-2000s and extended for years, indicated that the BASF product had problems. First of all, it was ugly; industry slang for the brushed nylon fiber was "rat fur," and generations of drivers had simply grown accustomed to something that looked like a dirty towel sitting above their heads. Hill quickly identified a variant of polyester that could be used to make a cleaner, more streamlined head-liner. He was confident about the product but had no idea how to enter the market. He didn't have any contacts among the big automakers and had heard that they were extremely risk averse and generally unwilling to take meetings with unknown companies that claimed to have some new revolutionary prod-uct. After all, if auto company executives took those meetings, they'd never do anything else. The headliner business, he soon learned, was more complex than the apparel industry. Any-thing that becomes part of a car is subject to a host of complex regulations, as well as enormously demanding quality control requirements and carefully managed prices. And, since the auto industry had moved to just-in-time manufacturing, deliveries had to be made within strict parameters. This explained why, historically, very few companies from other industries could enter the automobile supply chain and why BASF had been able to control the headliner business for so many decades.

Hill was having a blast. This project was perfect for some-one with his particular set of passions. He loved doing the sci-ence and the research, but he also loved being an underdog, taking on the big, established players in the market and out-maneuvering them. He relished being able to walk someone in the auto industry through his insights and watch as their dismissive skepticism gave way to delighted agreement. After Hill persuaded one executive at GM to meet with him, Glen Raven's headliner was chosen for GM's new truck platform, the GMT900, which forms the core of the Chevrolet Silverado, Tahoe, and Suburban; the GMC Sierra and Yukon; and the Cadillac Escalade. It was, at the time, the single most used vehi-cle platform in the world. Soon Glen Raven picked up orders from every single auto company.

The headliner business suggested a model for how Glen Raven could thrive in the twenty-first century. It was the oppo-site of a supply-chain commodity. Glen Raven didn't directly sell to the end customer—a car owner had no choice in the headliner installed—but it could persuade leading auto manufacturers that it could help them make the product that would most please the people buying their cars. Rather than produce endless spools of identical product, as it had in the past, Glen Raven had to develop customized solutions for each model and color of car and truck that used its headliners. No longer was Glen Raven simply earning revenue by selling textiles in bulk. Hill had helped shift the company from the commodity economy to the knowledge economy. Its real value was what it understood about its customers. This began with some broad, basic knowledge: people prefer a cleaner- and sleeker-looking headliner, if given the choice. That information led to extremely technical know-how. Glen Raven became expert at the interaction of fire-retardant chemicals and permanent dyes. The company learned the precise angles and shapes of the roofs of every major model of car and how to best adhere fabric to their insides. It also knew how to make those fabrics look smooth and contemporary. All of this knowledge would be extremely hard to replicate, which meant few other companies, if any, would be able to compete against Glen Raven. Just a few years earlier, the company had been competing moment-by-moment with dozens of other producers. Now Glen Raven had found a narrow niche that was served by few in the world.

The lessons learned from the automobile headliners were clear. Glen Raven would have to find other narrow, highly knowledge-intensive markets that weren't being properly served by any existing suppliers. Harold Hill and his team began scouring the world for other candidates, including industries that few people think have anything to do with textiles. One team researched the municipal-sized water-filter industry and developed a mesh screen that strained out pollutants far more effectively than any competitor's products could. One of Hill's engineers became obsessed with the mining industry, seeing all sorts of problems that could be solved by textiles.

Most mines are made up of dozens or hundreds of separate tunnels, most of which have been thoroughly dug and are no longer being used. Mines need to be ventilated by unimaginably massive and expensive air-conditioning systems. This is especially costly since so much air is wasted in abandoned tunnels. Glen Raven developed MineMaster, a thick, bendable nylon curtain that can cover the entranceways to abandoned tunnels and be bent into funnels to direct air right to working miners. MineMesh, another new product, is a thick polyester fabric with an adhesive coating that can be applied to the walls of mines to prevent cave-ins.

Gant had issued a decree that he didn't want to be in the apparel business. Apparel, he had determined, would always be a commodity. But Hill learned of one area of clothing that wouldn't fall into that trap: protective clothing for utility workers. Workers fixing electrical power lines or doing maintenance on oil refineries are required, by government regulations, to wear fire-retardant uniforms. DuPont had long controlled this specialized niche business. It seemed potentially perfect for Glen Raven: a highly technical textile product that had not seen much innovation in years. Hill ordered a research study of the end user, his customer, the utility workers themselves, to find out what they would want in a uniform. He learned that these workers disliked the DuPont product. It was thick and scratchy and didn't breathe at all. It was uncomfortable and, on hot days, when the men were working out in the sun, truly unbearable. Workers routinely took the uniforms off and did their job in T-shirts and shorts, even though this meant violating regulations. Companies were fined. It was a mess.

A team of Glen Raven chemists and engineers quickly determined that DuPont's product was designed solely for safety, with no consideration for comfort. After all, DuPont was selling to utility company managers, not the people who actually wore the stuff. Glen Raven's engineers, thinking of that end user, came up with a new recipe for a fiber that was just as fire-retardant but was considerably thinner and more supple. It even breathed. Sales of GlenGuard protective uniforms have been remarkable, especially in Europe and Latin America.

This exploration eventually brought Glen Raven into a business that Gant would have never envisioned when he'd made his declaration, one that the Bossman could have never fathomed: geotextiles, or the use of heavy polyester fabric to build concrete structures. Normally, concrete for the foundation of a building or the bones of a bridge is poured into a mold made of wood and metal. Building that mold is actually the most expensive and time-consuming part of erecting a concrete structure. Geotextiles offer a faster, cheaper alternative— a rigid fabric sheeting that can be bent into shape far faster than it takes to hammer and screw together a typical mold.

When Hill learned about this product, the industry was still small and dominated by a handful of specialty firms with no other experience in textiles. Glen Raven, with its expertise in textile manufacturing and the various coatings needed to create a water- and sun-resistant fabric, was able to enter the market and quickly dominate. Glen Raven's geotextile business reached its zenith only when Gant signed a deal to manufacture and distribute the product in India, a building-crazed emerging economy. Today, Glen Raven's products are among the most used solutions for new bridges in India. Gant recently signed another deal, this one with a company in Brazil.

This new strategy was perhaps best manifested by Glen Raven's decision to enter the design business. By the time Gant called for a transformation of the company, Glen Raven had one well-regarded consumer brand name, Sunbrella. This specialty awning fabric graced a majority of American backyard and patio umbrellas. Sunbrella was different from other products because it was made of a specially formulated fiber thoroughly impregnated with richly colored dye. Cut into nearly any colored fabric—your shirt, your pants, your sheets, your upholstery—and you will see that each thread has a thin coating of dye on its surface, covering a white or gray fiber. Gant enjoyed pointing out that traditional fabric is like a radish: the color is on the surface, but it's white underneath. Sunbrella is like a carrot: the color goes all the way through. This means that Sunbrella can be placed out in the sun and the rain for years, it can be bleached and scrubbed with industrial solvents, and it will still maintain its original bright color.

Sunbrella already had a substantial presence in the outdoor furniture and awning fabric market. By the 2000s, the company saw it as a solid business but with no room to grow—at least until Gant called for a brainstorming session and one executive asked, "Why don't we take Sunbrella indoors?"

Several people laughed. Since the 1950s, outdoor furniture and indoor furniture had been entirely different industries. They had different trade shows and different trade publications; they were sold in different stores. Glen Raven knew everything about the outdoor furniture world and had deep connections throughout it. Nobody knew anybody in the indoor world. They did recognize, of course, that it was massive—many times larger than the outdoor world—and that it was the only chance Sunbrella had at growth.

Gant asked a few of the Sunbrella staff members to research the indoor market. Their report was grim. The indoor upholstery market is, like the fashion business, built around design. People buying indoor sofas and plush chairs are offered endless swatches of seemingly infinite variety: stripes and flowers and solids in every shade and fabric imaginable. Well, nearly every shade. Nobody was buying indoor furniture made out of the standard Sunbrella outdoor colors, like forest green or beige. Also, the key selling point for most upholstery fabrics was comfort. Sunbrella awning fabric, on the other hand, was designed to be thick and hard. Worse, the upholstery companies in this market had a huge advantage over Glen Raven: they used uncolored yarns, which they could buy in bulk and then dye whatever colors or patterns happened to be popular in any particular season. Sunbrella's yarns had the color baked in, so the company had to commit to, say, ten thousand pounds of blue fiber several months in advance, and that blue could not, in turn, be dyed another color.

To compete indoors, Sunbrella needed to make its fabric softer and more supple, and it needed to be better at predicting color trends. Those were two big caveats, but Gant wanted to push ahead, even if it cost money, even if it cost time. He was convinced that Sunbrella had an ace up its sleeve. The Sunbrella team commissioned a series of research reports to answer some simple questions about their potential customers: Who was buying sofas? Who wasn't buying sofas but would if the right product came along? What do people want in a sofa?

What they learned was encouraging. A sofa is a huge purchase, often the most expensive household item after the house itself, and the upholstery, if it's done right, can represent half the cost of the entire piece. A huge segment of the market was composed of people who were either not buying new sofas when they wanted to or were buying cheap sofas when they really wanted a nicer one. By and large, these were parents or pet owners who feared that their six-year-old or their poodle was going to ruin the cushions. That, the team realized, was Sunbrella's advantage: their fabric could be cleaned far better than any other upholstery fabric. But to make it work, Glen Raven had to marry their technical expertise in the textile industry with some fast learning in the fashion business. Engineers had to figure out how to make a whole new set of cloth types, such as chenille and bouclé. They had to redesign their spinning process to create a looser, fluffier yarn and a more pliable fabric. Suddenly, their most important decisions would be predicated on something as immeasurable as "softness." It's called "hand feel" in the business, and there are no clear measurements. People just pick up a piece of fabric and rub it between their thumb and fingers to see if it feels nice. Engineers and operations-based managers are awful at this kind of gut-sense decision-making. Gant realized that he had buildings filled with scientists and factory managers but what he needed was a new kind of expertise. Glen Raven needed designers.

A team of nine designers was swiftly brought to Burlington and asked to develop a full line of Sunbrella fabrics to be sold indoors. Since it would take at least two years to develop new fiber colors and at least that long to reengineer the machinery that weaves the fiber into cloth, they needed to become expert at predicting what kinds of sofa coverings people will want to buy years into the future. Gant sent these designers to places no Glen Raven employee had ever heard of, let alone visited. They went, en masse, to the world's most important furniture show, held every April in Milan, the Salone Internazionale. But they soon learned that the furniture colors and design themes trailed behind the more quick-moving colors of fashion. Glen Raven, for the first time ever, began sending people to the big fashion shows in New York and Paris, where they jotted down inspirations. They consulted with the Color Association of the United States and tried to make sense of its annual forecasts, which predict the color trends that will dominate the market-place over the next few years. Each observation was accompanied by its very own "color story."

Today, Sunbrella is a standard upholstery product available in Crate & Barrel and Room & Board, as well as nearly every other mid- to high-end furniture retailer in the country. The company is thriving, even though its fabrics cost twice as much as most other upholstery options.

Just as Allen Gant, Jr., had hoped, Glen Raven has become an entirely different company. Looked at in broad outline, it seems almost incomprehensible that a company focused on making acrylic yarn for cheap sweaters is, today, designing and manufacturing bridges around the world, high-end sofas in New York and Paris, and the highest-rated protective uniforms for utility workers around the world. Gant says the transition was actually quite simple: instead of asking how to make the same things more cheaply, Glen Raven, as we've seen, began to ask what people actually wanted. If they wanted it, after all, they were going to pay a reasonably higher price for it.

Once Glen Raven began to think about its end user, it started doing all sorts of things differently. Previously, one of the key metrics of the company was making sure that all of its machines were running close to peak capacity for as many hours a week as possible. But customers don't care about machine utilization, and machines can be utilized 100 percent of the time making products that nobody wants. Every one of Glen Raven's leading products today—the geotextiles, the automotive headliners, the Sunbrella upholstery—involved experimentation and investment. That meant endless days of idle machinery and months of staff time devoted to ultimately failed research that brought in no revenue. That kind of patience is agonizing for people trained in an operations-focused world. It takes guts to continue to invest in new products that might not ever be profitable. It's even harder when the process is determined by imponderables like "hand feel" and "color story." No wonder so few companies made this switch earlier. As Glen Raven's head of marketing, Hal Hunnicutt, told me, "Most textile companies kept doing the same, safe thing, right until they collapsed."

Gant told me that the biggest surprise, on the other side of the big change, is that after abandoning the business model of his dad and uncle and grandfather, he didn't just survive; he's thriving. He also remarked that it is a lot more fun to run a customer-focused company. He is constantly surprised by the ideas that come bubbling up. "I had no idea we'd be making bridges in India, a few years ago," he says, smiling. "I have no idea what we'll be doing a few years from now."

# CASE STUDY: MORGENSTERN'S FINEST ICE CREAM

### DON'T COMPETE WITH MASSIVE COMPANIES;
### DO THINGS THEY CAN'T

Nicholas Morgenstern is tall, skinny, and looks straight in your eyes with an intensity that can be inviting (he is focused, fully, on you) but also a bit intimidating. More than anybody I spoke with for this book, Nicholas is the one who most thoroughly and visibly lives his passion. He works at his ice cream store in New York's Greenwich Village for eighty-one hours each week. He knows that number precisely, because he knows everything about his life with that level of precision. He just turned forty and has decided not to date seriously because he understands that the commitment he is making to ice cream would not allow for him to become a good husband or father at this time.

Nicholas's passion is to make the perfect American ice cream. For him, this doesn't mean he wants to create an ice cream that is especially tasty or that sells the best. He wants to understand the essence of this most American of desserts. He wants his customers to taste his chocolate and to instantly recognize that this particular version of chocolate—or vanilla or rocky road or banana split—is the most fully authentic expression of its essence. To achieve this, Nicholas has studied ice cream in every way imaginable. He didn't just read a book or two; he has devoted years to his investigation. That means, yes, reading every book written on the subject but also finding ancient recipes and reproducing them and traveling to every well-regarded—and many not-yet-discovered—ice cream shops around the world.

Ice cream, Nicholas believes, is essentially American. In a bite, one can taste the specific history and culture of this self-made, individualist, capitalist country. Ice cream's predecessors did begin in the kitchens of European royalty, as a showy, fussy dessert available to only a small handful of people. Back then, anything frozen couldn't travel far, which meant that people who didn't own cows could consume dairy only in the form of preserved products, like cheese and yogurt. This was primarily true in the United States until the mid-1800s, with much of the country's dairy farms at least a day or more removed from the big eastern cities. By the Civil War, though, primitive refrigerated train cars could transport fresh cream thousands of miles without risking spoilage. Some of those farms grew sugar beets, which allowed for cheap sweeteners, available even to the poor, for the first time in history. Early mass-produced, hand-churned ice cream makers—a favorite of Sears catalog consumers—meant that even the most humble of parents in New York tenements or on the Kansas prairie could whip up a delicious treat for the family. This was a first in human history. Poor people had never before enjoyed such ready access to so luxurious a dessert.

In the twentieth century, ice cream was being mass-produced in huge factories and shipped, premade, all over the country. There was no obvious reason why the rich array of flavors and home recipes gave way to a small handful of classics: vanilla, chocolate, strawberry. Later, more complex combinations entered the canon: butter pecan, rocky road, fudge ripple. (Nicholas says you can identify how old someone is by asking them one question: What is the classic flavor combination of your youth?)

Nicholas likes to study old restaurant menus and popular recipe books. He points out that various desserts have come and gone or have remained regional favorites but have never become national icons, like baked Alaska, shoofly pie, and chess cake. But, since the 1860s, everyone, everywhere in the United States seems to have loved ice cream and, especially, a handful of classic flavors and combinations. Yet, Nicholas believes, industrialization of ice cream has influenced most producers to make business decisions that have led to a dilution of the essence of the product. Factories inject stabilizers, like guar gum or cellulose gum, so that ice cream can be safely shipped all over the world. Inevitably, some ice cream will melt and then refreeze as it moves through the complex supply chain, but the guar gum prevents too many ice crystals from forming. They also use mono- and diglycerides or egg yolk and other emulsifiers to ensure that quickly made ice cream feels smooth in the mouth. More than anything, industrial ice cream makers inject lots of air into their products to minimize the use of actual ingredients and maximize profits. (Breyers' newest recipes are so distant from the original idea of ice cream that they are called "frozen dairy desserts.")

Ice cream shops, similarly, make compromises that have affected the experience of ice cream. They use giant tubs and leave them open so that customers can see the ice cream, but this dries out the product. Most ice cream is produced somewhere else and shipped to the retail store, requiring those various chemical additions. Major ice cream brands typically make a universal base—a recipe of cream and sugar and emulsifiers—in bulk and then add a bit of flavoring to produce chocolate, vanilla, strawberry, or whichever flavor. By working from one common base, big factories don't have to worry about maintaining an inventory of separate bases for each flavor, and they don't have to order different kinds of cream. It's much easier and cheaper to just use one base for everything.

Nicholas has obsessively avoided every one of these business-driven compromises. It's not that he is fussy (well, it's not only that he is fussy). Nicholas explains that emulsifiers change the flavor of ice cream, stabilizers change its texture, and all that air dramatically reduces the intensity of the taste. By using a common base for all flavors, mass-produced ice cream makers don't allow for the specific needs of each type of ice cream. Chocolate contains proteins that vanilla doesn't, so a chocolate base should have less protein in it, which means a less fatty cream. As a result of these many sensible industrial choices, ice cream makers are not producing optimal ice cream flavor, and thus most Americans have never been able to experience that perfect taste.

The first time I visited Morgenstern's, I had his chocolate and told a friend, "This is the perfect chocolate flavor that I didn't even realize I was missing." I was with my son, who was enjoying the perfect mint chocolate chip. It was wonderful. I think back on that moment with my boy with a smile and instantly remember going with my parents and my brother to an ice cream shop when I was a kid and how happy we were.

Nicholas had very little of the normal American childhood. His parents were lost, poor wanderers who took minimal responsibility for their son. They went through a bitter divorce when he was young, and Nicholas spent his youth living in a succession of marginal apartments—some scarcely better than squats—in San Francisco. Before he entered high school, his mother joined a cult and disappeared, taking his brother with her. He doesn't know where they are or what became of them. A few times, when he was young, Nicholas spent the summer with his grandparents in southern Ohio. They would often eat local ice cream together. Those were the best moments—maybe the only fully good moments—of his childhood.

Nicholas began working in restaurants when he was still in high school and, essentially, on his own. He went to culinary school and became a master pastry chef, eventually landing jobs in some of the finest restaurants in New York, including Gramercy Tavern, Nice Matin, and Gilt. Along with a partner, he opened his own place in Brooklyn, the General Greene, and began experimenting with ice cream. Soon ice cream became an obsession. He saw that there was a specific food experience—eating the perfect ice cream, preferably with family members—that he wanted to re-create.

Nicholas's ambitions are not modest. He wants to transform how people all over the country and the world experience ice cream. He wants to deepen our connection to the past, by making the ideal version of those iconic recipes. But he also wants to help guide ice cream into the future. He constantly experiments with surprisingly delightful novel flavors—burnt sage, cardamom lemon jam, avocado— introducing new ones annually. Nicholas does hope that, one day, his ice creams will be available in grocery stores everywhere. He has been approached by every major ice cream manufacturer and countless investors, offering to give him the resources to become a global brand. And, he says, he might take one of them up on it one day. But he's not ready. He hasn't nailed the flavors yet. He told me, recently, that when he pictures his perfect life, he isn't flying on planes to meet with investors and discuss distribution strategies and marketing plans. He is in the basement of his shop, coming up with new flavors, and then he's up on the line, seeing what his customers love and what they wish were a bit better.

A strong hunch tells me that Nicholas is not just making the right decision for his own quality of life but that he is also making a smart business choice by rejecting mass production and scale until he's fully ready. He is becoming ever better at understanding what large-scale production misses and what consumers most crave (even if they don't realize they crave it until they first have a lick). His ice cream is very hot right now. His flagship shop has been named one of the best places to have ice cream in the country by nearly every food writer who matters. He has opened a second shop, and both stores perpetually have lines of eager customers. He could sell for a decent payday based on his trendiness. But he is on a passion-fueled quest, and when he is satisfied that he has fulfilled his journey—or gotten as far as one person can—he will be more than just a trendy hotshot. He will be in a position to define how his ice cream—and, perhaps, how all ice cream—is made in the future. I expect that he'll earn plenty of money, but he'll achieve something even greater: he'll have delivered that perfect experience to countless others.

# CHAPTER 9

# DON'T BE A COMMODITY

*How a pencil factory in Jersey City changed my life and
could change yours, too*

I first stumbled across the single most important rule for thriving in the twenty-first century when I held a No. 2 pencil in my hand and listened to the man who had made it explain its particular history. At first, this pencil appeared ordinary. It was yellow and hexagonal, with a stamped metal band—the ferrule—encasing a pale pink eraser at one end. It looked exactly like the pencils I had grown up with, back in the 1970s, when I used No. 2's to fill out Scantron bubble sheets on standardized tests. The only difference with this new pencil, it seemed, was that it was bafflingly expensive: it cost around the price of a whole set of pencils at the nearest Staples. Yet it was selling like hotcakes. General Pencil Semi-Hex No. 2 wasn't a novelty item. I was holding it, in fact, at General Pencil's beautiful headquarters overlooking the Manhattan skyline, on some of the more expensive real estate on earth.

How was General Pencil doing so well? For months, I couldn't get this puzzle out of my head. Pencils are the ultimate commodity: for the vast majority of us, one pencil is just about as good as any other. The pencils I used decades ago in the New York City public school system are indistinguishable from the ones you might currently find in classrooms in

Toledo or Tashkent. Pencils are also a perfect example of what economists call the law of one price, which suggests that all identical products should cost about the same amount. And pencils, after all, have also become something of an outdated technology in and of themselves. These days, most of us do the majority of our writing by typing with our fingers and thumbs. If you were to visit a college lecture hall or high school class, chances are that you'd see many of the students taking notes on a device that hadn't been invented when I was a kid. The more I thought about it, the less it made sense: How was General Pencil still around? Why was it doing so well? What was going on?

It took some doing, but eventually my questions were answered. Moreover, lessons I learned in this building were not just specific to the pencil industry. I came to think of them as exemplifying the single most important rule for thriving in a twenty-first-century economy. The rule applies to manufacturers, but also to bankers and artists and teachers and middle managers at large corporations. The rule is simple: Do not be a commodity. Do not be easily comparable to other people who have, roughly, the same set of skills and the same background. The rule may be simple, but its history and implications are incredibly rich.

Let's start with a review. A commodity is something for sale that is pretty much identical to everything else like it. A sack of white rice is a commodity; so is lumber at a hardware store and a chicken breast at a discount supermarket. For most of us, accountants are commodities—we figure any one will do our taxes about as well as any other. Airlines desperately try not to be commodities, but most of them are. Commodities fit a few key criteria. They are undifferentiated. That means that people who buy them don't see any qualitative difference between competing versions. Instead, commodities are bought based on price and convenience. Most people gravitate toward buying the cheaper dish soap, the cheaper lumber, or the cheaper light bulb instead of the more expensive version on the same shelf. And the very existence of commodities shows how much our economy has changed in the last two hundred years.

For most of human existence, shopping was an exercise in absolute scarcity. People didn't have a range of choices of rice or lumber or clothing or, of course, light bulbs. They were lucky to have a chance to buy anything at all. Only the wealthy or the minority who lived in crowded cities were able to comparison shop. The word "commodity" has existed in English since the 1400s, but its meaning, for centuries, was simple: something of any value at all. It wasn't until 1842 that there was a need for a new word to express a new kind of economic arrangement, one that would revolutionize all of our lives.

Joseph Dart had no intention of transforming the world. Quite the contrary. He spent most of his life looking for a more reliable way to make a living. Dart was born in 1799 on a small farm on the Connecticut River. Joseph's life was made even more difficult because his parents kept having children. Joseph's sisters had a hard time finding husbands, so the house was filled with hungry stomachs. When he was twenty years old, Joseph moved just about as far away from home as it was possible to go at the time without leaving the United States, to what was then called the Northwest Frontier—Buffalo, New York. It was a rough town, a place where the wild fur trappers of the Canadian north brought their pelts to sell to merchants, who then shipped them south to the big cities of Boston and New York. These delivery routes were over land, requiring a traversing of mountains and travel through unsettled territory in which bandits often preyed on passersby.

Joseph arrived in 1821, got a job in a store specializing in hats and fur, and eventually became a partner in the business. He figured that all those trappers from the north and merchants coming from the south and east would want a nice, firm hat to protect them from the rain and the wind. His business did not do all that well. The people in Buffalo, like him, tended to be poor and didn't want to spend a lot of money on new hats. Joseph passed much of his days idling outside his shop on Main Street, which happened to be right in the path between Buffalo's port on Lake Erie and the main market for grain in the center of town. The grain business was, as one would expect in a forgotten frontier town, a sleepy affair. Farmers from northwestern New York and the few habitable pockets of Ontario would amble into town with a mule or two carrying a few sacks of wheat. Occasionally a boat would arrive, ferrying farm produce from as far away as Toledo or Detroit, on the far shores of Lake Erie. But there were few midwestern farmers then, and what few there were saw little reason to incur the expense of shipping their goods all the way to some muddy town in the wilds of New York State.

Then, on October 26, 1825, something happened that would transform Buffalo and, eventually, America and even the world. After nearly a decade of construction, the Erie Canal opened. It was, at the time, among the greatest engineering feats in history, a man-made canal that ran 363 miles through granite and mountains, connecting Buffalo with Albany, New York, the Great Lakes with the Hudson River. The cost of shipping a ton of grain from Buffalo to New York City fell from one hundred dollars to ten dollars, and the time it took was cut in half. It meant that any farmer within a mule ride of a Great Lake could quickly and cheaply ship his goods to New York City and on to Europe. The canal would play a crucial role in transforming America from a poor nation of isolated farming settlements into a national economy and a global economic force. It also helped New York City replace Philadelphia as the nation's economic center of power, though that was at least a decade away.

At first, actually, the Erie Canal had a lot of trouble. It had serious leaks all along its 363 miles, and its bed was too shallow, forcing barges to travel far more slowly than hoped. It was mocked as Clinton's Ditch, a dig at DeWitt Clinton, New York's governor and the lead proponent of the project. Finally, more than ten years after its unfortunate opening, the canal was enlarged, at enormous expense. As the canal gained in success, farmers from New England and northern Europe began moving into previously remote corners of the American Midwest, knowing they could buy land cheaply or, as homesteaders, get land for nothing at all, and ship their goods to Buffalo and then on to the rest of the global market.

Joseph Dart watched all this happen from in front of his struggling millinery. As he would describe it later, he noted that the slow movement of grain on the backs of mules steadily increased until there were too many mules to count. Dart saw that the entire system was wildly inefficient. Grain arrived via mule or boat in burlap sacks. Longshoremen would carry each sack, one by one, to a central area. A buyer for a grain company used a sharp knife to cut open the sack, grab a handful of grain, and offer a price. The seller and buyer would then haggle, after which the sack would be lugged back onto a cart and dragged by mule to the canal, where it would be hand-loaded onto a barge. It was tedious, costly, and time-consuming. (And, to Dart's great frustration and bewilderment, nobody seemed to want to buy any hats!)

Like nearly everybody in that age, Dart was familiar with Oliver Evans, the brilliant, self-taught engineer who revolutionized flour milling by figuring out how to use a high-pressure steam engine to automate a mill. Mills were already using steam power to perform tasks like grinding the grain, sifting the output, and filling the sacks with the finished goods. Evans was the first to realize that the biggest cost was all the people lugging material from one machine to the next. He created a system of buckets and conveyor belts that took care of moving the materials around. Introduced in 1790, his mill automation soon made Evans wealthy and famous.

Looking back, it's quite surprising that nobody, including Evans himself, thought to apply his bucket system to other parts of grain transportation. Not until Dart had an "Aha!" moment watching grain-heavy carts pass as he struggled to induce the citizens of Buffalo that they needed hats. Dart bought some land situated right between Lake Erie and the Erie Canal; then, working with an engineer, and cribbing from Evans's now fifty-year-old bucket system, he created the world's first automatic grain elevator. Buckets would scoop grain out of the holds of the lake ships and convey it to an enormous elevated grain crib. From there, aided by gravity, the grain could flow via a massive wooden shaft into the canal barges.

Dart was not immediately recognized as a genius. According to newspaper reports, a crowd of people jeered at him, mocking his plans for this bizarre device, that was first used on June 12, 1843. How could this weird contraption, rising fifty feet above the water level, possibly grab all the grain that arrived? That first day, the schooner *Philadelphia* arrived with a huge load of grain in its hold. Dart's elevator emptied it before dark, and the *Philadelphia* was quickly off. All of the longshoremen of Buffalo, working long and difficult days, were no match for Dart's elevator, which could handle more than fifty thousand bushels in a day. Buffalo quickly became the grain center of the country. A few years earlier, Buffalo had seen around eight thousand bushels a year in grain. Within a year of the invention of the grain elevator, three million bushels were coming through town annually.

Dart's invention was quickly copied and improved upon. Within a decade, there were massive grain elevators in Toledo, Philadelphia, New York City, and, most important, Chicago. This grain elevator system arrived alongside further developments in transportation: more canals were being dug, and rail lines were spreading across the country. The United States was soon the breadbasket of the world, producing billions of tons of wheat and corn and rye, which flowed to whichever global markets were willing to pay the best price. This huge demand for grain inspired millions of people to move farther and farther into the American frontier. Ambitious people, unsatisfied by their conditions at home in Ireland or Germany or Russia or China, were drawn by the stories of America's growing wealth, and, indeed, countless people were able to move from bare subsistence and centuries of feudal-like misery to something that, at the time, felt like wealth. There were, of course, losers. The longshoremen didn't see the change coming, and their way of life quickly disappeared, though many found that they could get even better jobs—higher pay with less damage to their backs—in the many industries that exploded alongside the grain elevators.

No wonder so few saw the change coming: it was profoundly radical. Grain and other crops had been sold for millennia in markets in medieval England or at the trading posts along the Silk Road in ancient Assyria. Each bundle of goods was evaluated on its own merits, and prices were negotiated, often over long periods of time by men who slowly drank tea or coffee, stormed off, or raised their voices in the middle of negotiations, and prided themselves on fighting as long as it took to get the best deal. That way of buying and selling seemed an inextricable part of commerce.

Soon after Dart built his elevator, traders realized they had a new problem. The grain was coming so fast that they couldn't possibly negotiate a distinct price with each farmer or, even, each barge owner. The solution came in Chicago, on the floor of the Board of Trade. Traders, surrounded by grain and cut-open burlap sacks, spent all day, every day, offering prices, negotiating as quickly as possible. Yet, still, the piles of unpriced grain piled high, with farmers sometimes waiting days to find out how much they would be paid for the grain they had brought to market. It was unworkable—a plug in the great flood that was fueling American economic growth.

So a group of traders met and came up with a simple, elegant solution, one that is still in use today. They created five grades of quality and set prices for each. Now every bit of grain that arrived in a sack or a barge or a horse-drawn wagon would be quickly graded, the price set. Grains that were plump and unbroken would be given top billing, grade 1. Those that were a bit thinner, with some broken pieces in each handful, would be grade 2, and so on. Each load of grain could be fairly quickly graded and sent to the proper storage site. The price would be standard. If your wheat was grade 1, it would get exactly the same price as every other bit of grade 1 wheat. It didn't matter if you had carefully tended your crop in Minnesota while another sack came from a lazy farmer in Kansas. Once they were graded, all grains become economic clones, their unique stories disappeared. It was the birth of commoditization.

Commoditization was such an elegant solution to the problems of early industrialization that it quickly spread through basic goods. Lumber and cuts of meat and iron and steel all became commoditized. They were given set quality levels and fixed prices. This allowed huge volumes of the stuff to be produced and traded quickly and efficiently.

Commoditization also provided more financial security and predictability. Soon farmers could not only buy and sell actual grain that they brought to market but could sell grain futures—a promise to deliver grain a few months or even a few years later. This allowed them to plan better. They would know, before they planted a single seed, how much money they would make when their crops were harvested. This preselling allowed farmers to invest in more land, more equipment, more fertilizer.

Another remarkable benefit of commoditization came with the development of futures markets. Within a decade after the Civil War, the Chicago Board of Trade had developed a mature futures market. Farmers could sell a contract to deliver grain six months or a year or three years in the future. This allowed them to get cash, today, for a crop they hadn't even planted yet.

Some farmers would also buy grain future contracts from other farmers, so that they would be certain to have a big enough harvest even if their crop was attacked by insects or hail. Bread manufacturers could buy grain futures to ensure that they would have a steady supply at a predictable price.

Before too long, there were futures contracts in beef and pork and almost every kind of grain. (For obscure reasons, onions are the one major agricultural crop that cannot be turned into future contracts.) While financial futures can seem exotic and dangerous—people are forever warning about the destabilizing impact of speculation—they have largely provided stability to American farmers and food manufacturers. Commodities ensured that businesspeople could plan properly, insure themselves against disaster, and generally think more long-term. However much this book dismisses commoditization as a strategy for most people today, it would be wrong to think that it has always been a negative. Commoditization helped create the modern world and made us rich enough to begin to imagine an economy built not on commodities but on passion.

General Pencil, the company that is still making writing implements in New Jersey, has its origins in the tail end of the European Middle Ages. In 1823, when Edward Weissenborn was born in Rheinbach, a small town in what is now western Germany, pencil making was an ancient craft. Master pencil makers would be required to complete several years of apprenticeship before being deemed expert enough to mold carbon rock into a thin slab and glue a wooden casing around it. Every region had its own pencil styles, and each master had his own personal techniques. Pencils in southern Germany tended to be a bit shorter and stubbier. English pencils tended to be longer, with thick carbon slabs.

As a young man in Germany, Weissenborn worked at the I. I. Renbach Lead Pencil Company, one of the world's first factory-based pencil manufacturers. He became an invaluable assistant in the engineering department, developing plans for new machinery to grind graphite and shape wood to produce finished, machine-made pencils. Weissenborn was not a member of the wealthy Renbach family, however, and he realized that he would never be able to rise in a country still shaking off aristocratic rules. So, like many bright, ambitious young men from the wrong families, Weissenborn set sail for America. His first job, in the 1860s, was assisting in the design and construction of the USS *Monitor*, a warship commissioned to fight in the Civil War. Weissenborn made enough money from this job that he was able to open a pencil factory in Jersey City.

At the time, machines that could make pencils automatically were the height of technological innovation and seen as something of a miracle. Weissenborn, a savvy marketer, made sure to get his products into the hands of the most powerful political men in the country, so that they could attest that his pencils were far more uniform and reliable than the ancient version made by hand. (This is the nineteenth-century version of working with Instagram "influencers.") He received, and proudly displayed, letters from four members of Abraham Lincoln's cabinet, the mayor of New York City, and the governor of New York State. With his fast-growing family, Weissenborn helped to develop the suite of automated machinery that made pencils incredibly quickly and cheaply, including the giant mixers that combined pulverized graphite rock with clay and other additives; the industrial furnaces that baked the resulting mix into pencil lead (which contains no actual lead); the machines that dug a groove into cedar slats to create space for the graphite; and the shaping machines that turned those slats into hexagonal stalks. General Pencil was among the first to adopt the yellow paint that, by the 1890s, had become the universal symbol for a quality manufactured pencil. For a time, General Pencil, situated on a hill overlooking Manhattan, was the largest and most advanced pencil factory in the world.

As Weissenborn passed his company down to his son and, eventually, his grandson, the U.S. economy was undergoing its own transformation. The development of massive batch processing paved the way for huge economies of scale. In the 1910s, the conveyor belt dramatically increased the throughput of even the most complex machinery, such as the automobile. In the 1920s came the fully modern corporation, with its middle managers and widely understood hierarchies. Every decade brought huge new advances—the airplane, the truck, the highway system, the computer, modern chemistry, and plastics. Every day brought smaller advances, too. These technological breakthroughs meant that the American economy was becoming increasingly productive. Every hour worked resulted in far more output. For most of the twentieth century, companies grew so fast that they needed to hire huge numbers of workers, so they competed by raising wages. Workers, making more money, bought more things, which meant the companies did even better, paid more money, and the virtuous cycle continued. For many Americans, it was a golden century. Companies got bigger and richer by making goods more cheaply. The average American's purchasing power skyrocketed, and our lives got better. People became more literate, and since they went to school for a longer period, they also needed more pencils. At the turn of the century, less than 10 percent of Americans attended high school; by the 1950s, nearly everyone did.

All this meant that there was a huge demand for pencils. In New Jersey alone, the number of children in schools skyrocketed from a few thousand in 1900 to 2.2 million in 2000. Every one of those kids was using a lot of pencils. Fairly quickly, General Pencil had so many orders from so many school districts that it no longer needed to be at the cutting edge of innovation.

The American pencil business had by then become what economists call a mature business. It was a stable one in which several dozen American manufacturers held fairly fixed shares of the market, based mostly on geography. Since pencils were a fairly cheap product, it wasn't economical to ship them very far, and customers didn't see much point in trying to squeeze their suppliers to save a few pennies here or there.

Edward ran the company until the 1890s; then one of his sons, Oscar, took over; he was in charge of the firm until 1927, when he handed the reigns to Oscar Jr. In 1979, when the fourth Weissenborn to lead General Pencil, Jim, became the boss, the company he ran was a lot like the one his great-grandfather had started. There were never more than fifty employees. In the basement, the graphite mixing drums purchased in 1875 still turned at sixty revolutions a minute, nearly every minute of the day. They were rotated by leather belts, installed in 1904, which were powered by an ancient diesel motor brought in sometime during World War I. Technology and speed were no longer major factors in General's success. Having long, deep relationships with school districts was the essential competitive tool that ensured that hundreds of thousands of pencils would be ordered every month.

This sleepy world was overturned in the 1990s when something entirely new began to happen. Ships arrived in the nearby Port Newark with huge containers filled with pencils made in China. These pencils looked identical to the ones General made. They were yellow and had the same No. 2 graphite, the same metal tube and rubber eraser at the tip. But there was one huge difference: these pencils cost a fraction of General's. Public schools could buy a gross of pencils—144 of them—for $1.50. General's cost about $1.50 a dozen. Fairly quickly, Jim Weissenborn's relationships with school districts around the country, built over a century, disappeared. First the Kearney district called and said, sorry, they just couldn't keep buying General's pencils. With the savings from the cheap ones from China, they could spend more on educating children. Then came calls from Trenton and Asbury Park. Before long, the calls didn't come at all. Districts simply stopped ordering. The hardest loss came when Jersey City—the home of General Pencil and the district where Jim Weissenborn, his parents, his kids, and nearly all of his employees had gone to school—canceled its order.

The news in the Writing Instrument Manufacturers Association newsletter confirmed that the same thing was happening all across the country. Dixon Ticonderoga moved most of its operations to the source of all the trouble: China and Mexico. It seemed clear, Jim thought, that this would be the end of the story for General Pencil, too.

Jim Weissenborn had always assumed that he would be the last member of his family to run General Pencil. While his daughter, Katie, had loved coming to the factory as a little girl—often grabbing charcoal that was still warm from the kiln—she seemed to lose interest in the business as she got older. When she went off to college, she told her dad that she had no interest in figuring out how to squeeze another fraction of a penny from the machinery, or how to get the throughput of pencils per hour up by 8 percent. Then she sat in on a marketing meeting and realized that she would love to spend her days drawing and figuring out how to tell the General Pencil story to shopkeepers and customers.

One day while she was shopping for art supplies, Katie noted that the store had only the really cheap pencils—the dozen-for-a-buck imports from China. Katie hated them. She resented that those pencils had destroyed her family's business, but she also hated that they contained subpar filler for their graphite, which led to a weak and inconsistent line. She hated that they were made with cheap wood from Vietnam, which was more likely to splinter and possibly ruin a child's love of drawing forever. The only alternative was the professional drawing pencils, scientifically engineered in Germany, that cost more than two dollars apiece.

In that moment, Katie realized that she had come upon an enormous hole in the U.S. pencil market. She couldn't pos-

pany. Sure, she enjoyed the process of developing those kids' kits, and it was always fun to visit the factory, but Katie was far more of an artist than an industrialist. Her passion lay in sketching nature, not in looking at spreadsheets, worrying about the rising cost of graphite and the bottleneck at their Midwest distributor. That was stuff her dad loved and would never be for her.

But while working with her dad developing the pencil kits, she found herself becoming fascinated by some of the very things she assumed she'd hate. Distribution, she realized, isn't just a dull corporate word; it's the way she can get pencils in the hands of children and artists. Finance isn't a deathly dull spreadsheet; it's a language that allows her to make better decisions about the experiments she wants to conduct, and it guides her as she invents different kinds of kits and assesses which ones have successfully found a market. She would never make distribution and finance the core of her work. General Pencil has plenty of experts in those areas. But she learned that there could be as much joy and creativity in business as there is in art. Well, maybe not quite as much, but enough to make it worthwhile. As her dad, Jim, got older and found the day-to-day burdens of running a pencil business too exhausting, Katie was shocked to realize that she wanted to take over. She has never had more fun in her life.

# CHAPTER 10

# THE WORLD IN A CHOCOLATE BAR

*When a Jesuit and an agnostic navy pilot team up
to transform the candy market*

I watched a video of a man named Denis Ring describing the joy of stretchy, creamy caramel, the kind that makes your fingers sticky as you eat it and coats your mouth with its combination of melted sugar, browned butter, and heavy cream. He did so with such a quiet intensity—a smile on his face, love in his voice—that I concluded that this was not just some ad for his candy company but an expression of something deeper. I called Ring, the founder of OCHO Candy, which makes, among other things, a chocolate caramel bar, and, boy, did I ever learn how deep it goes.

OCHO Candy is a small but fast-growing maker of candy bars in Oakland, California. Denis is a tall, slender sixty-three-year-old with a gentle manner and a soft, slow, precise way of speaking. It's easy to imagine him as a pediatrician or a yoga instructor. He founded the company with a younger friend, Scott Kucirek, who is, behaviorally, Denis's opposite. Scott speaks fast, walks fast, provides a torrent of information. It's easy to see how the partnership works. OCHO Candy began as a feeling Denis had, a passion that—as we'll soon learn—was driven as much by a spiritual yearning as it was by a quest for profits. He represents the gentle, quiet spiritual core of the business. Scott is the enactor, the energetic force that oversees the operation, manages the staff, runs the numbers, and generally ensures that OCHO's candy is available everywhere people might want a quick treat.

OCHO Candy could not have existed at any earlier point in history. There simply wasn't the right kind of technical know-how, machinery, financial instruments, and supply-chain structures to turn a passion like Denis's into a product available on shelves all over the country. There have always been people who dream up a particularly wonderful kind of candy, and many of them have been able to sell it to a small crowd of local fans. But everything that went national or international—Snickers and Twix, M&M's and Reese's Peanut Butter Cups—was not the result of an individual person's unique passions. They were industrial products, designed—engineered, really—to be mass-produced quickly and cheaply. When you taste a Snickers (which is, of course, pretty delicious), you are tasting industrialization, the output of a series of compromises based on the cost and availability of raw materials, the chemistry of highly processed foods, the physical requirements of machine-made bulk candy, and the creation of a global supply chain. When you taste an OCHO Caramel & Peanut bar (which is even more delicious) you are tasting a physical manifestation of one man's lifelong passionate quest.

Denis says he was about as typical an Irish-American teenager as existed in the United States circa 1970. He grew up east of San Francisco but had almost no awareness of the social revolution occurring just over the hills and the bay. It's not that his family was so religious or conservative; they were simply ordinary Americans who had more in common with small-town midwesterners than the free-sex-and-drugs carnival that was so close by. His dad was a lawyer, his mom a homemaker. He played sports, not especially well, and was an adequate but unexceptional student. His family went to church each Sunday, and then they spent zero time thinking about faith during the rest of the week. Today, looking back over the decades, he thinks that the one hint of his future life path was the time he spent watching the stream behind his house flow gently; then he would sometimes find himself reciting a prayer he had heard in church.

In 1974, Denis went to Santa Clara University, a Jesuit school an hour southeast of San Francisco. It was a wild time to be a college kid. The counterculture had, by then, lost its ideological and spiritual ambitions (however unclear they had always been; what, exactly, is an Age of Aquarius, and what would happen if we lived in one?) and had become focused more on immediate pleasures of the flesh. Slowly, Denis came to see that he had a profoundly passionate soul, one that craved something real. He saw the other college kids smoking marijuana and taking pills, knew about their sexual promiscuity, and felt repulsed. It wasn't moralistic conservatism that angered him; it was that it all seemed so false, so desperate, so sad and immaterial. Everyone around him laughed a lot, talked about their crazy experiences, but they didn't seem happy, really happy. They ran from quick buzz to quick buzz.

Many of Denis's teachers were Jesuits—priests who had taken a vow of chastity, poverty, and obedience to the church. These were, of course, the precise opposite of the prevailing values around him. Yet so many of his teachers seemed to be deeply, profoundly happy. This did not mean they were giddy and giggly all the time, or that they constantly shared their latest grand adventure. On the contrary, they were quiet and reflective. When they did express exuberance, it was often about an intellectual or spiritual insight they had come to through careful study and prayer.

Denis realized that this Jesuit version of Catholic faith was quite different from the one he'd been raised in. When he was a kid, church felt like a one-way experience. Mass was like a premade package, designed by people far away and long ago, that Denis was supposed to simply and passively accept. It made him think of his parents and their comfortable middle-class life. They, too, believed that having a nice house, two cars, and a vacation home was all they needed for happiness. Church, house, drugs, sex: in one way, these were all the same to Denis. They were supposed to be preapproved sources of happiness, and nobody stopped to ask if these things made people happy and, if they didn't, what would.

He was learning that the Jesuit approach was not to seek out one prepackaged solution and then expect to be happy. The Jesuits saw their entire lives as a journey of continually discovering the source of true, deep happiness—which, for them, was God's love. Denis's most profound moment came when he encountered a book, *Seeds of Contemplation*, by Thomas Merton, a Trappist monk. Denis read the book again and again and realized this was the kind of faith he had been looking for. This, he realized, would serve as the essential guide for the rest of his life. It described a life rooted in the idea that God truly loves people and that if people truly engage that love, it will provide an eternal happiness that no other source can match. The thing is, love is not always easy to find and requires real dedication. In the Trappist tradition, like the Jesuit one, one must devote specific times of the day to prayer and actively seek out the presence of God's love in the world. Trappists are more insular than Jesuits, though, living as monks, away from society, and they seek out God through the things they do in their monasteries— through prayer but also through simple tasks like baking bread or making cheese or wine.

By the time Denis graduated from college, he was ready to devote his entire life to engaging God's love through spiritual practice. He became a Jesuit. This meant moving into a home with other Jesuits and embracing the required vows. It is no simple step. The Jesuits require potential novices to undergo a series of psychological screenings and intense spiritual conversations to ensure that only those truly ready for this challenging life are admitted. Denis was a natural. Like all Jesuits, he woke long before dawn and spent the first hour of the day in quiet prayer. Then he and his fellow Jesuits would gather for breakfast and, typically, hold a broad discussion about whatever they had been reading or thinking or praying about. There were expert breadmakers and chefs who saw preparing wholesome, delicious meals and being at table together as central to their spiritual connection to God's love.

Jesuits, unlike Trappist monks, believe in being present in the world, directly serving people in the public. Denis worked as an orderly in a hospital; then he served food to homeless people; and later he taught at a Jesuit high school. He planned to become a priest, which meant he was expected to get an advanced degree. He went to Fordham University, a Jesuit school in New York City, and studied for his master's degree in philosophy. Although the Jesuit life is committed to obedience to the church and all Jesuits must adhere to certain rules, the order also encourages each Jesuit to find his own spiritual path. While at graduate school, Denis began to believe that food was central to his religious path. When he thought of his most precious days, he always recalled meals lovingly shared with the Jesuit community. He came to think of good, healthy food as a direct connection to God. It was, quite literally, taking a bit of God's loving creation into your body, and each meal offered you an opportunity either to open yourself up to God's love or to blindly wolf down whatever happened to be on a plate, perhaps loaded with enough sugar or salt to give you a momentary thrill. This interest in food led Denis to another passion, a fascination with the spirituality and ethics of business.

Too often, he thought, business is seen as completely cut off from spiritual concerns. Yet business dominates our lives. We work in a business and buy from other businesses, using money we made from a business. It is absurd, he thought, to imagine that we shed our spiritual selves when we walk into the office or a store and then put them on again when we leave. A mentor of his, a Jesuit priest with a PhD in psychology encouraged Denis to go to business school. A priest with no knowledge of how business actually works would have no credibility and, therefore, no influence with businesspeople. Denis liked this idea and soon enrolled at the Yale School of Management. He learned a great deal about business, which helped him in his next job: teaching undergraduate business courses at Loyola Marymount, a Jesuit university in Los Angeles. He was twenty-nine, and his spiritual commitment to the Jesuit way had never been stronger. As he was about to begin the process of ordination to become a priest, he hesitated. He decided he couldn't do it. He knew in his heart that he wanted a wife and children.

Shockingly quickly, he left the Jesuits—left everything he had known as an adult, all his friends, his home, even his source of food. "I had been living under a vow of poverty for seven years," he remembers. "I didn't have a car or a suit or a bed or an apartment. I didn't have money. I didn't have anything." He called a friend from business school, who called his businessman dad, who hired Denis for a "strategy" job at a big telephone company. Within three years he was married and owned a home, and he and his wife soon had children. He maintained his spiritual practice by praying on his own, spending time with Jesuit friends, and serving on several boards of directors of Jesuit organizations. But in many ways he was living the very life he had, at one point, so intently hoped to avoid. He was working in an industry he didn't particularly care about, doing a job that felt entirely removed from his spiritual life. He decided to quit the telecommunications industry so that he could work in food. He gave up a lot of likely wealth by doing so, but he knew that he needed to follow his passion.

After a few jobs in supermarkets in the early 1990s, he became fixated on Whole Foods Market, then a still relatively new, small chain just reaching California. He loved that Whole Foods provided such a broad range of delicious, healthy, natural foods. The stores' very layout demonstrated a more loving approach to food than that of the typical industrial supermarket. But Whole Foods was so expensive—"Whole Paycheck," shoppers joked—that Denis felt it was out of reach of most people and, therefore, would not make a true difference. He happened to have a friend who was close with John Mackey, the founder of Whole Foods, and he soon found himself sitting in his friend's office, explaining his view to Mackey. Mackey challenged him: What would you do differently? Denis responded that he would create a Whole Foods private-label brand, a variation on the generic brands often sold in supermarkets at a deep discount. Mackey told him to go ahead, and, just like that, Denis was the founder and co-owner of Whole Foods 365, a company he owned along with the grocery chain. It created a full line of products that were made from natural ingredients, minimally processed, and meant to be sold at affordable prices.

Denis and his small team ran the company for its first five years, learned a great deal about the food business, and noted a clear trend. Healthier, organic alternatives to traditional food brands were doing amazing business, but with one crucial caveat: they had to taste really good. The comparatively joyless, taste-free natural alternatives of the 1970s and 1980s (my mom gave me carob-chip cookies that I was sure were made of sawdust) had never captured a large market share. Organic foods of the late 1990s and early 2000s, though, did very well. Honest Tea, Amy's frozen meals, Annie's macaroni and cheese, organic ice creams, and Bob's Red Mill products were not only better, they were more profitable and growing far faster than traditional brands.

This shouldn't be surprising. Traditional brands, the familiar names produced by P&G, Unilever, Quaker Oats, Kellogg's, and the rest, are mature industries. They had their period of explosive growth and now compete for small shifts in market share. It is unlikely that millions of people are suddenly going to find a previously unknown love of, say, Cheerios cereal or Lipton Tea. Rather, those brands are in something of a trench warfare with their competition, fighting to dominate shelf space at stores and devising messages to increase their share of an already saturated market. New brands, especially new brands that have a radically new approach to a familiar food, can achieve enormous growth. This was especially true of organic products. In a few short years, entire categories of buyers, dominated by the well-off parents, shifted away from traditional food brands toward products that contained fewer chemicals. It was a wide open space for growth and profit. The organic sector was also in the sweet spot for entrepreneurs: big enough to make real money but small enough to not be a major focus of the huge companies (at least at first).

Denis remembers one summer when he and his family were on a beach vacation. He developed a routine: when the heat was at its greatest, he went to an ice cream vendor and bought a few frozen Snickers bars for his children. One afternoon while they ate the candy, he read the wrapper and could barely stop himself from yelling about all the unnatural, highly processed ingredients. Why was there so much artificial flavoring and partially hydrogenated soybean oil (a source of trans fats, which are among the least healthy foods we eat)? There on the hot sand, he proclaimed that somebody was going to make an organic alternative to the Snickers bar that would taste better, use more healthful ingredients, and sell like crazy. He just never considered that it might be him. (Since then, Snickers has stopped using many trans fats in its products.)

It is worth pausing a moment to study the Snickers bar and its various cousins: Twix, Nestlé Crunch, Chunky, Charleston

Chew, York Peppermint Pattie, Heath bar, KitKat, Reese's Peanut Butter Cups, Almond Joy. Like so much that has become part of the regular fabric of our lives, the chocolate bar is a relatively new invention, a widget that was made as part of the widget economy. The Snickers bar was created in 1930 as part of a battle between two giant industrial companies, Hershey and Mars. Hershey was dominant. It had become expert at buying up chocolate from all over the world at the most discounted prices and developing the machinery that could turn that chocolate quickly, and cheaply, into a solid bar.

In Minnesota, a wildly ambitious but so far unsuccessful father and son named Mars watched Hershey with angry envy. (The Mars family would later break up, with father and son at different firms bitterly competing with each other.) Frank and his son, Forrest Mars, had a small candy manufacturing company in which long rows of Scandinavian immigrant women, the wives of farmers, would make a wide range of small candy pieces, which would be sold by the ounce in stores within a short drive of their shop. That was not enough for the Marses—they wanted to be as big as Hershey; no, they wanted to be bigger, the dominant candymakers in the country and then the world.

It was the son, Forrest, who crafted their original plan. He knew that their existing process of making their confections by hand was too slow and too expensive to allow them to compete. He had two major insights that would transform how Americans consume sweets. The first was that Hershey was making an expensive mistake by creating *solid* chocolate bars. Chocolate is a temperamental material that was proving challenging to work with in industrial conditions. It required a great deal of time to melt chocolate down so it could be poured into a mold and then chill it so that it would become solid. Even worse, during the process of shipping the chocolate to distributors and then retailers, the stuff could melt and become unsellable. The second thing Forrest realized was that chocolate was expensive and hard to buy, and as a company became industrial-sized, chocolate actually became more expensive because it required sourcing the cocoa beans from ever-more-remote locations, so Hershey was making things difficult for itself.

Forrest envisioned a bar made up of a thin layer of chocolate surrounding a much cheaper and easier-to-produce filler material, one that didn't require all that cooling and that wouldn't melt in transit. Forrest experimented with all sorts of fillings—coconut, a minty cream, peanut butter—and landed on the recipe we now know so well. There is a layer of nougat, a layer of caramel, some nuts, and then the thinnest possible coating of chocolate. The chosen ingredients were far cheaper and bulkier than chocolate, allowing for a plump bar that looked a lot more substantial than the thin Hershey's bar.

Nougat was an obscure choice. According to the book *All Kinds of Nougat*, by Marie Josèphe Moncorgé, the first reference to nougat is in a thousand-year-old cookbook from Baghdad. Later, the sweetmeat spread to Spain and Italy, where it is known as *turrón* and *torrone*, respectively. It is traditionally made with melted sugar, egg whites, vanilla, citrus or other flavorings, and some tasty filling, like nuts, dried fruit, or chocolate. It is chewy, rich, and complex. The idea is to mix several unlikely flavors together to create a surprising taste. That is not what appealed to Forrest Mars. His nougat is a nearly flavorless mass-produced product, made using milk powder and protein extracted from eggs. It was designed purely to be a thick, cheap, easily produced filler that would provide some texture and bulk.

The caramel layer is a similar industrial widgetization of a traditional sweet. In its original form, caramel is a sticky liquid, made from melting sugar, which can be poured on top of a dessert like flan. Later, on the American prairie, milk was added to make it thicker. In Laura Ingalls Wilder's *Little House in the Big Woods*, Laura recalls pouring a kind of warm syrupy caramel that her mother had made onto a panful of snow, resulting in a chewy candy she loved. For Forrest, though, caramel, like nougat, needed to be firm enough to be cut by fast-moving circular saws—the sort designed to cut wood in sawmills. The bar-sized filler could then be pushed through a waterfall of melted chocolate to form the outer layer of a Snickers.

When Forrest Mars first designed the candy and the machinery that would produce it, Americans were overjoyed. Here was a cheap candy, made safely and consistently and available wherever people shopped. You could toss one in a bag and know that it would taste great hours or even weeks later. Snickers bars were launched for a nickel during the Great Depression; they offered consumers a large, substantive candy that could almost replace an entire meal. It was something of a miracle. People liked it. By developing the perfect widget bar, carefully designed to be made quickly, Mars is now able to produce fifteen million each day, seventy every second.

But the reason Snickers became the most popular bar in the country and, then, the world was not its flavor. Many candy bars do better in taste tests. Snickers is the most popular candy because Snickers is everywhere.

It wasn't enough just to produce a huge number of Snickers bars. Mars had to find a way to get the bars into every shop in the country that sold candy, which meant they had to entice countless thousands of local candy distributors. Every town had one, and big cities had dozens of small family firms that bought candy wholesale and then sold it to sweetshops and local pharmacies, groceries, and other stores that retailed candy. This was hard work. Mars had to employ hundreds of salespeople to maintain relationships with all of those small distributors. Each distributor had to employ several of their own salespeople to constantly visit all the small retailers to check on supply and order replenishments.

Once built, Mars's sales and distribution operation became both famous and formidable. It intimidated potential rivals. Anybody who wanted to compete against Snickers or, later, M&M's, Twix, or Mars's other candies, would have to first build their own massive distribution network. For Mars, their huge network was self-reinforcing. Because they were able to sell candy in every appropriate store in America, the company had a lot of revenue. That revenue allowed Mars to continue to grow larger, continually investing in increasingly cost-effective candy manufacturing, buying or building bigger and faster and all-around better machines. As the company grew in size, it was able to get steeper discounts on its raw materials, like cocoa powder, nuts, and egg whites. This meant that each candy bar cost less to produce, which allowed Mars's managers to offer deeper discounts to distributors and stores that promoted their candies. It also gave them the funds to launch major advertising campaigns.

The bigger the company got, the bigger it would stay. Mars's focus on mass production and distribution allowed it to surpass its old rival, Hershey, and become the world's largest candy manufacturer, a position it has maintained. Mars was the ultimate widget business. It made a surprisingly narrow range of products. Just three brands—Snickers, Twix, M&M's—accounted for more than half of its sales. Innovation came slowly, if at all. A Snickers bar today is pretty much the same as one that came off the line in 1930. M&M's have had some meager innovations. Launched in 1941, the candy had the iconic printed *m* added to each piece in 1950; in 1954, a peanut version was created. For decades afterward, the only changes to the product were in its colors; orange and blue got added and tan and violet were dropped. As a classic widget product line, M&M's remained very stable; executives focused nearly all of their innovation on improving the line's internal production, figuring out ways to make the exact same thing for less money. Today, this lack of fundamental innovation is on display at every candy retailer: small variations on the same product created in 1941. Now there are pretzel M&M's, ones with caramel or dark chocolate, but no true advance.

For much of this time, as was typical of the widget economy, the Mars ecosystem supported hundreds of thousands of decent jobs. Its machinery required huge numbers of workers, who were kept busy hauling big bags of peanuts, moving trays of nougat, and carefully monitoring every step of production to ensure that each candy bar was exactly like every other. Similarly, the company's distribution required many hundreds of thousands of workers: Mars salespeople; buyers and salespeople at the distributor companies; retailers, who often owned their own shops; truck drivers; peanut and sugar beet farmers; and on and on. Over the course of the twentieth century, hundreds of thousands of people owed their decent livelihood to the Mars company and its widget-making excellence.

Mars had competition. A handful of large companies, such as Hershey, competed nationally and, later, internationally. And many regional candy manufacturers competed in local markets. There was Sky Bar in New England, Goo Goo Cluster in the South, Brown & Haley Mountain Bar in the Pacific Northwest. Their products were good and, for many people, far better than Snickers. But the local companies could never get their products wide distribution. Their bars were more expensive to manufacture, and the companies couldn't compete with the massive Mars distribution network.

If Denis Ring had dreamed up his OCHO bar in the 1930s or 1950s, or even the 1980s, he would have been lucky to become a local player in the Bay Area candy industry. More likely, he would have run a small, not especially profitable chocolate shop in Oakland. Since he came up with the idea in the twenty-first century, in the Passion Economy, he has been able to become a major nationwide phenomenon. OCHO offers the perfect case study in the many changes to our economy that allow passion to compete directly against a widget.

Denis launched Whole Foods 365 in 1997. It was created as a separate company, co-owned by Denis, his team, and Whole Foods. Five years later, it had become a huge provider of goods to the supermarket chain. Whole Foods decided that its off-shoot was so vital, it wanted to move it fully in-house and offered Denis a buyout, which he took. Suddenly he found himself with some money and a whole lot of time. Because Whole Foods 365 did not actually make anything—the company contracted with manufacturers around the country to produce the line of foods and other supermarket staples—Denis had picked up virtually no experience in that area. He understood the efficiences of mass production but couldn't accept the compromises large confections companies have to make for speed and cost. But how could he judge Mars if he had never made quality products at scale? That was when he started thinking about candy bars again. Once he started, he couldn't stop. No one else had come along with better candy bars, a truly good food product made lovingly, using natural ingredients. It seemed like it needed to be him.

One day, after dropping his kids off at school, he began talking with one of the other dads, Scott Kucirek. Scott had been a navy pilot, flying the notoriously challenging and huge Sea Dragon off amphibious warfare ships. Naval aviators like to point out that they are different from air force pilots. In the air force, pilots have one job: to fly planes. Naval aviators, though, can't just fly. On a cramped ship, each person needs to be working full-time to justify a bed, so navy pilots have to take on a host of non-piloting jobs. Scott says his various non-flying navy jobs provided the perfect series of lessons for honing the skills necessary to run a company. Most memorably, he ran three divisions of the maintenance department of his helicopter squadron, overseeing two hundred sailors responsible for purchasing and inventorying the countless number of tiny parts needed to keep helicopters flying. It meant overseeing highly skilled repair people and also some of the least motivated and least skilled folks in the navy—people who had been shunted aside into warehouse jobs. "I learned that you can get people to work twenty hours a day if they believe in the leadership and the mission," he said. "And these same people will work four crappy hours if they don't."

He had to learn how to connect warehouse workers' admittedly boring, routine jobs with the greater mission of keeping helicopters safe so that people don't die and so that the navy can keep America safe. He learned that there were unimaginably complicated, overlapping rules and practices governing every job in the maintenance department. Far too many of the people under him were spending their days filling out paperwork and following procedures that made little sense and did nothing to ensure aircraft safety. Scott streamlined the process and spent much of his time making clear to each of his staff members how their specific job played a key role in ensuring the safety of naval personnel and, therefore, the country. His maintenance facility rose dramatically in official ratings. Then he commanded a recruitment station in San Francisco, which, he says, provided some amazing training in sales. There was a standard navy recruitment patter, laying out all the educational and career options available to people who enlist, but Scott learned that the best thing for a recruiter to do is shut up and listen. People have lots of reasons to enlist, and they will tell you what those are.

Scott had planned a lifelong career in the navy, but after a decade he came to realize that he was not seeing his family nearly enough and that the higher an officer's rank, the less time he seemed to have for his family. He left the navy and enrolled at the University of California at Berkeley business school. Right away, he noted that so many of his classmates complained about the same thing. They were finding it unbearably difficult to buy a house. Scott spoke with a few brokers and soon saw something that reminded him of his old navy maintenance unit. The home-buying system was filled with an overwhelming amount of absurd paperwork, outmoded practices, and rules that got in the way of what everyone wanted, which was to transfer ownership of a home in the most efficient way possible.

Sellers want every relevant home buyer to know that their house is for sale; buyers want to be able to see every home they might be interested in buying. The system, alas, had evolved into one in which most homes were represented by exclusive brokerages. This meant that a buyer could see only the houses of whichever broker they worked with and sellers could reach only that broker's clients. Scott thought this was ridiculous and ran counter to the core mission of home buying. He also thought that the Internet could provide a solution. He and a classmate, Juan Mini, began sketching out a vision for what an ideal system might look like. Before long, they developed ZipRealty, the Web's first major real estate site. It was an enormous undertaking. The company created brokerages in three dozen cities and accumulated the largest collection of homes for sale on the Internet. Scott used the same techniques he'd learned in the navy to keep his staff focused on the mission: getting buyers and sellers the best possible sale, rather than jealously guarding commissions by hoarding listings. It worked well, and the company thrived. Scott made a decent amount of money. ("Enough to start a candy company, not enough to retire," he told me.)

When Scott and Denis first met—the former naval aviator and the former Jesuit, the always-moving enactor and the deliberate contemplator—they, quite miraculously, realized that they could make a great team. They were near-perfect complements of each other, precisely because they are so wildly different. Scott goes to church a few times a year, but faith is not an important part of his life. ("Denis always says, 'CrossFit is your religion,'" Scott told me with a laugh.) Scott did not find some of Denis's more spiritual reasoning behind wanting to make a better candy bar to be particularly compelling, but he easily grasped the essentials. People are eating candy bars all the time, including his own kids. Those candy bars are filled with unhealthy, unnatural ingredients. The many outmoded, unhelpful systems that separated the people who wanted a good, chemical-free candy bar from the people who might make one reminded Scott of problems he had tackled in the poorly functioning helicopter repair maintenance department and the maddening home sales business. This was exactly the kind of problem Scott was perfect at solving.

The OCHO Candy factory sits in an unremarkable warehouse district in Oakland, across the street from a high wall that only partially blocks a view of a scrapyard. The outside of the factory is gray, low, boxy, and surrounded by a tall barbedwire fence. From the outside, OCHO could be any kind of factory—a ball bearing manufacturer or a metal fabricator. Only the brightly colored "OCHO Candy" sign out front hints that something very exciting is happening behind its windowless walls.

The day I visited, I was encouraged to squeeze my car into the overcrowded parking area, protected by those fences, because there was a car-theft problem in the area. I was with my six-year-old son, who had overheard me making plans to visit a candy factory and insisted on coming along. Once we were inside, Scott ushered us past a few small offices to a room where we donned booties, gowns, and head coverings (so as not to contaminate the candy) and then entered the factory floor. This was, indeed, a magical realm. My son was overwhelmed with delight at every turn; I was, too. A few dozen people in sterile garb tended to different stages of the candy-making process. In one corner, a man was pouring sugar, butter, and cream into a massive copper vat, mixing up a fresh batch of caramel in a process that seemed almost ostentatiously designed to be the opposite of the Snickers industrial method. The OCHO caramel is made by hand with natural ingredients—organic cream and butter, raw sugar, and vanilla beans—all in contrast to the highly processed dairy and vanilla powders used by Mars and other industrial candymakers. Not far away, some workers were preparing a huge tub of organic raspberry jelly, using raspberries from a nearby farm, for the OCHO PB&J bar.

The real marvel, though, was the machine at the center of the plant that combined various ingredients to make the OCHO bars. It was about as long as a couple of school buses and operated in a way that the Mars family and the Hershey Company could never have imagined. Those mass-produced candy bars are made by enrobing a solid, firm center with soft chocolate. The OCHO machine starts out by pouring high-quality liquid chocolate into molds, then stamps the chocolate with freezing-cold metal rectangles, instantly turning the liquid chocolate solid. This creates small, lidless chocolate boxes that will hold the bars' centers—peanut butter and jelly, caramel, coconut, and all the others. In this way, the centers can be gooier, more luscious than those made in the mass-produced method. The next step is the trickiest. After the fillings have been added, the machine has to just slightly heat the tops of the chocolate box walls to allow a new layer of chocolate to adhere; then it instantly cools that top so that it doesn't melt into the soft center.

It is a fussy, time-consuming process in which the machine has to perform several steps in a precisely timed ballet to produce each bar. It takes longer than a minute to make each tray of a dozen OCHO bars, an average of five seconds per bar. Five seconds might not sound like a huge amount of time for a bar, but it means that OCHO is essentially in an entirely different business from Snickers, whose machinery produces seventy bars per second. One way to think of this is that each OCHO bar has to pay for a much larger percentage of the company's costs—labor, machinery, real estate, shipping, and the rest. The expense is compounded by the fact that OCHO uses more expensive ingredients. The company buys higher-cost chocolate, peanuts, and jelly. Everything is organic. It makes its own caramel, which means it has two dedicated workers mixing sugar, cream, and vanilla in those giant vats all day long.

Those costs are not what is most strange about OCHO; there have always been high-end, luxury candymakers. OCHO, however, unlike those predecessors, does not sell its wares in a small handful of boutique candy shops or limit its sales to the surrounding Bay Area of California. You can buy OCHO at Walgreens pharmacies, Whole Foods, Albertsons, Costco, Target, and countless other nationwide big-box retailers. OCHO is still a tiny company whose distribution division is largely made up of three people who know how to run a UPS and FedEx account, and yet it is able to put its candy alongside Snickers bars in major retailers. That is a change in how our economy works. It is a passion candy competing directly with a widget one. It is passion at scale, and that is entirely new.

The OCHO Candy story is part of a major trend in the sector of the economy known as consumer packaged goods or fast-moving consumer goods (usually referred to as CPG or FMCG). These are the things you might buy on every trip to the supermarket or pick up on an impulse while you're in the checkout line: items like hand soap, laundry detergent, breakfast cereal, cigarettes, soda, ice cream, and, of course, candy bars. It's just about anything you buy that comes prepackaged and is made by a recognizable brand. CPG has become a bedrock of the U.S. and global economies. It is a $800-billion-a-year industry in the United States—one of the largest—and worth nearly $10 trillion worldwide. Those numbers represent the direct sales of goods. Trillions of dollars are also spent on industries that support CPG, like advertising, warehouse and distribution, trucking, and retail.

CPG is the iconic widget economy industry. There were no mass-produced consumer packaged goods until that economy,

but then they flourished, zooming from nonexistent to dominant. Mass-produced packaged goods with familiar brands have
saturated the CPG market for a very long time, but now they
are facing steadily mounting challenges as we transition to a
Passion Economy. That is because CPG, as it has historically
existed in the United States, is something like the antithesis of
passion.

From a consumer's perspective, CPG products are just fine.
Most people stick to the same products from the same brands,
knowing they'll be available wherever and whenever they need
them. From the manufacturer's perspective, CPG offers some
distinct benefits and costs. One chief benefit is that, once established, a brand can produce a steady stream of income. Consumer behavior—a field of study that was born and grew up
alongside the growth of CPG—doesn't change all that rapidly,
so the brands can count on reliable purchases. They can use
advertising, distribution, and pricing to increase sales. CPGs
didn't traditionally focus much on innovating new products.
The whole point of CPGs for the widget century was to make
sure the products were consistent. A lot of change could only
scare off otherwise loyal customers. The New Coke fiasco of
1985 is the iconic example. Coca-Cola found a new soda for-
mula that, in blind tests, people seemed to prefer to the old flavor. But once it was launched to actually replace the old Coke,
the product was a disaster. Nobody wanted that classic bever-
age messed with, and less than three months later, New Coke
was tossed into the dustbin of history.

Innovation, for CPG companies, was more about making
the same exact goods more quickly and cheaply. It was innovation in manufacturing, producing faster, more reliable machines
that used more automation and allowed the companies to use
(and pay!) far fewer people.

For the big CPG companies, the widget economy was an
amazing time of ever-growing strength and ever-increasing
profits. The bigger they got, the more they could spend on

machines to produce more goods more quickly, which allowed them to get even bigger. They could also spend more on advertising and on building their distribution networks, ensuring even more growth. Even better, as Americans got richer, they bought more and more CPG products. Bigness, in itself, became an insurmountable competitive advantage. Like Mars, every major CPG company was able to produce more goods, more cheaply, and distribute them to more stores than any upstart competitor. Sure, there were the occasional new firms that tried, but they were making more expensive products that fewer people had heard of and that couldn't get shelf space in supermarkets.

The Passion Economy has not destroyed the big widget CPG companies. The top ten global CPG companies—including Nestlé, Procter & Gamble, Unilever, and Mars (their onetime rival Hershey is much smaller these days)—each sell nearly $20 billion in CPG products each year. The global CPG industry is becoming increasingly top-heavy, with those biggest ten companies making up more than half of global sales.

These companies drive an even larger widgetized CPG ecosystem. Collectively, they spend hundreds of billions of dollars each year in advertising. And CPG companies are the single largest customers of transportation companies, shipping their goods on trucks and trains and giant ships. They are among the world's major purchasers of agricultural and industrial products.

Despite growth, the era of CPGs supporting millions of decent-paying jobs around the world, jobs that could become lifelong, continually improving careers, has ended. Today, the CPG widget economy, like so much else in the twenty-first century, is a story of two extremes. A handful of executives, entrepreneurs, and investors are profiting from this bigness, while far more of the people who work directly for CPG companies or allied industries are losing out to automation and outsourcing.

This is the point of the Passion Economy. It's not that passion products, like OCHO candy, will always beat out widget products like Snickers. OCHO's incredibly ambitious plan is to reach $100 million a year in sales. That would represent less than one-third of 1 percent of Mars, Incorporated's sales. But Scott and Denis don't need to rival Mars. They are growing rapidly and having a wonderful time doing it. They are paying their workers well, providing a safe and enjoyable work environment, and donating money and candy to local Oakland nonprofits.

Of course, OCHO is not alone. We are in the midst of an explosion of passion alternatives to multinational CPG products. Walk into a Whole Foods or a Sephora, Google whatever category of sweet, snack, or cosmetic product you like, and you will see countless examples of passion products. It is almost certain that you will find one of those passion products to meet your desires more precisely than the widget one available in your local Walmart. Whether or not they are worth the premium price is, of course, up to you. (I will always pay a premium for unusual chocolate but wouldn't pay anything extra for a unique piece of gum.)

A passion candy can be sold everywhere and doesn't require nearly as many consumers as a widget sweet does. That means it can appeal to an extremely narrow audience, those buyers who share the creator's passions. Those people will be willing to pay a much higher price for a product that so heartily appeals to them; therefore, the product can be made more slowly, with more expensive ingredients.

In a strange twist, the widgetization of the world's many support industries offers enormous opportunity to the Passion Economy, because those same industries can be enormously helpful to the passion producers. Passion Economy innovators can reach more customers through cheaper advertising, and they can get their products into those customers' hands through cheaper shipping. They can make their goods more cheaply by using advances in design software and manufacturing technology.

But perhaps the greatest benefit to passion companies is the transformation in how they can find money to finance their ideas. Scott and Denis began OCHO Candy by pooling far more of their savings than they felt comfortable with, renting a warehouse building, buying some used restaurant equipment. It was a costly process. After not too long in business, they learned two things. Lesson number 1: People absolutely love their chocolate bars. They find them more delicious than the competition's and are willing to pay more than twice as much as the competition charges for that quality and for a bar with organic ingredients (and, at just about $1.99, their bars are still highly affordable to most consumers). That made Scott and Denis think they had a successful business on their hands. Then there was lesson number 2: They were losing money on each bar. The more successful they were at selling, the more quickly they'd run out of money.

It is, not surprisingly, wildly inefficient to make chocolate bars by hand. It is a slow, messy business. That's why hand-made chocolates are typically sold in tiny boutiques that charge a fortune for a small box. Denis and Scott could have opened a small shop in San Francisco and made a modest living selling extremely expensive bars to rich people. But they wanted to go big. They wanted to sell to everyone who was frustrated by all those chemical-filled, mass-produced bars.

Scott tallied up the cost of buying the machinery that would allow them to produce bars at a faster clip and soon understood why chocolate bars have a hard core and a soft, mushy chocolate ribbon. The machinery used to produce such a product is fairly cheap and easy to buy. When I typed "chocolate enrobing machine" into eBay, I found one for $1,900 and another for $3,000. But Scott and Denis didn't want to enrobe chocolate; they wanted that hard chocolate bite. To obtain that, they would have to custom-order a special machine from Europe.

These machines use a new and complex technology, requiring a fair bit of computing power that would have, in itself, cost a fortune just a few years ago. Essentially, the machine automatically and quickly does what Scott and Denis had been doing by hand. It pours chocolate into a mold, where it is frozen instantly with a metal form attached to computer-controlled rapid-cooling technology, allowing the creamy center to be poured in and then another layer of instantly cooled chocolate to be placed on top to form a full, sealed bar. This is far faster than doing it all by hand—pouring the chocolate, taking it to a freezer, waiting nearly an hour for the chocolate to freeze, then pouring in the center, and then adding more chocolate and more freezing time.

The thing is, there aren't any used chocolate insta-freezing machines on eBay for a couple of thousand dollars. They cost hundreds of thousands of dollars. Once you buy one, you need to be extremely careful about your recipes. You need to have a consistent thickness of both the chocolate and the creamy center—whether it be peanut butter, nougat, mint, or whatever—because machines like predictability. That means you also have to invest in better chocolate warming and tempering equipment and a more advanced kitchen in which to prepare the centers. (OCHO still makes its centers by hand but uses temperature-control gear to keep the mix consistent.) Once Scott added up all the equipment required, he realized they would need to rent a much larger factory to accommodate it, and they would also need to pay their workers more so that they would feel invested in the level of quality. Even these two well-off guys found it impossible to fund the business they had dreamed of. If *they* couldn't do it, who could? Who could offer a healthier, more delicious alternative to Snickers?

Scott and Denis Googled around, trying to find venture capitalists and other investors who might fund a small chocolate company with big dreams. The problem was, their dreams weren't quite big enough. Typical investors in candy start-ups want to hear one thing: your exit strategy. They want to know how quickly you plan to sell your company to one of the big guys and how much you think you'll get for it. That's the whole model of venture capitalism. Scott and Denis wanted to make money, but they didn't want to sell the company. They were on a mission to make a healthier, more natural, and more delicious candy bar for the foreseeable future. And they understood that once they sold, that bigger company would, almost surely, start diluting their dreams.

OCHO's particular set of passions were seemingly incompatible with the particular set of needs of the large venture firms—until they stumbled upon CircleUp. Working with a company like OCHO was precisely what CircleUp was designed to do: help passionate entrepreneurs get access to the money they need to fulfill their dreams. It had been founded by two men whose very different paths had led them to the belief that the existing financial system was set up to best help those who least needed it, and that there was a huge opportunity for profit and for social improvement by making it easier for people with great ideas but not enough money to find the funds they need.

Ryan Caldbeck, CEO of CircleUp, looks like the actor a casting agent would choose to play the role of successful, visionary finance entrepreneur. He is tall, clean-cut, and handsome, with an easy confidence. He grew up in rural Vermont, his childhood like something out of the nineteenth century. He ran around the woods, in snow and in summer, often barefoot. His parents and neighbors never locked their doors, and the world of high finance and modern technology seemed quite far away.

Caldbeck noticed that most of his friends in his small, rural town assumed that the rest of their lives would be spent there. One of his classmates, a brilliant girl, was accepted at Dartmouth College, two hours away, but her parents told her she had to go to a far inferior college nearby. Separately, Ryan overheard the father of his best friend berate the boy for even think-ing of college. Why would someone pay money to go to school when he could get a job right out of high school? the father asked. Ryan's parents, in contrast, told him to follow his dreams wherever they took him. Ryan noted that his friends were just as smart as he was, just as capable, but their options were far narrower because of the homes they grew up in.

Ryan readily admits that he was a bit naïve, maybe even foolhardy, in his belief in his infinite potential. After he was admitted to Duke University, he wanted to join the school's world famous champion basketball team. But he didn't have the skills, so he became a volunteer assistant manager helping the basketball team. This meant sweeping the floor of the gym before and after practice, mixing big coolers of Gatorade, and serving the team in other ways. He signed on; he went to every practice, worked as hard as he could helping the team, and then, once they left, he ran drills on his own, all by himself. He did this every day. His teammates and the coaches eventually noticed. By his sophomore year, he was being asked to cover for absent teammates during practice. During one midseason game, the coach called Ryan onto the court. He played for pre-cisely one minute, never touching the ball, let alone taking a shot. But he was, officially and for the record books, a member of the storied Duke basketball team.

He never stopped trying to be better. He continued to work as hard as anybody on the team. By his senior year, he was still mostly sitting on the bench, although he played a few minutes here, another few there. He rarely took shots and even more rarely scored, but it was thrilling to be part of such a magnifi-cent team in one of their best years ever—the year they won the national championship.

Shortly before graduation, Ryan asked the Duke basketball coach, Mike Krzyzewski, for advice. Ryan didn't know what he was going to do with his life. He had gone to the career services office, and a counselor had suggested that he get a job at a consulting company; most such firms paid well, and they recruited students like Ryan who had good grades, played a sport and had good extra-curricular activities. Krzyzewski told him that the most important thing was to identify his core passion and follow it. Ryan didn't know what his passion was. He liked that coaching combined specific short-term tasks with grander ambitions about leading a better life. He liked that Krzyzewski was able to simultaneously make each player feel individually special while making everyone understand that only through collective success could they be their best. Ryan had no real path to being a coach, so he ignored Krzyzewski's talk about passion. He was offered a summer job at Boston Consulting Group, a prestigious consulting firm, and accepted it.

The job at BCG was fine, though boring. He was on a team of young people putting together spreadsheets of data for a senior partner's presentations. Sure, somewhere high up in the hierarchy of the firm, people were deciding which companies to buy and how much to pay for them, but Ryan spent his days looking at data on a spreadsheet and preparing boring reports. He figured the problem was that particular company, so he got a job at another one. It wasn't much better. He noted that the people on a partner track, the ones who seemed to be doing more useful work, had gone to business school, so he applied and got into Stanford's. After business school, he got a job at a firm in San Francisco—and hated every single second of it. The culture was vicious, with every associate trying to crush every other one to get ahead. The work wasn't even interesting. He desperately wanted to work somewhere with a better culture and, soon, found himself at Encore Consumer Capital, another San Francisco private equity firm, this one with the ideal culture for Ryan. His boss was a mentor out of the Krzyzewski school. There was an emphasis on teamwork. Ryan had everything he thought he wanted, and yet he was still unfulfilled and unsatisfied.

Ryan's girlfriend at the time (now his wife) gave him something of an intervention. She told him that he wasn't happy because he wasn't doing something he loved. He had taken the first job he was offered after college and become a consultant. While there, he kept hearing that the best thing to do after being a consultant was to go into private equity. Then he heard he had to get an MBA; then he had to rise up the private equity ladder. He kept doing what other people told him was the right thing to do, but he never once thought about what he truly wanted to do. He realized that he had faced a crucial test the day Coach Krzyzewski had told him he should identify his passion, and that he had failed that test. He understood now that he had completely missed the point. He had pursued the external trappings of success; Krzyzewski had been urging him to pay attention to those things that made him truly happy, that fed his passion.

Ryan's girlfriend had an idea. She went to a stationery store and bought some giant Post-its and, every Saturday, she and Ryan would sit in their living room and write down what Ryan loved. At first, she told him not to worry if it was serious or silly, thoughtful or absurd. One of the first things he jotted down was "buffalo wings." That initial list also included "working out," "basketball," "teamwork," and "helping others."

It took a few months, but it became clear that Ryan was happiest when he was directly helping a team of people achieve something great. He enumerated jobs that might allow him to spend most of his days engaged with something he was passionate about. He thought about teaching, coaching a team, going into politics. He was pretty sure that if he had done this exercise ten years earlier, he would never have gone into private equity. It wasn't that he hated private equity. It was that so much of his days was spent doing boring work, on his own, that had little direct impact on anyone else.

As he rose in the field, he acquired more power. Like

other private equity executives, he was tasked with identifying companies that could be bought, improved, and then sold at a profit. Some of that work was thrilling. He loved getting together with a team of junior analysts to go through the pros and cons of potential target companies. He especially liked it when the private equity firm bought a decent but stagnating company and Ryan was able to help its executives figure out how to turn their failing business into a thriving one. The problem was that those joy-filled, passionate moments were far too infrequent. He realized that fully 95 percent of his days were spent in drudgery, going through endless data sets, looking for information about companies, running through calculations of profit margins and likely future cash flow.

We generally think of the widget economy as the result of all those inventions that made it possible to manufacture the same product more quickly and cheaply: steam power, electricity, railroads, conveyor belts, and automatic lathes. Perhaps more important has been the financial innovation that allows those ideas to become funded. For most of human history, there weren't many ways for someone with a bright idea but little money to get someone else to give them money to pursue their idea. Surely there were countless people in ancient Rome or medieval Europe who dreamed up fascinating inventions, but money was held by a hereditary elite who had little interest in figuring out how to automate the work of peasants and were unlikely to hand their funds over to some ill-born inventor with an unproven idea.

In the seventeenth and eighteenth centuries, as the aristocracies in England, Holland, and other European nations lost power, there rose a growing middle class of self-made merchants who began to invent new ways of sharing risk and funding good investment ideas, regardless of the station of birth of the person with the idea. For example, James Watt, the Scottish inventor, credited with the world's first fully functioning steam engine, owed his success to decades of funding by Matthew Boulton, his business partner, who sought out investors in Watt's ideas. A century later, Henry Ford, the automotive inventor, needed longer to perfect the financing of his business than it took him to perfect his cars. His first lead investor, a wealthy lumber baron named William H. Murphy, was too controlling for Ford's taste, so he abandoned the company (which was then renamed Cadillac) and started a second car company with new, less pushy investors. The stories go on and on. Nearly every great inventor whose name is known by all was funded by investors whose names have been lost.

As the widget century entered its full force, no longer would an inventor have one generous benefactor. He could use the stock and bond market to sell shares to countless thousands of investors, whose money, collectively, would fund the business. Just after World War II, a new financing idea transformed the world further.

Georges Doriot was born in Paris in 1899. His father was an automotive pioneer, helping to develop the fastest cars in the world for Peugeot. He was also a daredevil driver, racing cars all over Europe. Georges fought in the French army in World War I and then decided to go to the United States to attend business school. He remained and became the dean of Harvard's business school and a leading expert in logistics and operations. He was naturalized as a U.S. citizen, and when World War II began, he enlisted in the Quartermaster Corps. Using scientific principles, he was able to transform the ability of the U.S. army to deliver everything from screws to tanks to food and water to every place on earth where soldiers needed them. He was soon named a brigadier general and the Quartermaster General of the U.S. army.

In 1946, Doriot went back to Harvard and thought of all the many brilliant soldiers he had worked with, people who were bright and inventive and would now just return to a civilian world that didn't know how to properly use them. Doriot suspected that many of them could run their own companies if only they had funding. He created American Research and Development Corporation, which would become known as the world's first institutional private equity fund, though nobody used that term at the time. Doriot's idea was to get a lot of investors to each chip in a bit of money, which would then be given to discharged soldiers with promising business ideas. He figured that some of the ideas would succeed and some would fail, but by pooling money together the investors could take more risk and, therefore, were likely to get a much higher reward than they would if each investor chose one company to put his money in.

ARDC was a triumph. Doriot's single biggest success was putting $70,000 of his investors' money into Digital Equipment Corporation and receiving more than $300 million back a few years later. The idea caught on, and by the time Ryan was in the business, there were thousands of private equity firms, each with its own strategy and approach.

The popular media has focused almost exclusively on high-tech private equity and venture capital, its close cousin. The average news consumer might have thought that the only types of companies that private equity companies invest in are tech start-ups, like Facebook, Google, and Twitter. Ryan was never interested in tech private equity. Early on, when he was considering the field, he came across a series of studies that showed that tech venture capital and private equity were wildly over-hyped. A handful of firms had made a fortune, from a handful of deals. The early investors in Google, Facebook, and some other companies became wildly wealthy. Outside of ten or so deals, though, the rest of the industry actually lost money. Ryan saw it as akin to playing the lottery.

Ryan had always worked in the consumer packaged goods private equity field. He focused on products that were sold at supermarkets or online; he would buy a promising company, help it improve its sales and market share, and then sell the company at a profit. It was unsexy and rarely got media attention. Being in San Francisco, Ryan sometimes felt like a second-class citizen, with the high-flying tech guys looking down at CPG firms like his. All the while, he was seeing humble packaged goods businesses that were growing and bringing in real income. The people who worked in CPG private equity often made a lot more money than those who invested in high tech. There were a handful of wildly successful high-tech venture firms, but most don't earn anything like the returns of CPG-oriented investment companies. "It wasn't even close," Ryan told me.

Ryan started to wonder what it would look like if he could keep all the things he loved about private equity and none of the things he hated. What if he could spend most of his days doing the things he had real passion for—identifying good companies to buy, helping guide company owners to better decisions—and never had to do the tedious work of reading countless prospectuses and industry reports, pulling out data, putting it in spreadsheets, and assessing the information?

Ryan shared his thinking with one of his closest friends, Rory Eakin, from Stanford. Ryan was a lifelong Republican from a tiny town; Rory was a Democrat from Washington, D.C. Ryan is tall and athletic, with a loud voice and a big personality; Rory is shorter, quieter, nerdier. Still, in certain ways, they felt as if they were clones of each other. They both had a remarkably systematic way of analyzing issues by assembling data, constructing hypotheses, and testing them. Even though they often had radically different opinions, they both enjoyed engaging in long, fact-based discussions about business strategy or political issues or the ideal way to structure a society. They had the same method of analyzing information and coming to conclusions.

As Ryan climbed the private equity career ladder in the mid-2000s, Rory was living in South Africa, working in a humanitarian program to help promising black students. The Mellon Foundation, founded by the children of industrialist and political figure Andrew Mellon, funded Rory's work with the US.ZA Education Initiative to help students who had studied at horribly funded all-black high schools and hadn't been exposed to the basic academic requirements needed to succeed in college. Rory learned that he was a decent teacher and was capable of hard work in difficult conditions. He also learned that he was quite good at running the overall operations of a newly created nonprofit. A mentor told him he had a gift for thinking strategically and executing his vision, that he should get better at it so that he could have a greater impact. Rory left Africa and enrolled in the Stanford Graduate School of Business.

After graduating, Rory went to work for Pierre Omidyar, the billionaire founder of eBay, and his wife, Pam. Rory worked at their charitable investment arm, which invested in groups seeking to improve the lives of people in sub-Saharan Africa. He spent part of the year in San Francisco and part in Africa, assessing the groups that received funds. He began to notice something that surprised him. The for-profit companies were having a far bigger impact on poor people's lives than the nonprofits. Rory saw that, in Africa, nonprofit organizations might spend years and millions of dollars researching some community's needs, planning some big intervention—a new school, a health clinic—and then there would be a grand opening, complete with a ribbon cutting and tedious political speeches and photographers capturing the moment for brochures that would ask for money from rich people somewhere else. Then, a few weeks, even a few days, later, the community would seem precisely the same. There was no radical change. A few locals would make some more money, largely by working at inflated salaries for the nonprofit. Too often, the nonprofit would lose funding, or its interest would be diverted elsewhere, and those jobs would disappear and everything would go back to the way it always had been.

Meanwhile, Rory did see lives improved and transformed regularly in Africa. He met people in small, poor towns who had grown up illiterate, with access to barely enough calories to survive, and who developed into entrepreneurs who were able to feed their families, pay for a concrete floor, sometimes even afford electricity, and send one or more of their kids to a private school. Rory could identify several people who had achieved something no nonprofit could offer: they had left misery and put their families on a path to sustained economic independence. In nearly every case, it was because of profit. A woman would run a stall in a market, selling inexpensive meals she started cooking before dawn to passing construction workers. She would save up enough to buy a cheap fridge and a small generator and would then be able to sell cold cans of soda. That would give her the profit to build a small canopy and some chairs. Soon enough, she had a small but hugely popular restaurant, one that her children and cousins could work in. Because of that, she had enough surplus income to lend money to others, to send her kids to school.

Rory, who remained devoted to changing lives, became an idealistic capitalist. When he heard Ryan's vision for a democratization of venture capital, he immediately saw the potential. One simple reason why poor people often stay poor and the rich get richer is that the rich have capital; they have money to invest in new ideas, money to take risks with, to use to build a new business. Perversely, since they already have capital, they are offered even more capital, in the form of investments and loans, by other people with capital. Rory realized, though, that investors were not making fully informed choices. They were investing with people who had capital because that seemed less risky. People with capital—rich people—are more likely to pay back loans; they're more likely to know how to get their goods and services to market, to generate profit that can make an investment flourish.

That drove Rory nuts. He believed that rich people who

lend and invest in other rich people are being shortsighted. They should be investing in people with great and promising ideas, and, as far as Rory could tell, poor people have just as many great ideas, maybe even more, since their needs and desperation can fuel more creative thinking. If poor people's ideas could be evaluated alongside rich people's, using some set of objective metrics, then the people with great ideas would see them funded, and they'd use that money to build businesses that would thrive, that would yank them and their families out of poverty.

Rory's passion for using capitalism to end poverty met Ryan's passion for helping a wider group of entrepreneurs thrive. The problem Rory identified was the same problem Ryan had identified. The process of matching people with money to lend and invest was so inefficient, so costly in time and effort, that it was a luxury good. If it were made more efficient, cheaper, it could become something available to all.

It would be ridiculous to call Denis Ring and Scott Kucirek poor. They are both successful entrepreneurs who had made enough money to buy comfortable homes in the Bay Area, send their kids to great schools—and decide to invest some money in a new start-up idea of making organic but delicious candy bars. In the context of the consumer packaged goods industry, though, they are ants in a world of elephants. Their entire combined net worth wouldn't equal a few minutes of value created on any Snickers production line. Still, they had decided to take on the big players, and there was no way that they could scale up without financial help.

CircleUp's analysts were able to quickly (and at almost no cost) run OCHO through their artificial intelligence engine. While OCHO had a small audience, it had generated enormous enthusiasm, which CircleUp's computers had automatically registered by scanning comments on Twitter, Facebook, and other social media platforms, as well as reviews on various candy review sites (there are a surprisingly large number of them). While still tiny, OCHO had enough sales to show a sharp upward trajectory. CircleUp's software showed that OCHO could grow dramatically. CircleUp had created an investment platform powered by artificial intelligence that they called Helio. Helio could proactively find, track, and evaluate over 1 million brands in the United States by ingesting hundreds of data sources ranging from nutritional information to product reviews to retailer locations. This data would feed into machine-learning algorithms to predict which brands had the highest likelihood of future growth. These algorithms were used to help CircleUp make swift and informed investment decisions and help entrepreneurs yield insights about their own businesses.

Since CircleUp's algorithms are so fast, so detailed, and so inexpensive to use for any one company, its analysts are able to identify prospects traditional venture capitalists might overlook. Take OCHO. Scott and Denis have a dream—one they're not sure they'll ever achieve—of making $100 million a year in sales. Food manufacturers typically have fairly high profit margins—around 30 percent—which means OCHO could bring in $30 million per year in profit. To most of us, this is an unimaginable sum of money. But to many venture capitalists, this is a sum barely worth analyzing. It would cost hundreds of thousands of dollars in analyst time just to determine if OCHO is a company worthy of investment. Then investors would actually have to tie up capital in a firm whose greatest dream is to bring in what a successful high-tech startup might make in a few hours.

The reason venture investors want the opportunity to make ten times as much money is that they are taking huge risks. Most of the companies they invest in will not succeed, and the investors will lose their money. CircleUp, though, feels confident that its software takes a lot of that risk away. Since OCHO received funding, CircleUp has also now raised a series of internal funds to provide capital directly to companies like OCHO, with more speed than traditional venture capital funds. According to CircleUp's calculations, a company scoring as highly as OCHO did is a good bet, so investors should feel comfortable with a lower return, since they're not taking on the same risk.

The other great thing about CircleUp is its speed. Rather than months or even years of research and investment decision-making, CircleUp evaluated OCHO in minutes and in less than two weeks had identified investors who loved OCHO's mission, believed that CircleUp's analysis was right, and were ready to cut a check. CircleUp is the reason OCHO was able to acquire that huge custom candy machine—the very first of its kind in the United States. Soon after, OCHO was able to take on a dozen new retailers. The company's sales had outperformed its ambitions. OCHO's bars quickly became a highly popular item at Whole Foods, which makes sense. Whole Foods is filled with shoppers willing to pay a premium for more natural food. But it's the fact that OCHO got orders from Walgreens, Safeway, Target and other mass-market retailers that really makes the company stand out. It turns out that the desire for a perfect organic candy bar with a hard chocolate exterior and a creamy center, all made with natural ingredients, isn't limited to the customers of Whole Foods. It is something that at least some people who shop at the largest chains crave, as well.


Ever since I met Denis and Scott, I've noticed, I shop differently. When I walk through Whole Foods or Walgreens or any supermarket, I find my mind quickly categorizing the products. Which are the result of some person's passion? Which are trying to speak to some specific audience that will be unusually receptive, and which are hoping to please everybody passing by? It's hard, I find, not to be a bit judgmental of those crowd-pleasing, passion-free products made by marketing teams at large consumer brands. Nobody centered their spiritual life around producing more Sprite or designing the latest iteration of the Snickers bar (now with darker chocolate).

I find myself selfishly thrilled that we are just at the beginning of the Passion Economy. The fundamental shift that allows for the flourishing of OCHO Candy will lead to so many other unique products. With technological advances and low-cost access to global markets, it will continue to be easier for those with a particular vision to create products they love and feel confident others will, too. Even if those others are thinly spread around the world, those enthusiasts will be able to support a sustainable business.

When I imagine the Passion Economy in the future, when it's more fully developed, I picture a supermarket. Supermarkets, today, can give the illusion of variety. There are countless thousands of products on shelves. But there is an underlying base of sameness. Most of those products are made by a small handful of global corporations whose food recipes are engineered to appeal to everybody and, therefore, are special to nobody. Supermarkets everywhere are remarkably identical, with the same products available to everyone. Supermarkets today also stock a lot of the same products they did a decade or even three decades ago. Imagine, instead, a shop filled with products like OCHO: passion-based goods that are made to appeal powerfully to a smaller but far more engaged audience. Those shelves will become explorations in themselves, with surprises awaiting. Some products will become your favorites, while others won't appeal at all to you but will catch the eye of the next person walking down the aisle. Mass-produced global brands won't disappear. There will always be a benefit to scale, allowing big companies to cut prices and market aggressively. But the trend is clear: those big players will represent an ever-diminishing share of our products. Far more of what we buy will be passion-based goods. We will love the things we buy more. And, as more of us buy those goods, they will be produced with ever-greater efficiency and fall in price. The companies that make the things we buy will have to compete by offering a continuously improving suite of products, each one designed to delight some specific group of people. I can't wait.

# CASE STUDY: BREAKTHROUGH ADR

### *THE DAMALI MOMENT*

It would be hard to craft a better career for a lawyer than the one Damali Peterman walked away from in late 2016. She was an award-winning lawyer and senior manager at Deloitte, one of the world's largest accounting and advisory firms. As an Assistant General Counsel, she supported Deloitte entities throughout the world, working alongside Deloitte consultants, guiding some of the largest companies through their most challenging business and legal matters. Damali loves challenges—the tougher, the better—and had experienced some of the biggest. She was one of the talented attorneys at Weil, Gotshal & Manges LLC to work on the dissolution of Lehman Brothers, the investment bank whose collapse spurred the financial crisis of 2008. While Lehman was no longer operating as a functioning firm, it had left behind trillions of dollars in obligations, unreceived revenue, and complex contracts with companies spread around the globe. She likened herself to the character Olivia Pope from the television series *Scandal.* Unflappable, strategic, and able to get the best for clients in trouble, she was on track to be among the most powerful lawyers in corporate America.

After the 2016 presidential election, Damali faced a personal crisis. She saw that the United States was fracturing, with seemingly unresolvable anger from every side. Damali has her own personal political views—though she will never share them publicly—but her concern wasn't that one party or another had won. She hated that her nation was experiencing a degree of internal upset that she had previously seen only in other countries. Damali decided that she could no longer solely devote her life to helping large corporations resolve commercial disputes, no matter how fascinating and challenging the work was. She wanted to return to her roots as a mediator and conflict resolver.

Damali says she was a born mediator. She was the oldest of

seven children in a family in Washington, D.C. Her stepfather, a cop, worked long hours, and Damali had to help her mother rein in the chaos of her rambunctious siblings. She attended Spelman College, a historically black women's school that encourages students to improve not only themselves but also society. She took this message seriously and went on to receive an MA in International Policy Studies, with a focus in conflict resolution, from the Middlebury Institute of International Studies at Monterey. She imagined that she would become an official at the United Nations or some other international agency. She thought a law degree would help, so she went to Howard University School of Law, another historically black institution with a strong focus on social engineering.

As happens to many idealistic law students, Damali got an internship at a corporate firm and was quickly identified as a rising superstar. She took to the law and found herself able to wade through the complex technical issues in a corporate conflict and identify solutions that would be acceptable to all sides. Her first job led to a promotion, and then she was recruited by Deloitte, where she spent two years in a senior position.

Shortly after the election, Damali realized why she suddenly felt unfulfilled. She had followed her talents, taking whichever job she seemed most able to perform well. But now she needed to follow her values. She sat down with a yellow legal pad and wrote down all the things she was good at. It was a long list. Damali is no braggart, but she doesn't have time for false modesty, either. It took her a few hours to list her various abilities. Then she circled those things she loved doing, the things for which she felt passion. The results were striking and impossible to ignore. She was spending far too much of her time doing things she didn't really love. She realized that she wanted—she needed—to focus her time on resolving conflicts and teaching others how to mediate.

Within days, she quit her job and started the groundwork for what would become Breakthrough ADR LLC, a firm that helps companies, nonprofits, government agencies, educational institutions and individuals manage and resolve conflict. ADR stands for "alternative dispute resolution," which means finding ways to solve conflicts without lawsuits or other adversarial processes. In this litigious time (and country), small disputes between businesses, collaborators, or employers and employees can easily blow up into protracted court battles with punishing legal fees. On top of that, the relationship between the two parties involved almost never survives the process.

Mediation is not a new idea. Breakthrough ADR, however, works to not just resolve a dispute but resolve it in such a way that all those involved feel heard, respected, and satisfied with the outcome. Breakthrough ADR's methods have proven so successful that the company now teaches communication, negotiation, and conflict resolution skills to businesses, educational institutions, government agencies, nonprofits, and individuals.

Damali decided to leave corporate law for dispute resolution because she wanted to feel a deeper sense of satisfaction in her daily work. She assumed that this change would come at some financial cost. That isn't how it turned out. She quickly found that Americans are hungry for her faster, more mutually satisfying approach to resolution. Clients came knocking. Within two years, she was already making more money than she had at her well-paying corporate job. Her business has been growing steadily since.

I have come to use the phrase "the Damali moment" to describe a process that is invaluable to anyone seeking to move into the Passion Economy. Write down what you do for a living and then circle those things that bring you real joy. You don't have to be thinking about starting your own business—this exercise can help you become happier and more efficient in your workplace. It can help you adjust the work you are currently doing, or it can steer you in the direction of a different position. Damali shows us that it is possible to have a career in which everything you do is circled.

# CHAPTER 11

# THE NUDGE

*How Google and science helped demonstrate the profit in happier workers*

Jessie Wisdom did not set out to transform the nature of work in America. She just wanted to understand why so many people—including herself—struggled to eat better. We all know that eating poorly can harm us, even kill us. Yet it is so hard, at any given meal, to choose the healthier option.

For Wisdom, this question was far less of an abstraction than it is for others. Jessie's family on both sides has a predisposition to high cholesterol and heart disease. Her mother's most painful memory goes back to when she was a little girl: she was watching television with her dad when he suddenly fell into her lap. She thought he was asleep. He wasn't; he was dead of a heart attack.

By the time Jessie was in grade school, the family was so concerned about her vulnerability to heart disease that they had tested her cholesterol. She was only six, weighed less than forty pounds, didn't eat particularly poorly, and yet she had the high cholesterol of an obese fifty-year-old junk-food addict. Jessie was supposed to limit her sweets. "At snack time," she remembers, "they would bring cookies for the other kids and I had my peaches."

Jessie's mom was in almost every way a fabulous mother.

She was loving and supportive and a lot of fun to be around. There was only one major issue: Jessie's mom was a secret eater, especially of ice cream. One time, Jessie called her mom when she was running an errand and a stranger answered, explaining that the cell phone had been left on a table in the Häagen-Dazs shop. Other times, Jessie would monitor the Häagen-Dazs container—there always was one—in the freezer and notice that it had become empty overnight. Her mother had eaten all of the ice cream but didn't want anyone to see the empty pint in the trash, so she'd put it back in the freezer.

Jessie realized from a very young age that her mom was constantly putting herself at risk of a heart attack. "I was so scared for my mom," Jessie says now. "I didn't want anything to happen to her. And I kept asking myself, *Why does she eat things that she knows she shouldn't eat?*" How did her mom choose, so often, to do the very opposite of what she knew would be good for her? Looking back, it's clear that Jessie was a decision scientist at seven.

When Jessie was in college, at Brown, she knew that she wanted to devote her life to helping people like her mom make better choices about their lives. She studied psychology but quickly realized it wasn't for her. The courses she took were about clinical psychology, in which a psychologist works one-on-one to help individual patients. "That was not up my alley," she says. It felt so slow, working with one person at a time, slowly solving their problems. There had to be other, more comprehensive solutions that would reach a lot of people quickly.

When she graduated from college, she was a bit lost. She had thought her life would be focused on helping people make better choices, but if she didn't want to become a psychologist, how would she do that? She had no idea. So she followed her boyfriend (now her husband) to Pittsburgh, where he was getting a PhD in computer science, and took the one job she could find, as assistant manager of an office building. She hated every minute of it. She had to be at work before eight, which meant she had to be outside, at the bus stop, by six-thirty. She'd stand there, freezing in the dark on winter mornings, waiting for a bus that never seemed to come on time, finally squeeze herself into the thick crowd on board (there was never a chance of a seat), and spend an hour being jostled, just to get to a job that was mind-numbingly boring. There, she would sit at her desk, staring at the door in front of her, and try to wait a full hour before checking her watch. Once, she checked it to find that only six minutes had gone by. She often promised herself that she would look for another job; but she didn't. Once again, she was confronted with this mystery: Why do people choose to do things (or, in this case, not do things) that work against their own interests?

One day, her boyfriend came home and asked if she had heard of something called "social and decision sciences." He had stumbled across the discipline and learned that there was a department at Carnegie Mellon devoted to it. "This is what I've been looking for," Jessie recalls thinking. "Literally seeing those words and reading what the different professors are studying gave me the motivation." Jessie remembers running to the computer, checking out the website, and deciding right in that moment that she was going back to school.

Jessie's precise field of study is called behavioral economics; it is a new discipline—or, more precisely, a new configuration of several older disciplines. For most of the twentieth century, the fields of academic psychology and economics rarely had anything to do with each other. Sure, psychologists and economists both studied human behavior, but their approaches were irreconcilably different. Psychologists, generally, thought many economists were mistaken in assuming that human beings are rational creatures who, for the most part, make decisions that maximize their well-being—an idea that is hard to square with actual human behavior. Economics, generally, recognized that individual human beings can act in wildly self-destructive ways but believed that taken as a group and averaged out, human beings do tend toward economic rationality.

This shift began quietly and obscurely in the 1970s, when some economists and psychologists started to realize that instead of clashing, they could help each other. For economists—at least those who embraced this new collaborative approach—psychologists were able to reveal crucial ways people behave that had been undiscovered by decades of economic study. For example, people tend to value the immediate far more than any logical, mathematical system would suggest. If I offered you a slice of pizza right now but told you that I'd give you two slices and a can of Coke tomorrow, you'd be highly likely to grab the slice now. Similarly, most of us know that our lifetime happiness would be increased if we took, say, one hundred dollars each week out of our paycheck and put it toward our 401(k). Yet far too few of us actually do this. We value the immediate pleasure of whatever it is we can buy now over the increased chance of a perilous future. People don't always behave like rational robots making precisely the accurate, logical choice. The economists were able to learn that people are, well, a little crazier than previously thought.

It can seem absurd from the outside, but for some in the two disciplines, the idea of psychologists and economists working together was radical and infuriating. Why not have aerospace engineers work with poetry professors or physicists merge with some painting school? At many universities, this was not just a theoretical problem. There was a real nuts-and-bolts question: If economists and psychologists want to work together, where will their offices be? What department will they be in? Which classes will they teach? Which graduate students will they tutor? It would cause too much uproar to have a bunch of psychologists transferred into an economics program or to send some economists to work for a psychology department. So at a handful of universities around the country, new departments were created for the two disciplines to come together. A host of new terms were coined to describe these collaborations: decision science, behavioral economics, behavioral finance.

Jessie knew none of this history. She wasn't aware that the department she was entering was a by-product of a long-simmering war between ways of thought. She just knew that she had always wondered why people—specifically one person—make decisions they know they shouldn't make and what, if anything, could be done to help them make better choices.

In graduate school at the decision sciences department of Carnegie Mellon University, Jessie became enthralled with the idea of a "nudge." The nudge is one of the most important and impactful ideas to come out of the collaboration between economists and psychologists. It shows that it is possible to change people's behavior in life-altering, grand ways through a tiny change in the context in which they make decisions. It is a by-product of one of the most persistent biases in the human brain: the instinct to value the immediate over the long-term.

The science of nudges can help explain why so much of what we do, each day, is *not* rooted in our own passions, as well as why the widget economy thrived in the twentieth century and why we allowed widget products, widget companies, and widget jobs to dominate. One of the first scholars of the nudge was Thomas Schelling, an economist and game theory expert who worked for President Kennedy and helped develop the theoretical underpinnings of the Cold War—the idea of mutually assured destruction, in which the Soviet Union and the United States were prevented from attacking each other because any attack would lead to the total destruction of both nations.

Schelling was a heavy smoker and had wanted to quit for years. He knew, of course, that smoking was disastrous to his health and made it harder for him to play with his children, because he would quickly get out of breath. Smoking was one of the most destructive, negative forces in his life. Yet he didn't quit. Over time, though, he used the same analysis he had applied to the Cold War to his own behavior. He saw that at any given moment, he didn't truly face a choice between quitting smoking forever or not quitting smoking forever. Rather, he faced a smaller choice: Do I have this one cigarette? He was able to convince himself, each and every time, that having that one cigarette was fine, since he was planning to quit the very next day. Of course, the next day he would convince himself to have one more cigarette and then one more and then one more. He likened this to the United States or the USSR considering using just one little nuclear bomb in, say, the Korean War. It would be just one bomb—how much damage could it do? Through mutually assured destruction, though, both nations realized that any one bomb would quickly lead to an all-out nuclear war, so they never used the one bomb. Schelling decided to create his own mutually assured destruction. He sat his children down and promised them that Daddy would never smoke again; and, he said, if they saw him smoking, they should no longer respect him. He knew that, for him, losing his children's respect was the greatest price he could pay. He had created the conditions under which smoking even one cigarette would be devastating.

This idea came to be called a Ulysses contract, named after the ancient Greeks' mythical figure of Ulysses, who had himself strapped to a mast to avoid the temptations of the Sirens. Today, websites offer Ulysses contracts, in which a person can, say, agree to have her money sent to a political group she despises if she doesn't quit smoking or if she stops following her diet.

I find this way of thinking to be helpful in understanding how we allowed our economy to become widgetized. Most of us, given the choice, would rather lead passion-fueled lives in which our work fulfills us. But most of us aren't presented with that choice. We enter the workforce in our late teens or twenties when we need a job to pay the rent, and we take what is offered. That job leads to another job, and that one leads to the next. Before most of us feel we've made any choice at all, we find that we're in our thirties or forties and thoroughly ensconced in some profession. It would be enormously costly to leave the field in which we have experience and a network of connections and start over somewhere else. We never chose a widget job; we just made a bunch of smaller choices that led us there.

The field of nudges is rooted in and elaborates on the work of Schelling. It was created by two scholars: Richard Thaler of the University of Chicago, who went on to win the Nobel Prize in economics, and Cass Sunstein, now of Harvard Law School. They developed a gentler approach to the same problem Schelling had described, in which people routinely make short-term decisions that go against their long-term desires. Thaler and Sunstein hypothesized that it would be possible to make little shifts in our environment that would guide us— nudge us—toward making a better decision. Thaler initially had the idea in the 1970s when he was hosting a party for a group of economists. He had put out some nuts, and the economists were eating so many, he feared they wouldn't have an appetite for dinner. So he moved the nut bowl to another room and, immediately, the economists stopped snacking. This is the kind of observation that most people find obvious but economists can see as earth-shattering. If someone wants nuts, they should be willing to walk a few steps to another room to grab some—yet none did.

Over time, Thaler and Sunstein were able to show that we could make far better decisions if we simply shifted the context in which we decide things, raising the cost—just a bit—for making the choice that goes against our long-term goals and lowering the cost of making the right choice.

One of the first great studies of nudges concerned retirement savings. For decades, human resources departments, retirement fund companies, and personal finance writers had lectured people about how important it is to save more for retirement. Most of us have seen the graphs that illustrate how relatively small savings today will transform our lives in the future, and most of us have ignored those graphs and saved far too little. Are we stupid? Do we need to have it explained ever more clearly and starkly? No.

Under the guidance of some decision scientists—meaning economists and psychologists—the Deluxe Corporation, a giant in envelope making, changed its retirement fund rules. In most companies, when a new employee is hired, she is informed that she has the opportunity to deposit a portion of each paycheck in a retirement plan. Around 40 percent of new employees don't do so, leaving themselves in a vulnerable position when they retire. In 2008, Deluxe changed the default option so that each new employee was automatically signed up to deposit 5 percent of her salary in a retirement plan, with a 1 percentage point increase each year. Each employee was free to opt out and stop receiving retirement savings, but very few did.

This struck the world—at least that small part of the world that considered such things—as a bizarre finding. What could be more important than retirement savings? People who have adequate retirement funds are able to lead much fuller lives, with far less stress, than those who don't. It should be in everybody's interest to put aside enough today to have a good life later. Only telling people this—even hectoring them, warning them—has little impact. Then along comes a really minor change—a shift in the default option on some paperwork for new hires—and it has a revolutionary impact on people's lives.

Jessie's own life shows how the same approach—a gentle nudge—can shift someone from a widget-like existence to a passion-based one. She knew that she was miserable in her work, and she understood that if she didn't change, she would lead a considerably less happy life. At any given moment she could have researched her options, sought out advice from others, and begun the process of identifying a more satisfying job. But that was overwhelming and scary. Where would she start? Who should she talk to? What could she do? It was easier to stick with the familiar routine, even if it left her miserable. Then there was one tiny change, a minuscule one: she learned a new phrase, "decision science." She was able to Google it, find a list of people to call, and soon had transformed her life. Looking at this moment through the lens of, well, decision science, it's actually a bit odd. What could be more important, more worth spending some time engaging in, than the very quality of one's life? Yet Jessie took no action until she was given that phrase.

One major cause of the growth of the Passion Economy is as simple as the lesson Jessie teaches. Being able to Google a phrase makes it so much easier for us to find work we might be passionate about.

As it happens, Google changed Jessie's life in more ways than this one. Once she was in graduate school and saw that decision science was, indeed, her dream vocation, a friend showed her a small ad in one of the academic journals: Google was looking for behavioral scientists to spend a few months as interns in its human resources department, helping the company improve the lives of its staff. Jessie thought it might be fun to see the giant company from the inside, so she applied and was accepted.

At the start, she told her supervisors at Google about her background, and they mentioned that there was a problem in their offices they had long wanted to address, one that was especially familiar to Jessie: employees were making some really bad food choices, and it was affecting their health. Google, rather famously, provides free food to all employees. It doesn't just offer snacks and a basic meal plan; it provides cupcakes and taco trucks and gelato and pizza and waffles and dumplings and pies. The food was made with top ingredients by excellent chefs and was, in general, very, very good. This, however, had led to something people called "the Google fifteen." New employees gained weight really quickly. They ate more than they usually would because the food was delicious and always available. Most of us have had the experience of seeing our co-workers swarm a couple boxes of free Friday morning doughnuts. Imagine if those doughnuts were a massive fantasy buffet available every minute of the day. If you're just a little peckish, you're going to eat. If you're stuck on a tough problem, or you just want a reason to leave your desk, or if you are kind of bored, you go and eat some more. Jessie was tasked with seeing what she could do to help Google employees make better choices.

In graduate school, Jessie had administered lots of tests and conducted lots of surveys designed to figure out what works and what doesn't when trying to get people to make better decisions. She had spent hours standing outside fast-food restaurants, asking questions of people who had just left so that she could better understand what choices they'd made and what had influenced them. It might take months and thousands of dollars to get a sample size of two hundred people on a certain subject. At Google, she could do almost whatever she wanted and instantly try it out with the tens of thousands of employees, yielding immediate results.

Jessie's training had taught her that it's best not to take away choice—by, say, offering a selection of only healthy foods. It would be far more effective to nudge people toward healthier decisions, often without them even knowing the nudge was happening. Jessie noticed that there were big glass jars filled with M&M's. It was a Google tradition. Jessie replaced the glass jars with opaque metal jars. The new containers were labeled to communicate the presence of the M&M's yet lacked the bright, visual cue of all that delicious candy on display. People were still free to eat as many M&M's as they liked, but they wouldn't be able to see the candy and, presumably, wouldn't be as tempted. She measured the M&M's in spots where they were in glass containers and in spots where they were in opaque containers and, sure enough, people ate far fewer when they couldn't see the M&M's. In one Google location—the New York headquarters—this one change to the jars containing M&M's led to more than three million fewer calories consumed over a seven-week period.

Jessie tried another experiment in some of Google's cafeterias. The company had long offered two sizes of plates, small and large. Jessie put up signs informing Googlers that people often eat more if they use a bigger plate. Soon, use of the smaller plates increased by half. A third of diners were eating less food because of a small, simple sign.

When her summer internship was over, Jessie returned to Pittsburgh and graduate school and realized, pretty quickly, that her entire life purpose had shifted. She had always assumed that once she got her PhD she would find a job teaching at a university, writing academic papers. If she wrote enough papers that made a splash with other academics, she could get tenure and eventually run a department. That had seemed a wonderful goal—until Google. In just three months as a junior intern, she had been able to have a major impact on tens of thousands of people's lives. As an academic, she would run small studies— a dozen people here, maybe a hundred there—over several months and then spend more months, maybe years, drawing on that data to write an article for an academic journal. If the article was truly interesting, some academic or other might take the idea a bit further. All this seemed so small now—so slow, so lacking in impact—compared to working in a large company where she could have an immediate influence on thousands of people's lives.

It had taken Jessie years to realize that she even had a passion. She had known that she was upset about her mother, and that she had questions about how people behave, but she would never have thought to call that a passion, let alone one that could become a life's mission and a benefit to others. It would never have occurred to her that she might one day follow her questions toward a set of solutions that would allow other people to identify and pursue their own passions. To fully engage her unique passion, Jessie would need something else.

As it happened, she would need to meet another person whose childhood had been filled with his own sadness and concern about a loving mother who couldn't quite get her life together. A man whose approach to the relationship between company and employee was the reason Jessie had been able to conduct her work in the first place, the reason Google treated its employees the way it did. She had to meet Laszlo Bock.

Bock reminds me of Charlie Brown. He shouldn't, really, since he's the opposite in many ways. Laszlo stands erect and has an easy, fluid charm. He can talk to anybody, confidently, about anything. He walks into a room or joins a conversation with a kind of earnest curiosity that infects everyone. Nonetheless, I always think of Charlie Brown when I think of Laszlo. Part of the Charlie Brown connection is certainly the big bald head, though Laszlo's is more chiseled and handsome than poor Charlie's. The key, I think, is that Laszlo has this permanently bemused expression on his face, as if he is in the world but also, somehow, just outside it, observing it, and noticing that everything doesn't really make perfect sense. It's as if Charlie Brown grew up, stopped letting Lucy take advantage of him, got over his crush on the little red-haired girl, and became confident.

Laszlo, of course, is no Charlie Brown. He is the single most respected leader in the field of human relations. He has transformed how companies understand how to motivate workers to do their best. He doesn't brag, he doesn't lecture, he doesn't dazzle with complex analysis. He keeps things remarkably simple: he asks basic, uncomplicated questions, takes in and considers the answers, and follows up with more basic, uncomplicated questions. What conditions make a person do his best work? What does a company need to understand about its workers and communicate to those workers so that they, and the firm, can excel? Happily, as Laszlo soon learned, the answers are not only good for business, they're morally good.

Laszlo is now at the top of his profession, but he started life in pretty bad circumstances. He was born in 1972 in a small city in Transylvania, Romania, with several strikes against him. His father was ethnically Hungarian and his mother Jewish in an authoritarian Soviet country that allowed only ethnic Romanians to attain any sort of decent job. When he was two, Laszlo's family snuck out of the country and landed in a refugee camp in Austria with nothing more than a handful of diapers. Eventually, the family made its way to the United States. Laszlo's parents were educated: his father had an advanced degree in engineering, and his mother had a master's in English literature. But moving from a poor, Communist nation to the United States was a difficult adjustment.

"My mom, I love her, she couldn't hold a job," Laszlo remembers. "She was too kind." She would routinely become close with the most troubled employee at a company, often a single mother or a recent immigrant, befriend that person, and encourage the company owner to be kind and generous. She would fight so hard for them that she would get fired along with them. Then she'd get another job, find someone floundering there, and repeat the pattern. Laszlo recalls that this happened three or four times, right when the family was facing its own economic troubles after his parents divorced. His father, too, struggled to grow his own engineering business, and Laszlo's younger brother was having a hard time fitting in. Laszlo distinctly remembers coming to the realization, when he was a freshman in high school, that his entire family's survival might depend on him. "I was going to have to support my mom," he remembers thinking. "I was going to have to support my brother. And I was going to have to support my dad."

In middle school, Laszlo had been at the bottom of the social hierarchy, an awkward immigrant who was picked on. When he entered high school, he began a self-improvement project that would—later and with far more sophistication—become his life's work. "I didn't plan to be the coolest kid in school," he says. "I wanted to move from being strictly a nerd to maybe the middle of the pack." Laszlo didn't have the right natural instincts. He didn't have any fashion sense (he still doesn't, he assures me) and never knew what to wear. He wasn't sure how to behave around higher-status teens. However, he did have something that might be more valuable: Laszlo has a natural belief in the ability of people to improve their conditions through small but impactful choices.

He read somewhere that standing straight would help with social acceptance, so he paid a lot of attention to his posture. "And it worked!" he remembers. "Things got better. I got picked on less." When adolescents did make fun of him, Laszlo didn't just feel miserable (though he definitely felt miserable), he took note of what they said and sought ways to improve. For example, Laszlo recalls that he wore Grapevines shorts—the tight and too-short shorts that looked like the kind Magnum P.I. wore—long after they had gone out of style. He wore them to school every day. "I remember this guy, this football player, looking at me," Laszlo recalls, "the venom in his eyes as he took in those short shorts." It was awful, of course, but Laszlo made a mental note, got rid of the Grapevines, and bought new and more acceptable pants. Another time, a pretty girl who was with the popular crowd looked at an outfit Laszlo was wearing, laughed, and said, "You can't wear a vertical-stripe shirt with horizontal-stripe shorts." Ouch, sure, but lesson learned.

Step by step, Laszlo became more comfortable with himself and more accepted. He never became wildly popular, but he was no longer bullied and mocked. He even ended up dating that popular girl who'd laughed at his mismatched shorts and shirt. He went to college nearby and became confident enough to pursue a career as an actor in Hollywood (which, no surprise, actually meant making a living as a waiter at Olive Garden).

After college, Laszlo felt the pressure to get a more steady, lucrative job so that he could support his family. One day he found himself wearing an old suit with too-short pants while interviewing for a job in the management office of a manufacturing plant in an industrial section of town. The owner of the company sat tipped back in his chair, shoes on the desk, smoking so much that a thick haze surrounded his head. After peppering Laszlo with questions, the owner boasted about himself: "My W-2 last year was $2.3 million! I live in the Four Seasons! I drive a Mercedes!" At one point, the owner looked at Laszlo and asked, "Do you have any questions for me?" Laszlo blurted out, before he could realize it, "Are you happy?" The owner called out to another man in the office, telling him to come over, and then said to the man, "This kid wants to know if I'm happy? I made $2.3 million last year. I live at the Four Seasons. I drive a Mercedes. If that's what makes you happy, then I'm happy!"

To Laszlo's surprise, he was hired. The company made a kind of Styrofoam form that allowed concrete to be poured in preset shapes on a building site. The firm was run by two men— the owner and his chief operating officer—who were opposites, perfect archetypes of the worst and best ways to manage people. The boss, of course, was all bluster, yelling at Laszlo and everyone else, viewing the company as a big machine whose primary aim should be pleasing the owner and gratifying his ego.

The COO was the opposite. Toby was kind and modest. He didn't view the employees as his servants; he wanted to serve them and help them do better. He became a mentor to Laszlo and gently and generously tutored him about business. Laszlo realized that, growing up with immigrant parents from a Communist country, he had never learned much about American capitalism. He didn't know the names of big companies or how to think about the stock market. (In college, he had received an invitation to apply for a job at McKinsey & Company, the most prestigious consulting firm in the world. He'd assumed it was some sort of scam, a time-share or the like, and had thrown the invitation away.) "Toby had all this business knowledge that I didn't have," Laszlo realized. He decided that he had to go to business school and was accepted at Yale.

As a general rule, Ivy League MBA students don't pursue careers in human resources. HR executives rarely become CEOs, and they rarely achieve the wealth of Silicon Valley start-up founders. But Laszlo became fascinated with HR. He realized that human resources touched on the very things he cared most about: What makes people do their best work? What makes them happy? How can a company and its managers motivate workers? More than anything: Why was there this glaring disconnect between what business leaders espoused and what they actually did every day? Nearly every manager talked about how they wanted to empower workers and create a great culture, but so few actually did it.

After Yale, Laszlo—by now having learned quite a bit more about business—got a job at McKinsey, where he was immediately confronted with the gulf between word and deed. "At McKinsey, they talk about the 'obligation of dissent,'" Laszlo explained. Managers tell young recruits that they must speak up when they think someone higher up in the company is making a mistake. "The reality that I saw was that the first time you speak up, the partner is interested," he recalls. "By the third time, they just say, 'Get back to work.'"

Laszlo left McKinsey to pursue a career in human resources and landed at a division of General Electric. GE has one of the world's most well-regarded management and human resources cultures. The company popularized Six Sigma and a host of other now-famous systems for improving the ways its employees work. Laszlo thought he would learn the latest and most scientific techniques for managing human beings. But when he got there, he says, much of the human resource practice didn't seem sophisticated or highly technical. "It was still a lot of management by gut," he notes. For example, there is a formal talent review, called a Session C, in which someone from HR and a manager are supposed to analyze the workforce according to objective, metric-based standards. Instead, Laszlo found himself sitting with a senior leader who flipped through a list of his underlings, looking for the names of his friends; he would then talk about how great they were. "This process was viewed as the most sophisticated," Laszlo said. "But it was just the standard old boys' club."

Laszlo was reading obsessively about human behavior and management. He was studying the work of behavioral economists and other decision scientists and was struck by the fact that so little in the actual practice of management was rooted in validated studies. "There was very little, if any, science, applied to HR," he remembers concluding. "There are a bunch of things we do instinctively, but we are wrong." He found that there seemed to be two different streams of thought: the one used by academics who knew things with rigor but had little impact on actual practice and the one applied by practicing managers and human resources departments that amounted to, essentially, "just people making things up."

Laszlo read an article about IBM's research and development arm in Yorktown Heights, New York. It mentioned that forty PhD scientists were focused on some particular engineering challenge. Laszlo remembers thinking, *Man, if I could have forty PhD scientists trying to figure out how to measure and improve employee engagement, I could really get somewhere.* But, of course, no company would spend the tens of millions of dollars it would take to hire forty top scientists to see if some HR exec's hunch was right.

Then, in 2005, Laszlo got a call from Google. Or, more specifically, he got a call from a headhunting firm hired by Google to bring in a new human resources leader. Laszlo was hired and suddenly found himself working for perhaps the one company in all of human history that would most welcome his idea of throwing dozens of scientists at the problem of human resource management.

Above all, Google is a data-obsessed company. The whole firm's purpose is to assemble all of the world's data and make it usable. There was far too little data about workers. Think of any large company. People are doing, or not doing, all sorts of things. They're checking e-mail and talking to each other and starting projects and finishing or not finishing them. They're going to meetings and making phone calls and hiring some people and firing other people, and bosses are trying to motivate workers, and workers are trying to convince their bosses to do one thing or another. At the end of the day, all that activity *is* the business; that's what helps a company make a profit or forces a company to declare bankruptcy. But which of the things they're doing are productive and which are a waste of time or, worse, cost the company money? What are those people feeling and thinking, and how do those feelings and thoughts affect their work, and how does their work translate to the bottom line?

If you think of any place you've ever worked, chances are you have some gut instinct about all of this, but you've had very little data. Are meetings helpful or do they hurt? Which meetings help and which ones hurt? Is there an optimal amount of time to talk on the phone? Are there specific questions in a job interview that really do predict who will thrive and who won't? Should managers be kind, indulgent, mean, insistent? For data scientists, answers to questions like these had largely been a black hole with no substantive information. Laszlo suddenly had the budget and the authority to hire those PhDs he'd dreamed of; he hired twenty, then forty, then forty more. He had so many scientists, he could assign some to figuring out how to get workers to drink less soda and others to determining the optimum length of meetings. (Zero minutes is the optimum; meetings turn out to be, almost always, a waste of time and resources.)

By the time Jessie joined Google as a full-time employee, Laszlo's team of data scientists was extensive and well established. Jessie remembers the first time she presented some of her research to a large group of executives that included Laszlo. Beforehand, she was warned that he would be very nice but would ask questions you never would have thought of yourself; they would be simple but smart, and it was no use trying to predict them. Only Laszlo, people said, seemed able to ask those Laszlo questions. Sure enough, he asked her basic questions, such as how people felt after eating less food. Did they know that Google was conducting this experiment? Did they feel manipulated or well taken care of? He asked how such a model could be spread throughout the company, to other functions. Jessie couldn't quite answer in the moment, but she told him with confidence that she would figure it out. Laszlo, in time, recognized that Jessie was exactly the kind of scientist he wanted to collaborate with: she was driven and obsessively rigorous in her research, but she was also imaginative in thinking about problems and coming up with novel ways of getting answers.

People who work at Google are very lucky. They are typically top graduates from top schools getting paid large amounts of money for elite jobs. They get all that free food, plus free transportation and free drinks in the evening. They get to tell everyone they meet that they work at Google, which, in Silicon Valley, is about as cool a thing as someone gets to say. In fact, life is so good at Google that the company has the opposite problem of almost every other firm in the country. Most companies have too much turnover; qualified workers leave for other opportunities too often, forcing the companies to eat the cost of hiring and training someone new. At Google, Laszlo realized, very few people were leaving, because life was so great. He had to come up with ways of gently nudging poor performers out the door without being so tough that it spooked other employees.

In the first several years, Laszlo and Jessie were excited just to be part of the world's first human resources team using real science at scale to motivate workers. They came to call what they were doing "people analytics," and it soon became its own field of study. You can now get a degree in it, and hundreds of companies have people analytics departments—all because of those simple questions Laszlo was asking and the answers scientists like Jessie provided.

Laszlo's ever-growing team of scientists conducted complex studies, made all sorts of rigorous data-based recommendations, and helped transform Google. The science was an extension of Laszlo's instincts. There is observation: progressively more sophisticated ways of studying what people are doing at work and how they think and feel about their jobs. There is analysis: taking all that data and coming up with models and theories about what is working well, what might need to be changed, and how, precisely, to change it. Then there is action: using that data to change the way people work so that they will work better and feel more motivated.

It became clear that three core values made work more satisfying for employees and, simultaneously, made them more effective at their jobs. One: people want to feel some sense of autonomy over their work, feel that they can make choices that will have an impact. Two: they want to feel a sense of belonging to the organization they work for. Three: they want to trust their company and their bosses. Together, these three components make people happier at work and better at their jobs in clear, measurable ways. These are also attributes that I've noticed at most Passion Economy businesses. Passion businesses are, by their nature, driven by a founder's vision to connect, deeply, with a specific set of customers. Employees who thrive in such businesses often share the founder's passion, or at least share the joy of that more profound connection with clients. In short, these employees trust their leadership, they feel a sense of belonging to the passion business, and they understand how they can add to it. This is not to say that all passion businesses successfully achieve these satisfactions or that non-passion business—widget-oriented companies—can't achieve them. There are terribly run passion businesses and widget firms with amazing corporate cultures. But if someone wants to feel satisfied in their work, they have a much better chance at a passion company.

Laszlo and his team learned that even within the same company, there can be pockets of satisfaction and pockets of misery. In their data gathering, they found that there were some managers whose teams scored off the charts for all of those positive values and that those teams also performed far better than similar types of employees doing similar work.

There was a bit of a culture clash, at times, between Laszlo's vision and the core values of Google. Google had been started by two computer scientists studying at Stanford University who wanted the company to work like a graduate school: individual computer scientists should be able to move easily between projects. If they didn't like their manager or they found a particular project boring, they could go somewhere else. Good managers would, presumably, attract more and better employees. In practice, though, the managers at Google didn't really matter all that much. What mattered were the projects, the computer scientists, and a system that quickly and easily adjusted.

While Laszlo's vision was not to create a profoundly hierarchical culture, he did believe that good management, in and of itself, was essential. In part to prove this, he launched Project Oxygen, an effort to identify the best managers at Google. That allowed him to show, through data, that there were some managers whose teams always performed at a high level and also felt enormous trust, autonomy, and belonging at Google. When those managers moved on to a new project, the high scores moved with them. What's more, Laszlo was able to demonstrate that, with a bit of coaching and training, the previously underperforming managers could actually get their teams' performances higher and raise their level of general happiness, as well.

One of the best managers Laszlo ever saw, a man whose team regularly scored in the very top of performance at Google, was Wayne Crosby, a computer scientist who ran a number of major projects, including the Google Slides presentation tool and Google's G Suite of productivity applications, which many companies, large and small, now use for mail, documents, and other cloud-based tools.

Wayne became manager of the teams at Google researching artificial intelligence. He soon realized that, with the AI revolution underway, we could end up in a world in which nobody needed to be employed. This created an existential crisis for him, and he began to question the deeper motivations behind why human beings work. In the end, Wayne came to believe that we, as humans, actually like to work. There is something fundamentally human about coming together and accomplishing something that we couldn't have achieved by ourselves. So, while the nature of work is going to transform dramatically due to advancements in AI, the fundamental human need to belong and to contribute to something bigger will never go away. Yet several macro forces at work in today's widget labor market contribute to dehumanizing workers and leave workers unfulfilled with their work. Wayne wanted to play a role in bringing the human elements of work back into the labor market, something that is at the center of the evolving passion economy.

It's one thing to want to change the world of work; it's something else entirely to engage workers. Wayne says he wasn't a born manager; in fact, he was pretty lousy at it for years. One of his first jobs was at a company that happened to be run by a former marine drill sergeant whose managing style involved frequent yelling and awarding demerits when people arrived a few minutes late or didn't turn in their paperwork with the proper formatting. After reading management books and seeing that Google was able to accomplish far more with a much more humane culture, Wayne realized that he was thinking of the role of manager completely wrong. He had assumed that the manager was the main engine of a team, choosing the path, pushing the team forward, forcing stragglers to get back in line. He eventually understood that a good manager is more like the coach of a track and field team. She doesn't win the medals, doesn't cross the finish line, doesn't get all the glory. Rather, the coach needs to understand each team member and her individual motivation, and create the conditions under which each person can do her best. Sometimes a coach has to be tough— removing one team member, reprimanding another—but that is the exception. Most days, a coach's job is simply to understand each member of the team and help her achieve the success she wants.

Top managers at Google were awarded a celebratory trip to Hawaii. At one year's festivities, Laszlo and Wayne chatted on the beach outside the resort hotel they were staying in. They came to recognize that they wanted to achieve the same thing and that together they could do more than either could alone. They both wanted to understand how best to motivate workers and their managers, using data and their similar sense of values. Laszlo had the ability to ask those basic questions and keep a large team of scientists focused on what mattered most. Wayne understood that Laszlo's quest required an incredibly complex computer infrastructure, especially if it were to be deployed outside a company like Google, which already has all the computer backbone anyone could need. Wayne realized that Laszlo's quest was a natural extension of the work he had done on Google G Suite and in AI. He began to imagine intelligent productivity software that could actually help improve employee behavior and morale and strengthen corporate culture.

Soon after Wayne and Laszlo began talking, they brought Jessie in. The three began to imagine how wonderful it would be if far more people around the world—people who didn't work at a company as well resourced as Google—could have the benefit of thoughtful people analytics.

Eventually, the three left Google to create Humu, with the goal of democratizing the people science that only the wealthiest companies, like Google, had access to.

Imagine that you want to find out how much the people who work at a large organization trust their management, how much they believe that they belong at that company, and how much autonomy they feel in their jobs. In short, you want to know how happy they are and what factors of their work would need to change to make them happier. You could, of course, just send an e-mail to every employee, asking them to fill out a questionnaire in which they rate, on a scale of one to five, how much they trust their bosses, how much they feel they are making a difference. But, of course, the less the workers trust their bosses, the more certain they'll be that those bosses will read their results and then judge them for it. If a company or a team were to score very high on trust, would that be because there is real trust or merely because of the fear of being honest? Similarly, you would probably want to know how the answers to such questions correlate with actual performance. Do teams with high degrees of trust work harder? Do they perform better? Do they add to the bottom line?

There are several overlapping problems in trying to get honest answers. A survey company like Humu needs to convince employees that their answers will absolutely be anonymous. That means developing highly secure software and hardware. To validate the responses and compare them to actual performance, you need to take in a great deal of objective data: the hours employees work, the amount of sick time they take, the output of their team. You have to match that data while still maintaining complete anonymity. These turn out to be enormous computer science challenges, requiring the very best in computer engineering. That's the job of Wayne's team.

At the same time, the survey questions need to be carefully crafted, and the analysis of the answers needs to be conducted according to the highest degree of scientific rigor, to ensure that the results are meaningful and can lead to real change. That's Jessie's team's job.

Overall, the operation can't get lost in the details. It can't become so overly complex that the core purpose is obscured. All that data gathering and data protection needs to lead to one simple goal: to improve the happiness of workers by increasing their feelings of trust, belonging, and autonomy, so that they can perform their jobs better and the company can make more money. That is Laszlo's job.

Humu's offices are in Mountain View, California, a town that has become synonymous with the largest giants of Silicon Valley. It's within throwing distance of Google, LinkedIn, Microsoft, and 23andMe. But to find Humu, I was told to look for Fu Lam Mum Chinese restaurant, whose large sign—not to mention the reviews and menus taped to the windows, partially blocking the views of its soaring interior—can distract a passerby from the small glass door with the tiny plate informing visitors that Humu is upstairs.

One flight up, Humu occupies one large office space, just about enough room for its fifty employees. The deep, open space is, at once, playful and also clearly focused on business. There are no foosball or Ping-Pong tables, but there are free snacks. Several pods of three or four desks are attached in a flower-like pattern, the desks poking out from a central stalk. Each person can position a desk at whichever height he wants. Some are standing desks, some are meant for taller seated people, and some are at conventional desk height. Somehow this relatively minor adjustment to the usual open-plan office creates a sense of intimacy and personalization that counters the oppressiveness of the usual cubicle farm. The desks are reassigned every few months, so, over a few years, every worker will have spent at least some time working in a desk pod with everyone else, fostering unexpected collaboration and a strong group identity.

Once a week the entire staff gets together to share what they're working on, as well as anything important from their own lives. It happened that I was visiting on the first anniversary of Laszlo's brother's suicide, and in the group discussion Laszlo mentioned that it was a tough day for him and that if he seemed a bit distracted or short, he hoped everyone would understand why. I was struck by the admission. It could have been overly maudlin, even a bit self-indulgent, for the boss of a company to tell employees about his personal pain. Laszlo handled the moment elegantly, with a touching mix of matter-of-fact business-appropriate clarity and just a bit of emotion. It was an example of Laszlo modeling the kind of culture he wants for his employees. It is a tricky balance. Laszlo was sharing a personal, emotional fact about himself—making clear to his employees that he wanted them, too, to feel comfortable being honest about their emotional states—but he was doing so in a way that was conducive to work, not egocentric or disruptive.

In my time with Laszlo, Jessie, Wayne, and the Humu team, I realized they were reshaping how I understand a Passion Economy business. Some companies are, well, passionate in everything they do. I think of Jason Blumer's firm or the factory floor of OCHO Candy. There is a palpable feeling of the company's mission. It's impossible to go an hour without someone mentioning the purpose of the firm and its connection to its clients. Much like nudges, though, Humu's approach shows that a passion-based business can use a subtler, quieter touch. Yes, Humu has a grand mission, and its employees talk about it a fair bit. But they also spend a lot of time thinking about more mundane matters, issues that are rarely seen as connected to a passionate mission. The thoughtfulness around where people sit (or stand) when they do their work and how they talk about themselves are embodiments of precisely what Humu is designed to do: to use data, science, and a strong sense

of values to thoughtfully tweak a work space so that it can operate well and, essentially, provide the workplace happiness, trust,
and engagement that is core to Humu's mission.

Humu's changes can seem minor, almost timid, compared
to some of the radical ideas that have swept through corporate
America since there's been a corporate America, particularly in
Silicon Valley. In a time so thoroughly dominated by corporations, it's hard to remember that the very act of gathering a
whole bunch of people in one company and asking them to
work together is a very new phenomenon, one that would have
puzzled our great-grandparents and every ancestor who came
before them. A handful of institutions in history have brought
thousands of people together to perform some shared task—
armies, various religious orders, the Chinese government
bureaucracy—but most human activity for most of human history has been done in relatively small groups; the typical clan
size is thought to be around 150 people, small enough that
everyone knows everyone else. It was only in the nineteenth
and twentieth centuries that single companies had tens of
thousands, even, in a few cases, millions of employees, whose
actions were directed by a tiny group of corporate leaders, who,
of course, would never meet most of the employees.

Human civilization is facing a new challenge, the need to
direct the activities of huge numbers of people spread around
the globe. Corporate leaders have struggled to address this
challenge in various ways. Some of the first large companies
were rail lines that hired military personnel to demand strict,
blind adherence to a company's many, many rules. In the 1880s,
a new wave of corporate leaders had the model of a medieval
village in mind. Companies like Pullman, which made railcars,
and Kohler, known for toilets, would build entire company
towns, in which workers would live their entire lives. They'd
work in a company factory, buy food in a company store, sleep
in a company bed inside a company house. On Saturday night,

they'd drink in a company bar, and Sunday morning they'd hear a company-paid preacher try to save their souls.

Over time, and after some horrible, violent fights, companies and workers reached a bit of a truce: the company would get the workers' days but leave their nights and weekends alone. This still left the challenge of coordinating all the activity at work. There were strict hierarchical firms with a small group of leaders sending orders through an army of middle managers. There were multidivisional firms, in which different divisions acted relatively autonomously and even competed against one another. Eventually, there was a penchant for flatter organizational structures and the lean movement, where workers were empowered to make choices for themselves, albeit within strict parameters. More recently, there have been more radical experiments, such as Holacracy, pioneered by Zappos, in which there are no titles, no job descriptions, no externally imposed structures of any kind.

Most of these corporate experiments were, more or less, top-down and fairly mechanical, viewing an organization as something akin to a machine that could be tuned to work more efficiently and, therefore, produce more goods at a lower cost and make a bigger profit. Humu's approach is almost precisely the opposite. It is focused on improving one key variable: how happy workers are. Having studied a rich set of data, Laszlo, Jessie, and Wayne believe they can prove that when workers are happier, the company will achieve all of its goals. If the company starts with profitability as a goal, it will quite probably make its workers less happy and, therefore, less likely to deliver a maximum profit.

Of course, give each employee a huge raise, a free car, and forty-two weeks of vacation and they'd probably say they were very happy (and the company would disappear instantly). The folks at Humu talk a lot about the meaning of the word "happiness." Psychologists differentiate between two very different kinds of happiness. Hedonic happiness is the immediate rush of joy that comes from getting something pleasurable: candy, money, a kiss. Hedonic happiness can feel exhilarating for a moment and then disappear, leaving little lasting trace. By contrast, eudaemonic happiness (derived from a Greek word that means the state of having a contented spirit) can be less immediate, without the sudden highs, but it is enduring and provides an entire lifetime of meaning. A one-night stand is hedonic; a long-term marriage that survives challenges is eudaemonic. An ice cream sundae is hedonic; achieving a long-held goal of running a marathon is eudaemonic. Humu wants to increase eudaemonic happiness at work. Humu's core, data-backed principle is that having a rewarding, satisfying work life is a key pillar in any person's overall life satisfaction, along with family and personal acceptance.

It is one thing to spend time trying to make work deeply satisfying for highly paid engineers at a company that is rapidly changing the world; it's something else entirely to help workers at the opposite end of the career ladder.

# CHAPTER 12

# ALL IT TAKES IS A QUICK REMINDER

*Humu's technological solution to promote human passion*

When I first walked into a Sweetgreen, I was pessimistic. The workers seemed to be engaged in the most mundane tasks: chopping vegetables, scooping those vegetables into bowls, and serving them to a long, impatient line of customers. I did note that the workers seemed a bit, well, happier than I might have expected at such a place, but I wondered how much meaning, how much enduring life satisfaction, they could find. Then I met Venus Paul.

Venus, twenty-four years old, spent her childhood in a small, poor village in Guyana, the tiny country nestled next to Venezuela and Brazil in South America. Her family struggled. Her father tried to make a living as a farmer, but after three consecutive years of drought, he had to sell his minuscule tract of land and seek work in the city. Her mother had a genetic deformity in one leg that meant that walking more than a few minutes exhausted her. Following a cousin's prompting, the family decided to move to Brooklyn, to see if they could make it there. It wasn't easy. Venus's mother never could find work that didn't tire her out. Her father got a job as a security guard on a construction site, making minimum wage. Venus left high school before graduation so she could make some money, too. She worked at a flower shop down the block from their small apartment, where she was paid cash, under the table, and made less than minimum wage. She then got a job screening bags at Kennedy Airport, which paid minimum wage but was rough going. Venus is tiny, barely hitting five feet; she is shy; and, having grown up in a tropical jungle, she hated that the job required her to go in and out of the cold during New York winters.

For someone in New York City like Venus, an immigrant with minimal education and work experience, the challenge isn't to find a job. As New York City has become much richer, it has developed a near-insatiable demand for low-paid service workers to make coffee, sell burgers, maintain the shelves at department stores. Venus has done it all. She worked at McDonald's and Staples and Dunkin' Donuts. She raised money for Greenpeace on a street corner. While each employer was different, each job was quite similar. She would do whatever it was she was told to do, often with little supervision, and then would get a paycheck reflecting her minimum-wage salary. She always took home less than $300 a week, barely enough to help her parents with the rent and groceries. It was always easy to get a new job. The problem was moving upward. There was no career trajectory, no clear way to earn a raise or a promotion or to have any feeling that the future might be different from the present. She would work at a place for a while and then she'd get bored or have an issue with a co-worker or decide that she wanted a shorter commute and she'd quit and find another job. She never stayed anywhere for more than a few months because it didn't seem to matter if she did or if she didn't. She felt destined to be stuck doing minimum-wage work for the rest of her life, like her father.

There were managers at all these places, of course. In some of them, the managers barely made more than the line workers, though they had to take on a huge amount of additional responsibility and stress. In others, the managers seemed to be well paid, but they hadn't been promoted from the line staff. They'd been hired as managers.

When Venus walked into the Sweetgreen on Court Street in downtown Brooklyn, she didn't have any particular hope that this job would be any different from all the others. Her interview, however, took a lot longer than usual. She didn't just fill out a form, answer some perfunctory questions, and then learn what day and time she should report. The manager sat with her for forty-five minutes, asking her about her interests and her background. That was nice, but Venus didn't put much store in it. She mentioned that she loved to cook food at home, and the manager told her she'd be a great fit in the kitchen.

At first, the work wasn't all that different from what Venus had done before. Her job was to chop raw vegetables, a mundane task that quickly becomes repetitive. Over time, though, Venus noticed that the place felt kind of nicer, happier, than any of the other places she had worked.

The kitchen was bigger, cleaner, and brighter than the kitchen in a McDonald's. The work wasn't quite so hurried. She had to work hard each day, but not with the kind of frenzy she was used to at other places. Workers at Sweetgreen actually make the meals; they don't just open up big bags of precut onions, premixed sauce, and preformed hamburger patties. They take raw, full-sized vegetables, big hunks of meat, a bunch of spices and oils and vinegars, and combine them to make spicy Thai salads, curry chickpea bowls, and the ever-changing mix of other dishes the restaurant prepares.

There was definitely a lot different about this new job. There was far more clarity about what Venus could achieve if she proved that she was good at her job, if she continued to learn how to do other tasks. She could move to the saucing area, mixing all the various dressings and sauces the restaurant makes fresh each day. With some more training, she could work in the cooking part of the kitchen, where meat is grilled, chicken broiled, and fish fried. She felt she could learn a lot about working in a high-speed kitchen. And there was the chance to become a kitchen manager, all of whom were promoted from the line; even the restaurant managers who ran the whole place were promoted from the line. Venus wasn't sure she could become a manager, or even get to the hot side of the kitchen, but she liked that it at least seemed possible.

One day, while Venus was chopping vegetables, the store manager, Simone Swain, asked her what her goal was. Venus said she thought she would like to cook. Simone said she could become a cook; she could even become a manager. Simone remarked that Venus was on time, worked hard, and was always responsive to requests. Yes, she was a bit quiet, a bit shy, and didn't stand up for herself, but she had proven herself to be someone reliable, capable, and eager to be part of a strong team. She'd have to learn a few things to become a manager, but Simone thought she could do it.

I was in the Sweetgreen kitchen the day this happened. The interaction does not seem especially notable on the surface: a manager chatted with an employee and shared some encouraging words—nice enough, but not revolutionary. Only it turns out to have been a pretty radical moment. Simone meant everything she said, but the *idea* of saying it had not been her own spontaneous impulse. She had been prompted by a software program designed by Wayne and his computer science team, based on psychological research conducted by Jessie and her team. We normally think of automation and enterprise software as a force that removes our unique individuality, that would have us all become indistinguishable worker drones in a workplace machinery that cares nothing for our individual hopes and skills. This was the opposite. This was the automation of empathy, of targeted encouragement, of a very personal and direct appeal to one particular worker, designed precisely for her needs at that moment.

Sweetgreen had hired Humu to solve a major problem the

restaurant chain, like all fast-food places, was facing: employees quit too quickly. Like Venus, most employees know they can get another minimum-wage job anytime they want, so they rarely stay anyplace very long. For many employees, it's not that big a deal—leave one job, start another. For the companies, however, the turnover is extremely expensive, as I mentioned earlier. It costs roughly $2,000 every time an employee leaves. First, there is usually a period of time when there aren't enough workers. Then there's the cost of hiring and training a replacement. Training typically requires several more experienced workers to spend a significant portion of a week training the new recruits, time in which both the trainer and the trainee are being paid. Sweetgreen is a relatively small company, with around four thousand employees, and about half the employees in fast-food chains will leave in any given year. That means that two thousand people could be predicted to leave Sweetgreen each year, costing the company $4 million annually. The company has around $60 million in revenue a year, with a roughly $6 million profit. If Sweetgreen could lessen the turnover by half, it would increase its profit by a third—a huge increase.

"Every three months of tenure is like one percentage point in profit," says Jonathan Neman, CEO and co-founder of Sweetgreen. "If I can get the whole company, all the employees, to stay, say, six months longer, I would be two percentage points more profitable."

Two percentage points might not sound that big, but the average profit of a fast casual restaurant like Sweetgreen is 6 percent of revenue. If Neman could increase that profit to 8 percent, he would instantly transform the company into one of the most profitable of its kind in the country. Sweetgreen, a privately held firm that is relatively small but growing quickly, hopes to compete with Chipotle and other multibillion-dollar empires. Increasing the profit margin by two percentage points would completely shift the company in investors' minds, guaranteeing that far more people would pay far more if it offered stock. With the extra money that comes from that investment, Neman could finance his growth far more quickly. Two percentage points of profit would be transformational. The problem is, the faster the company grows, the more people it would need to hire, and the more out of touch with those workers the senior leaders would be. To make billions of dollars, Neman needed to figure out how to make Venus Paul and workers like her happy, and he didn't even know who Venus Paul was or anything about her.

Neman's problem is not unique to him or to Sweetgreen. Every company on earth with more than a handful of employees has the same challenge. In theory, every company would make more money and avoid more risks if each and every employee were more engaged in their work, more motivated to excel, more able to be their best. But how in the world do you do that? Imagine that you are the CEO of a large business, one with thousands of employees you will never meet, never sit down with to learn their hopes, their frustrations, their aspirations. These employees are spread all over the country or, maybe, the world. Some are older, some young; some have big hopes, while others are just trying to make it through the day. You know they are so different from one another, and that each is different from you, and there is no way to come up with some slogan or some single approach that will engage all of them at once. So companies rely on a handful of far less than ideal options. They come up with cheesy motivational slogans and post them in break rooms. They resort to strict rules that each worker must follow or be terminated. Or they try to minimize the number of workers they need, replacing them with automation, since nobody has to worry about the happiness of robots and software programs. These "solutions," though, only cause more problems.

Walk into a McDonald's, say, and it is immediately clear

that you are not in a place of joy. McDonald's is a leader in work automation, having created machinery that can shape and grill a burger, cut and cook French fries, with a minimal amount of worker skill. This helps franchise owners handle the turnover problem. A new worker can learn all the fundamentals of the job in minutes and, therefore, will cost much less to train. But the more easily a worker can be replaced, the more the worker feels replaceable; and the more unmotivated and frustrated he is at work, the less pleasurable the restaurant is for customers, the cheaper the food has to be to get people to walk through the door, and the higher the employee turnover will be. This vicious cycle keeps many retail companies, fast-food restaurants, and other chain businesses in an ever-worsening state. I can think of a dozen chains I don't go into anymore in part because I dread entering a place that feels blanketed in an overwhelming sense of dissatisfaction. I see it in the workers' faces, and I sense it in the indifferent service.

A fatalism has settled over much of modern business. Customers, managers, and workers have all, somehow, accepted that this is the permanent, inevitable, and unalterable state: if we want lots and lots of inexpensive things, we have to accept big box stores and chain restaurants staffed by unhappy workers who pass that unhappiness on to customers. The thing is, it's not true—not anymore. In the twentieth century, this was an almost unconquerable problem. There simply was no technical way to do otherwise. But computing power has advanced alongside our understanding of the psychology of work, and that means that certain computer-based automation tools actually have the power to make us happier in our work.

Humu's solution is, in one sense, quite simple. When a company like Sweetgreen hires Humu, its staff, as always, sends out questionnaires carefully designed according to the best psychological research to elicit truthful and helpful (and fully anonymous) answers. Then Humu's software is able to begin to create special reports that help a company understand which areas are of greatest concern and which ones can most easily be improved. This is where employers learn how happy their employees rate in those three key factors affecting their happiness. Each company—often each division or even each individual store—might have its own answers and own areas of concern. A Humu engineer showed me a fascinating 3-D multicolored graph that illustrated the degree of happiness along those three key areas for every individual worker at a large multinational firm. I could see, at a quick glance, that some divisions and some managers had created an environment that supported highly engaged and happy workers while other divisions and managers had mistrustful, unengaged workers who appeared likely to leave as soon as they could find an alternative.

For Sweetgreen, the biggest problems became obvious quickly. At first, there was a large trust problem. Employees had taken surveys before and then turned around and seen those surveys used to reward some workers and punish others. They didn't want to take any more surveys. It was a long process to earn that trust back. Once employees trusted the company enough to fill out Humu's surveys, they reported that they did not feel the company cared for them, so there was little sense of belonging. Neman decided to offer more workers health insurance and a retirement plan. This had a huge, immediate, and positive impact.

Solutions like that could be made in bulk, but others have to be tailor-made to each worker. The biggest drivers of happiness in a fast casual restaurant are scheduling and a career path, and these must be customized. The ability to do that has been revolutionized by the tricky marriage of technological advances and psychological research. This, too, is part of the Passion Economy.

When I visited, Sweetgreen had seventy-five restaurants in the country, with a plan to add dozens more each year. Scheduling in each of them is a computational challenge. At any given time, each location has about fifty employees, who collectively

have to cover twenty positions during the rush hours of breakfast and lunch, and ten positions during quieter times. Each of
those fifty employees has her own general preferences (some
want short shifts; others want to work as many hours as they
can) and personal issues (jury duty, a sick child). Matching the
ever-changing needs of fifty people to the uneven demands of
the food-buying public requires a host of trade-offs. You can
have more people on staff, to cover every possible last-minute
problem, but that costs money. You can let people take off
whenever they want or work as many hours as they prefer, but
that, too, would cost too much money, leaving shifts uncovered
and customers unhappy. You can be insensitive to each worker's
needs and let them know they'll be fired if they take time off
to be with a sick child, but that will damage trust, happiness,
and belonging and, ultimately, cost money in turnover. This has
been the approach of many fast-food restaurants and big-box
retailers. They use "shift optimization" software that assigns
workers based on a computer program that cares zero about
each worker's needs and programs them to work according to a
strict, inflexible schedule.

Humu's approach is to marry automatic software processes
with human interaction. Shift assignment can never be fully
automated if it is also to be humane and thoughtful. What is
needed is for each store manager to understand and take into
account the specific needs of their store and their employees.
But this just kicks the problem up a level: How do you make
every one of hundreds of managers more empathetic, more
engaged with her workforce? Each manager, like every other
employee, has her own unique strengths and weaknesses. Some
might be naturally gifted at empathy and engagement but not
always the best at doing the complex math needed to make sure
every shift is covered. Others might be the reverse. Humu's
surveys tease out each manager's strengths and weaknesses and
identify their personality type and natural proclivities. None of
this is reported to the manager's own bosses. That is because

Humu can succeed only with absolute privacy. The Humu software does something the company calls "story generation." It takes the data it has about a manager—what the manager herself revealed in surveys and what employees said about her—and then generates prompts that will nudge the manager to do the important things she might otherwise forget to do. A manager who is great at scheduling and financial management but not so good at interpersonal skills might get a text message, right after the lunch rush, requesting that she randomly pick an employee and ask him how he's doing. A manager who is a natural people person but doesn't always remember to do the math might get a prompt, once a week, to check inventory and make sure he or she has ordered enough of the raw food needed for the following week.

This "nudge engine" is rooted in the work Jessie studied in graduate school. It is based on the now well-founded research that shows that gentle, regular nudges in the right direction are more effective than transformational change. When I learned about it, I was reminded of an experience I had several years ago after I had been quickly promoted from working as a reporter to managing a team. I was overwhelmed and, as a result, often brusque and angry. I yelled at the team more than once. These were wonderful people who were highly motivated and great at their jobs, and far too often, I made them feel unhappy and unable to do their best work. I discussed this problem with my own boss, and we both concluded that I needed to be permanently transformed from one kind of person to another. I then took a short, expensive course for bad managers. I spent three days in a conference room with a group of equally angry and incompetent managers as three psychologists trained us to identify our flaws and seek ways of becoming better. This experience convinced me that I wasn't a born manager, and I quit that job and swore I would never manage again. As it happens, I did become a manager several years later, just as I was researching Humu, and I was able to immediately apply this nudge concept. Instead of seeking to massively transform myself, I gently nudge myself, every now and then, to check in on the employees, ask them how they're doing, point out ways they are doing well, and subtly encourage them to develop other skills. So far, it's working well.

In Venus's case, those Humu nudges have added up to something transformational. To understand how, you need to know the story of her manager, Simone. She first managed a hotel in her native Grenada, then came to New York to get married. After some years of struggle, she, also, made the rounds of minimum-wage work. Simone became a manager of a higher-end chain that offered fast table service, but she was unable to be a successful manager there. The executives who ran the company were inconsistent in what they wanted each store manager to achieve. One month, it was profit; another month, it was to lower turnover; then they wanted to have a larger share of the local lunch business. Without clear direction, Simone didn't know what to emphasize: Should she over-schedule shifts to please customers and get more return visits or underschedule shifts to cut costs and raise profits? Also, that company, like many, had a two-tiered management track. Very few line workers—servers, bussers, kitchen staff—were promoted to management, and when they were, they were paid far less than the managers recruited from outside. Like other restaurants, management was overwhelmingly white and the line staff was overwhelmingly African-American and Latino. Simone herself learned that she was paid less than half of what the recruited, white managers got, even as she scored well on every one of the ever-changing metrics.

Simone took to Sweetgreen immediately. She has a big, welcoming personality, and it is obvious, as you follow her around the store, that she inspires trust in her workers. They like her, they respect her, and they feel respected by her. But Simone is the first to say that she can achieve this kind of relationship only in the proper context. At Sweetgreen, Simone knows what matters most to management. Yes, she has to turn a profit: she can't spend too much on food or be overly generous with shifts. She needs to run a popular restaurant, with strong customer loyalty, to get revenue. She also knows that the single most important metric to the company is the happiness of her workers. Thanks to Humu, she gets periodic nudges to make sure she keeps those workers happy.

Simone knew that Venus responded well to the idea that she could earn raises and promotions by acquiring more knowledge and by working harder. During the talk they had on the day I was there, I could see that Venus understood that she might actually have a way out of the minimum-wage loop she thought she was stuck in. She had a chance to become a store manager and, one day, a regional manager. That gave her a feeling of real purpose in her work. If she did get promoted, she might be able to buy a home and take a lot of the pressure off her dad. When Venus had a family of her own, she would be able to put her kids on an entirely different track than she has been on as an undereducated immigrant. Such dreams can be nurtured by small nudges along the way. Simone encouraged Venus to take some of the Sweetgreen training programs. Venus's main weakness is her shyness. It's ineffective to tell someone to stop being shy, but it is possible to encourage a shy person to learn the basics of customer interaction, and to encourage her to practice them, and to reward her if she steps outside her comfort zone and makes progress.

Similarly, Humu is able to nudge Simone around the particular challenge of encouraging shy workers. One nudge Humu developed addresses the very issue of shy people and scheduling. A manager like Simone might receive an e-mail on a Friday, the day she schedules staff:

Dear Simone,
As a manager, you're tasked with covering hours—and positions—at the Sweetgreen on Court Street. But as

new shifts and positions open up, how do you decide who to consider?

## TRY THIS
### Consider all your options

When new shifts or positions open up, start with a full list of team members rather than choosing the first person you think of.

Take a few minutes to go through all your options, instead of rewarding only the people who speak up about needing extra hours or wanting more responsibility.

**Why?** Sometimes qualified team members are hesitant to ask for more responsibility. By removing the burden on employees to speak up, you'll make decisions that are more fair.

I'm here for you if you've got questions,

Wayne at Humu

Each word in this nudge was carefully crafted based on psychological research. It begins by making clear that the person who wrote the e-mail (along with the computer program that sent it) understands Simone and her role, having studied the diagnostic analysis the Humu software conducted specifically on Simone and her team. The nudge then suggests a specific action. The nudge doesn't tell Simone to transform herself from an unfair to a fair person. Who could do that? It recommends a simple, doable tweak to an already required task and then explains why this will achieve a bigger aim. It will make employees feel that the company is more fair, because it will actually be more fair. Employees can trust that they won't be ignored simply because they're quieter than others.

One challenge in conveying the import of Humu's work is that it can seem so simple, so small. It's almost easy to dismiss it: Who cares that some restaurant manager in Brooklyn got an e-mail suggesting that she pay more attention to the quiet workers? But behind that simple e-mail is a revolution. It took dramatically cheaper computing power to achieve it, computing that allowed for a new kind of psychological research as well as a new way of questioning and encouraging workers and managers.

For Humu, this nudge engine is only the very beginning. The team is hard at work developing even more potentially revolutionary tools. Laszlo's dream is to have software that does a much better job of matching people with the work that is most likely to help them thrive. I imagine someone like Venus, who loves spending time experimenting with flavors in her own kitchen, being identified to be part of the recipe research and development team at Sweetgreen. Simone, I suspect, would be a highly effective trainer. She seems to understand precisely how to encourage her assistant managers to encourage the workers below them. The ultimate goal of Humu is to reframe the very nature of corporate America. Rather than have a set organization with set jobs and set job descriptions, something like the Humu engine can far better understand each worker's unique set of passions, skills, and constraints and re-form the organization around them or even direct employees to another company that would be a better match. Computer technology, artificial intelligence, and automation don't have to mean the soulless destruction of our individuality. They can achieve the precise opposite: passion-based organizations that promote individual happiness.

# EPILOGUE

John Maynard Keynes was the towering economic intellect of the first half of the twentieth century, and not only because he was six feet, seven inches tall. Keynes had a remarkable ability, throughout his life, to see the future with clarity. In the midst of the Great Depression, Keynes all but singlehandedly created an entire new school of economics—macroeconomics—that offered fresh tools that could explain and eliminate the horrible economic stagnancy that had taken over the world. After World War II, Keynes guided the creation of, essentially, the modern world, developing the World Bank, the International Monetary Fund, and the host of international agreements that allowed Europe and much of Asia to rebuild after the brutal war and essentially created the global economy.

In 1930, with much of the world experiencing the early, panicky stages of the collapse known as the Great Depression, Keynes wrote an essay in which he took a much longer view. Titled "Economic Possibilities for Our Grandchildren," the essay warns readers not to give in to the "attack of economic pessimism." "It is common," Keynes wrote, "to hear people say that the epoch of enormous economic progress which characterised the nineteenth century is over; that the rapid improvement in the standard of life is now going to slow down." No, he argued. "We are suffering, not from the rheumatics of old age, but from the growing-pains of over-rapid changes, from the painfulness of readjustment between one economic period and another."

Keynes was forty-seven when he wrote those words, and

he, like every person alive, knew how rapid the technological changes had been. He had been born into a world that still, largely, ran at the pace of a stroll. The telegraph and rail existed but were not a part of the average person's everyday life. The telephone, electricity, cars, airplanes, and mass production were all in the future. Most people never communicated with anybody they didn't see face-to-face. Most citizens continued to be farmers doing their work by hand or, if they were lucky, with the help of a mule.

Then, seemingly overnight, the world transformed. It became urban and industrial, with instantaneous communication across land and sea. People whose ancestors had farmed for millennia were working in jobs that hadn't existed a few years earlier. The change happened so fast, Keynes observed, that it caused profound "maladjustment," as the entire economy had to shift each time some major technology appeared. The telegraph alone was transformative, allowing business decisions across long distances to be made in real time rather than at the pace a horse could walk. It destroyed the long-standing economic ecosystem built around horse-based mail delivery: carriage makers and carriage drivers, carriage inns, not to mention buggy whip manufacturers. The conveyor belt and other inventions that allowed mass production destroyed the jobs of blacksmiths and other artisanal craftspeople. The loss of these jobs and the confusion that all of the rapid change brought were loud and inescapable. Keynes pointed out, though, that all that change brought with it something quieter, easier to miss, but far more important: a slow, steady increase in the quality of life. He estimated that increase to be about 2 percent a year, barely enough to notice. Over time, though, it was that slow, steady growth that made the most dramatic change. In 1930, Keynes predicted that by 2030 the average person in Great Britain would be four to eight times richer than their average ancestor a century before. He was right. By 2010, the average U.K. income was just over five times greater than the average in 1930, with twenty more years of growth to come. The United States saw even more growth, with the average income in 2018 nearly six times that of 1930.

Keynes would be the first to point out that this doesn't mean everyone is happy today. There is rising inequality as many of the economic gains of the past few decades go to only a small number of very rich people. Still, our lives are unimaginably better than the lives of our grandparents in 1930. Then, hunger was a real issue in the United States and the United Kingdom, infant mortality was far more common, and health care was only beginning to emerge from medieval superstition-based quackery. Taking the long view, as Keynes suggested, shows that we did adjust. As he wrote, "mankind is solving its economic problem."

The solutions did not come all at once, perfectly formed. They emerged chaotically and often looked more like desperation than problem-solving. The union movement ensured that workers would share in economic growth through better pay and working conditions. A variety of government and private-sector insurance solutions made it less likely that people who were old or injured would become penniless. Our education system grew steadily, improving the skills and earning potential of countless people. In most cases, the society-wide responses came only after profound crisis. Unions grew as a response to corporations that went too far in what they demanded of workers. Social Security and Medicare were responses to the cruel fate of so many impoverished elderly people cast aside during the Great Depression.

For all his foresight, Keynes seems to have underestimated how much change human beings were in for. We didn't just move from one stable economic system to another one. We now see that the pace at which technology advances is speeding up. The new system is one in which there is no stability at all. Whatever is happening today, and whatever jobs and businesses are thriving now, will be different tomorrow. That is scary—of course it is. It's also thrilling, or it should be.

I believe that our society will, like societies past, come up with grand, new solutions that operate at the national or international level. We will have new laws, new institutions that increase the number of people who can thrive in this economy and protect those who can't. We will have new forms of education, new social safety nets, new financial products, and new forms of insurance. These will take time. There will be mistakes and setbacks and loud, angry fights. Nothing will be perfect; nothing ever is. Eventually, though, we will all understand the rules of this new age and have more tools available to help us achieve financial and personal success.

Crucially, we don't have to wait. The opportunity exists right now for each of us to create the lives we want. We have tools, right now, that no human beings had before. We can use the very forces that upended the widget economy to thrive in the Passion Economy. We can use the full suite of technology— the Internet, artificial intelligence, robotics—and the increase in global trade to create special products and services and to find those people, spread thinly around the globe, who most want what we have to offer. Our work lives and our deepest passions can merge, happily, in ways that make us better off financially and personally.

Every person in this book has found their path to living wisely and agreeably and well. Each has lessons to teach us. Now it is up to each of us to find our own paths, to define, uniquely for ourselves, what we want and what we have to offer. For all the chaos of our age, we get to do these things that so few people in history have ever had the chance to do. Let's go.

# ACKNOWLEDGMENTS

Kris Dahl of ICM has been so much more than an agent (although she is an amazingly good one). She signed me, decades ago, when I had no business asking anybody to represent me. She saw something I couldn't see in myself and has been a constant sounding board, advocate, friend, and voice of reason throughout my career. We spent countless hours together, brainstorming the ideas that would, eventually, become this book. Then she took it to market and represented me with her gentle ferocity. No writer could ask for a better ally. This book would not exist without her.

Jon Kelly was my editor at *The New York Times Magazine*, where many of the ideas in this book first took shape. He saw that there was something bigger in the arguments I was making in my weekly column and helped me shape those thoughts into book-length form. He then served as my collaborator throughout the writing process. His hand is present on every page. (If there is anything you don't like in the book, blame him; it's probably his fault.)

The moment I met Jonathan Segal of Knopf, I knew I had to work with him. It wasn't that he was brimming with praise. It was the opposite: he identified some flabbiness in the proposal and told me I would have to remove it from the book. But he saw the core of what I was seeking to do and made it clear that he could help me eliminate everything that would get in the way. I put him through a lot. It took me far too long to finish this book, and there were false starts (we killed an *entire* book I wrote that wasn't, in the end, very good). He can be, rather famously, gruff and impatient. But don't let him fool you. He is a sweet man who cares deeply about his authors. There is also nobody more fun with whom to have lunch or to share a drink or three. He is wickedly funny and a great storyteller. (Sorry, Jonathan, for revealing your secret kindness.) He was true to his word; he understands what a book needs and what it doesn't. He kept me focused on the larger goals of this book while also being ruthlessly helpful with his pencil on every page.

The ideas in this book were the result of opportunities key people gave me at *Marketplace*, NPR, *This American Life*, *The New York Times Magazine*, *The New Yorker*, and *The Atlantic*. I also worked with a bunch of amazing people who helped me shape my ideas and improve my craft. These include Jon Lee Anderson, Alex Blumberg, David Brancaccio, Neal Carruth, Zoe Chace, Deirdre Foley-Mendelssohn, David Folkenflik, Ira Glass, Jacob Goldstein, Chana Joffe-Walt, Caitlin Kenney, David Kestenbaum, Eric Lach, Hugo Lindgren, Karen Lowe, Michael Luo, Pam McCarthy, Don Peck, Mike Pesca, David Remnick, David Rohde, Kai Ryssdal, Jake Silverstein, Robert Smith, Julie Snyder, Nicholas Thompson, Vera Titunik, Nancy Updike, Bill Wasik, Ellen Weiss, Kinsey Wilson, and Daniel Zalewski.

Adam McKay has been a great friend and creative partner. Working with him on *The Big Short* taught me so much about how to make complex economic information accessible and exciting to a broad audience. Our endless talks about every damn topic under the sun have been so crucial in shaping my thoughts. And thanks, too, to Shira Piven, Pearl, and Lili, for creating a home away from home in Los Angeles.

I explore the ideas in this book in the podcast of the same name, *The Passion Economy*, from Luminary Media. Laura Mayer, the executive producer, and Lena Richards, the launch producer, have made that show much better than I deserve. Jayme Lynes, Matt Sacks, and Kenzi Wilbur have been wonderful partners at Luminary. John McConnell of Workhouse Media made the deal possible.

Laura Mayer and I cofounded and, together, run Three Uncanny Four, a podcast production company that applies this book's lessons to a growing and passion-fueled industry. Laura has a unique combination of profound creative passion and thoughtful discipline; I learn from her every day. She and I are continually blown away by our entire team of passionate audio creators. Our company is a joint venture with Sony Music Entertainment, which may be the world's largest and most successful passion business. Sony Music's core purpose is to support artists so they can create their best work and then to connect them with their most enthusiastic audiences. It has been thrilling to learn from so many great businesspeople there. Rob Stringer and Kevin Kelleher are proof that it is possible to place the highest expression of the human soul at the center of a big, global company. I have learned so much from them, as well as from Neil Carfora, Amanda Collins, Brian Garrity, Dennis Kooker, Tom Mackay, Christy Mirabal, Emily Rasekh, Charlie Yedor, and many others. They all give me such hope for the future, as they prove that passion and global scale can work together to bring great work to the public.

I am grateful to the many inspiring businesspeople I spoke with, both those who are in this book and the ones who had great stories that I—sadly—wasn't able to use. I learned so much from all of you.

My parents, Aviva Davidson and Jack Davidson, showed me that a passionate life is possible and worth living. They did so in different ways. My dad identified his passion early and pursued it vigorously every moment of my life. My mom offers a remarkable model for others who bloom late. She decided to stifle her passions to raise my brother and me. In her forties, though, she began her life anew. She went back to school, ran a theater, then took over Dancing in the Streets, a wonderful organization that brought her to the South Bronx, where she became a central part of the hip-hop dance community. She has such a rich and passionate life. I wish I had her energy.

My brother, Eben, has been on a parallel journey during our adult lives. He has pursued his passion for film, television, and other forms of entertainment. Like me, he found satisfaction in straddling the business and creative worlds, though he has done it far more successfully and creatively than I could. I'm grateful for his constant generosity, advice, and, more than anything, being a great guy to talk with.

How in the world do I properly thank my wife, Jen Banbury? She has been my secret weapon, an incredible editor and writer who stepped in to turn messy thinking, lazy writing, and a ton of misplaced commas into a manuscript I was ready to submit. She saved this book many times. Of course, she saved me in more ways than one. We fell in love in Baghdad during a war, which showed us quickly that we could trust each other in a crisis and also trust each other's editorial sensibility. (It also showed us that we like each other.) We have encouraged each other's passions ever since. No other passion could compete with our greatest one: Asher Arrow Banbury Davidson, who is seven years old as I write this. Ash is a model of how to live a passionate life. He hurtles himself at whatever topic fascinates him, inhaling everything he can learn about tropical rain forests, Egyptian gods, all kinds of animals, coral reefs, or whatever he is up to by the time this book is published. I am so glad he will get to grow up in the Passion Economy.

# INDEX